BREAKING THE BARRIERS
TO
EVERYDAY CREATIVITY

A Practical Guide for Expanding
Your Creative Horizons

By Noland L. VanDemark, Ph.D.

Professor Emeritus and former Director of Research
Cornell University Agricultural Experiment Station
and
College of Agriculture and Life Sciences
Cornell University, Ithaca, New York

NURTURE

CREATIVITY

ISBN 0-930222-911

Published by
The Creative Education Foundation
Buffalo, NY 14224

ACKNOWLEDGEMENTS

The author and publisher wish to express their thanks for permission
to reprint and reproduce the following:

From the *American Scientist* and Dr. Ernest Harbury, for permission
to reproduce the map entitled *"The Island of Research,"* which
appeared in the *American Scientist* 54, 4. 1966.

From *The Power of Ethical Management*, by Kenneth Blanchard and
Norman V. Peale. Material from pp. 80 and 125. © 1988 by
Blanchard Family Partnership and Norman Vincent Peale. By per-
mission of William Morrow and Co., Inc.

From William G. Dyer, *Team Building*, © 1987, by Addison-Wesley
Publishing Company, Inc., Reading, Massachusetts. Table 10.1,
pages 108-109. Reprinted with permission of the publisher.

From *How to Solve Problems: Elements of a Theory of Problems and
Problem Solving*. By Wayne A. Wickelgren. © 1974 by W.H. Freeman and Company. Reprinted by permission.

Dedicated to

my wife, Beda,

who has taught me so much about relating to people

and who along with our children - Gary, Judy and Linda -

has shown me much love and devotion,

and to

the many students and colleagues whose

challenges, love, growth and enthusiasm

have contributed so much

joy and satisfaction to

my life and living.

CONTENTS

List of Tables 5
List of Figures 7
Preface 8

1. Creativity 12
2. Brain Power: The Base - Intelligence 32
3. Brain Power: The Sparks - Curiosity,
   Intuition, Imagination, and Perception 52
4. Attitudes, Emotions, and Feelings 62
5. Balance, Discipline, and Wisdom 80
6. Problem-Solving: Identifying and Finding Solutions ... 102
7. The Self in Creativity 132
8. The Impact of Others: Relational Power 152
9. Team Efforts: Group Influences 180
10. Societal and Environmental Influences 198
11. Personal Growth, Development and Self-Renewal 226
12. Leading and Managing to Foster Creativity 256
13. Organizational and Institutional Growth,
    Change, and Impact 288
14. Putting It All Together 316
    References and Suggested Readings 334
    Index 342

LIST OF TABLES

Table Title   Page

1-1 Some Characteristics of Creative Adults 25
1-2 Potential Interacting Factors Affecting
    the Creative Capabilities of the Individual 27
1-3 Various Factors that Affect Creativity 28
1-4 Some Participants' Thoughts in Facing
    the Difficulties of Overcoming Blocks to Creativity...........29
2-1 Some Generally Desirable Mental Capabilities
    of the Potentially Creative "Whole Person"
    Scientist (Individual) 43
2-2 Characteristic Results of Directed
    Versus Creative Thinking 46
3-1 Some Causes of Perceptual Blocks to
    Creativity and Problem-Solving 60
4-1 Some Generally Desirable Mental Attitudinal Qualities 63
6-1 Osborn's Suggestions for Self-Interrogation
    to Stimulate Coming Up with Ideas 118
6-2 Comparison of the Problem-Solving Approach of
    Osborn and Parnes et al, (1977) and the
    Salisbury (1951) Pattern for Scientific Research.............126
7-1 The Five Principles of Ethical Power for Individuals 140
7-2 Inner (Self) Barriers to Creativity 148
8-1 Factors Affecting Loving, Growing Relationships...........159
8-2 Levels of Communication 164
8-3 Blocks to Effective Communication 173
8-4 Fruits of Courage to Be Self and
    in Relationship to Others 175
9-1 Stages of Community Making 182
9-2 Essential Principles for Effective Groups 184
9-3 What the True Community Must Be 184
9-4 Some Advantages Provided by Team Efforts.............187
9-5 Common Problems in Group Efforts...............189
9-6 Factors Causing People to Dislike Working in Groups 191
9-7 Required Characteristics for an Effective Team 192
9-8 Group Impact on Creativity 194
10-1 The Way Our Parents (Caretakers) Treated
    Us May Carry Over into Our Adult Lives 207
10-2 Rogers' Principles of Learning 213

List of Tables (continued)

Table   Title   Page

10-3 Essentials for Facilitating a Learning Atmosphere 216
11-1 Erikson's Eight Ages of Man 229
11-2 Evaluating Your Potential Burnout Level 232
11-3 Ideas of Workshop Participants on Preventing Burnout ...233
11-4 Blocks to Personal Growth Suggesting
     Changes Are Needed 235
11-5 Forces Which Block Growth 236
11-6 Strategies for Overcoming Procrastination 238
11-7 Faith: The Force That Frees You to Succeed.................240
11-8 Forces Which Stimulate Growth 241
11-9 How to Beat the Time Trap 249
12-1 Historical Patterns of Leadership Attitudes 266
13-1 Characteristics of the Good Organization 293
13-2 The Five Principles of Ethical Power for Organizations ...299
13-3 Necessities in Order to Accomplish Group Changes 303
13-4 Guidelines for Managing Change....................................304
13-5 Encouraging Creativity Through Management
     and Organization...305
14-1 Some Measures of Maturity 324

LIST OF FIGURES

Figure
Number   Title   Page

1-1 The Self as the Center of Creativity
and the Anticipated Influences
and Hoped for Responses 26
2-1 Graphic Representation of Percentage of
Recall with the Passage of Time with
and without Reviews 38
2-2 Effect of Learning Period Breaks Every
20 to 40 Minutes on Recall and Understanding.................39
5-1 Requirements for a Balanced Creative Individual.............82
5-2 Conditions Affecting Our Ability to Respond
in Making Decisions for Change 90
6-1 Conceptualization of Solving Problems
and Contributing to Man's Stream of Knowledge 104
6-2 Conceptualization of Problem- Solving Pitfalls
and Diversions in Science 128
7-1 Factors within the Self in Its Central Role
in Creativity 134
7-2 The Hiearchy of Human Needs as Perceived
by Maslow...135
8-1 The Impact of Others on Individual Creativity.................153
10-1 Societal and Environmental Factors
Influencing the Creativity of the Individual 199
10-2 Negative Comments That Slow and Kill Progress 220
11-1 Average Percentage of Basic and Growth
Needs of the Individual That Are Actually Met 252
12-1 Example of the Many Programs, Persons
and Other Items Which a Leader Can
Expect to Demand Attention 259
12-2 Comparative Time and Difficulty in
Making Various Changes...265
12-3 Leader Behavior Can Either Enhance
or Restrict the Freedom of Subordinates 267
12-4 Characteristic Responses of Persons
Who Participate in Decisions Which
Affect Their Work...269

PREFACE

We all have dreams of living a better and more meaningful life. In a complex and competitive society this goal demands creative approaches. We can either learn to become more creative and attain some of those dreams, or we can remain at a standstill while the world passes by. From the cradle to the grave, we are buffeted daily by helps and barriers to our creativity. Understanding how to use, or avoid, and otherwise deal with these factors can increase our personal potential, and help us obtain more productivity and creativity from others. These benefits can be derived in our business or profession, from our students, our work force, our children and from the groups we associate with in a variety of ways. This book is targeted toward helping people discover their untapped creative resources and become more adept at turning problems into opportunities.

I am not sure that creativity can be taught outright, but I am certain, from long experience on many fronts, that we can do much to nourish and cultivate it. We can further our personal creative development through education and training. We can influence our environment by encouraging others to be creative. Creative breakthroughs are most likely to occur when individuals interact within a creative environment. We can also learn to be more aware of those things which inhibit, poison, or delay the development and growth of creative capabilities.

Each of us is unique with our own set of creative potentials. Genetic makeup and environmental influences set each of us apart. No one has ever been, nor ever will be exactly like us. But internal and external forces constantly push us to conform to standardized thought and behavior patterns. When people fall into such non-creative patterns they fail to capitalize on their full potential. MacKinnon's studies (1978, 186) suggested that to be creative we will likely need to develop a high level of effective intelligence; an openness to experience; a freedom from crippling restraints and impoverishing inhibitions; an esthetic sensitivity; a cognitive flexibility; an independence in thought and action; an unquestioning commitment to creative endeavor; and an incessant striving for solutions to difficult problems.

Some of the needs for creativity and the many influences affecting our creative capabilities are suggested in Chapter 1. Many of these start with our own intelligence (Chapter 2), intuition and imagination (Chapter 3), and the attitudes we develop toward ourselves and others (Chapter 4). We can use our wisdom, common sense, and discipline (Chapter 5), and become more adept at solving problems (Chapter 6), and learn to know ourselves better (Chapter 7).

All those with whom we come in daily contact can greatly influence our response and the opportunity and freedom we have for expressing creative capabilities (Chapter 8). Thus we are influenced greatly by immediate family, teachers, superiors, subordinates, mentors and peers, and by group (team) members (Chapter 9). So understanding interpersonal relationships is also extremely important to the creative process.

Understanding individuals helps us create a stimulating environment so that our upbringing, culture, education, and religion become positive rather than negative forces in bringing out our dormant creative abilities (Chapter 10). Understanding and utilizing the positive aspects of our internal factors and our interpersonal relationships can help us grow and develop in dealing with many negative and adverse situations (Chapter 11).

Leadership and management can also be major factors affecting our opportunity to express our creative capabilities (Chapter 12). Organizations, institutions, governments, and the groups in which we find or place ourselves can either be helpful or become "The Dead Hand on Discovery" (Chapter 13). We must each assume responsibility for ourselves and for the group, organization or institution to which we belong, sometimes against popular pressures and opinions. Becoming adept at doing this can greatly increase the possibilities of finding and exercising our own untapped creative resources as well as helping others to utilize theirs (Chapter 14). Several "thought" questions or suggestions, called "Aftergrowth Stimulators," are offered at the end of each chapter. These are intended to help readers implement and foster the continuing growth and development of their own and others'creativity.

This book has been many years in the making, for it stems largely from experiences over much of my life as a student, graduate student, teacher, scientific researcher, and administrator in an academic setting. However, I also learned many lessons from other experiences as an army infantryman, officer, counter-intelligence agent, and director of a post World War II over-seas livestock rehabilitation program in Austria.

My early childhood years in a rural poverty setting provided many lessons on how to make do with little beyond the bare necessities for living. I am grateful that during those years I had solid, hard-working parents and teachers who firmly believed in human rights and freedom, and were unwavering in practicing the "golden rule" and ethical behavior. These helped me forge a strong background that included belief in mankind and a divine being, a conviction that I should do the best I could with the capabilities I possessed, and that rewards would come if I deserved them.

I will be forever indebted to and appreciative of my wife, Beda, and our three, now adult, children - Gary, Judy and Linda. Each sacrificed by enduring my absence, time and time again, as I was busying myself with teaching, researching and administering, and giving them less time and attention than they so thoroughly deserved. Their love, devotion and encouragement never failed, whether I deserved it or not, in nearly four decades during which bits and pieces, now in this manuscript, were collected.

The basic aspects for this book were initiated (at the University of Illinois while a teacher and researcher) during the study of great people in science. From this base a course focusing on creativity was taught for 10 years at Ohio State University (as a teacher, researcher, and administrator). Then (for five years at Cornell University) a course on "Nurturing Scientific Creativity" was offered, along with seminars on "Managing to Foster Creativity" (also presented at numerous other locations). Both of these were presented at the University of Georgia (winter quarter of 1985). The book is an outgrowth of all these varied experiences.

There have been few people in my life that have not taught me something that has helped me in governing my actions and behavior, both for improvement and avoiding pitfalls. I am glad that one of my high school teachers, Ralph Brooks, taught me that even farm boys had brains and convinced me to go to college, and that T. Scott Sutton encouraged me to go on to graduate school.

Most of all in the academic areas, I am indebted to Glenn W. Salisbury, my mentor for most of my Ph.D. degree, who urged and helped me to develop a questioning and inquiring mind; who helped me to realize that freedom and responsibility must go hand in hand; and who later served as my chairman, co-worker, co-author, and colleague for more than 20 years and has been a best friend and model for nearly 50 years.

I am deeply indebted to the several hundreds of students, graduates, technicians, postdoctorates, and fellow scientists and teachers who had the courage to constantly challenge me to stay abreast of the times and new developments. As a result we all profited and went on to achievements beyond our original hopes and dreams.

To the several administrators, under whom I have served, who urged me to push on to wherever my ideas led me, gave me support, and got out of my way over the years, I owe much for their encouragement, consideration and friendship. A special thanks is due my former co-administrators who helped prove that respect and consideration for one another at all levels serves to build the most effective teams and lasting friendships.

Special thanks are due the several secretaries (especially Suzanne Bremmer) and others who served so faithfully over the years and without whom I would not have been able to collect and process much of the information contained herein.

I especially want to thank J. Robert Cooke, Joän Egner, the late Larry Ewing, W. Reginald Gomes, Ronald Kuhr, and Judy and Robert Lindamood (all in higher education from several states), as well as members of my immediate family for reading the first drafts of this book and making invaluable suggestions for improvements. Special credit is due James West for his editing and layout help, and to Susan MacKay of Suma Designs for the preparation and refinement of the illustrations.

For all of these people and those whose presence and participation in my classes, workshops, and meetings unknowingly taught me much about life and living, I will be eternally grateful. I am sure there were many more things I could have learned from them, but my human frailties surely caused me to miss some lessons that were presented. We never know what great lessons or discoveries (positive or negative) may be available unless we constantly look for them and put what we learn into action. This book focuses on becoming aware of many of these things in order to tap more of our own untapped creative human resources and at the same time help others to make better use of their capabilities.

Suggestions and/or comments on any parts of this book will be welcomed at 8801 Leesville Road, Raleigh, NC 27613-1012.

January 5, 1991

Noland L. VanDemark

CHAPTER 1

CREATIVITY

1- 1   Introduction
1- 2   The Certainty of Change
1- 3   The Need for Creativity
1- 4   Definition of Creativity
1- 5   Who has Creative Abilities?
1- 6   Creative Traits
1- 7   Factors Enhancing Creativity
1- 8   Barriers to Creativity
1- 9   Highlights of Chapter One
1-10   Aftergrowth Stimulators

1-1 INTRODUCTION

As individuals, we cannot possibly learn and handle all of the knowledge and all of the broad aspects of the universe in which we live. In fact, and at best, what is known of all that goes on in the universe, even by the most learned person, is infinitesimal as is the life span of each of us. As Ornstein (1972) said, "We cannot possibly experience the world as it fully exists - we would be overwhelmed."

Nature has spared us much of the danger of this agony by equipping us with filtering mechanisms. For example, we can only see the visible light portion of the electromagnetic spectrum. Think what life would be like if we were equipped to perceive even radio waves, let alone cosmic, gamma, and X-rays, and could see ultraviolet and infrared light waves. We only hear a limited range of sounds. We are aware of very little of what goes on around us and do not realize much of what goes on within our own bodies because of the built-in, involuntary filtering mechanisms.

Most of what we are has come about as a result of natural evolution and the need and urge to survive. Many of us tend to pay attention to little more than what is necessary for survival. For that reason many are never stimulated to seek to understand the unknown or learn much beyond what is needed for that survival. Swindoll (1987, 276) said:

> Mediocrity is fast becoming the by-word of our times. Every imaginable excuse is now used to make it acceptable, hopefully preferred....Incompetence and status quo averages are held up as all we can now expect, and the tragedy is that more and more people have virtually agreed.

If we aspire to no more than mediocrity we are not likely to contribute many creative advances to keep pace with needs, nor experience many broadening aspects of life.

Civilization has changed and progressed throughout history as problems have been solved by chance or as a result of deliberate efforts to find solutions. Today's society is dynamic and it is complex because we have discovered more and more ways to unravel the secrets of the universe. As a result, we seem to face ever-increasing complications in all aspects of everyday living. Such a situation calls for a more concentrated and deliberate effort to solve problems and seize opportunities, if we are to survive. Creative approaches are in ever greater demand. The question is, "How can we contribute individually?"

In addition to the need for creativity to meet the world's problems, all people find themselves challenged to adjust to the rapid changes that are occurring. To fail or even to delay making efforts to keep up can seriously jeopardize our future. Beyond these necessities we are all desirous of and in need of some degree of accomplishment, productivity, efficiency, happiness and fulfillment in order to be more fully human. Increasing our creative capabilities can help us gain greater control and satisfaction of life and everyday living.

1-2 THE CERTAINTY OF CHANGE

The universe, the world, and the people are changing constantly. Yet so many of these changes are so gradual that we often are not aware that they are occurring.

1-2.1 Unbelievable Changes - from "Status Quo" to Something New

To those of us living today it is hard to believe that the lives of even our great-grandparents could have been so simple. Toffler (1970) cleverly illustrated the magnitude of change since the known beginning of humanity. By dividing the last 50,000 years into 62-year human lifetimes, he pointed out that there have been a little more than 800 generations. He indicated that for 650 of these generations people lived in caves. Only during the last 70 lifetimes has one generation been able to communicate effectively with the next. In only the last six has there been printing. In only the last four has time been measured with any great precision, and we have had the electric motor just within the last two. He concluded by indicating that most of what we use today has come within the last generation.

Ten years later Toffler (1980) wrote of the changes and the clash of the waves of more recent changes from the original dominance of the Agricultural Revolution through the impact of the Industrial Revolution to the changes of today. He indicated that we are now into a third wave, a new civilization with its own jobs, lifestyles, work ethics, sexual attitudes, concepts of life, economic structures, and political mind-sets. From these projections and from our own experiences of recent years we know that we face dramatic and even drastic changes. It is almost impossible for most of us to grasp what some of the developments are, let alone envision what their potential and impact will be on our lives.

1-2.2 The Challenge

A report of the National Business Higher Education Forum on America's competitive challenge (Chronicle of Higher Education, May 18, 1983) pointed out that:

> The central objective of the U.S. in the next decade must be to improve the ability of American industry and American workers to compete at home and abroad.

The article highlighted three elements as being needed. These were:

1. Technological innovation — from basic research to commercialization of new products and new processes.
2. Productive capital investment.
3. Development of human resources.

These would seem to be basic needs for us for many years to come.

Jastrow (1983), who chaired the first lunar exploration committee, wrote an article on "Science and the American Dream" in which he cited some of the same issues as mentioned above. Jastrow pointed out that we can help to create wealth by enhancing human productivity. He said that America has the advantages of:

1. being an open society;
2. allowing an upward mobility that gives free reign to innovativeness;
3. believing human capital counts most of all in an environment and society in which human potential can be utilized to its maximum; and
4. possessing a final item of utmost importance-venture capital to invest at great risk in testing crazy ideas.

Obviously the collective efforts of government, business, education, and labor will all be needed to succeed in these efforts. However, the desire to learn and the motivation to be creative must come from all of us. We must get serious about longer range planning for things like finding more efficient ways of utilizing energy, of stopping the pollution of the environment, of reducing the threat of water shortages, of slowing up our use of non-renewable resources, of helping individuals to be more creative, and the hundreds of other items focused upon by many who have been looking to the future. Perhaps most important of all will be learning to change and finding how we can live with each other without letting greed, selfishness and disregard for the rights of others lead us to the point of destroying each other and our world.

1-3 THE NEED FOR CREATIVITY

Among the many major problems we face will be how to handle the increase in need for information:

- Can we learn more?
- What is our learning capacity?
- Can we learn faster?
- Aren't there better methods of handling more information so that it can be absorbed more rapidly?
- Can we discard more?
- What will we discard?
- How much information does each of us need?
- Can we broaden the limited capacities we have for absorbing and using knowledge and information?
- Who will be the creative persons coming up with the new ideas?
- Can we individually be creative enough to even keep up with the advances?

We need to be ready to make maximum use of the unbelievable developments in biology and medicine; with electronics, computers and artificial intelligence; with communications, glass fibers and laser beams. Before the 1930's, atomic bombs, radar, jet engines, laser beams and space travel were considered by most of us as wild imagination and few of us even had fantasies of them. Even more unbelievable then would have been that we could send people into space and satellites to other planets and receive back specific information concerning the nature of those planets. Even if such developments were suggested, they would have been considered so fantastic as to boggle our minds.

We never dreamed of the potential biotechnological developments in agriculture and medicine through the use of recombinant DNA, single cell protein formation, and cellulose digestion by microorganisms which may allow the production of sugar, liquid fuel, plastics, drugs, and rubber from plants which can be rapidly replaced in nature. Obviously, final developments with many of these may be years away from practical economical implementation, but the potential, again, boggles our minds.

If we are going to keep pace with developments and maintain our position in the world's science, industry, and education, we must be prepared for changes. With the complexity of things, it is obvious that no small group of our population can supply the brains to deal with all the many challenges. We thus must have planning, coordination, and education on many fronts. This will require the super efforts of many for years to come. Especially challenging will be finding ways to speed up exchanges between those who have been privileged to developments and those who have not. Even in circumstances where education and technological developments are available, some choose not to attempt to make these opportunities a part of their way of life.

It is important that all of us, and especially our leaders, realize that coping with the future will be dependent upon having an adequate number of creative, uninhibited thinkers. This can only be done by creative, productive people willing and confident enough to be individuals, but community-minded enough to work for the good of all. This becomes a major challenge for us individually and for working teams.

Overall, we will need creative individuals, effective teams, dynamic leaders, stimulating environments, and effective organizations. We must have unity of purpose. Individual creative minds will determine whether this enormous challenge will be realized or whether civilization is doomed to facing severe and possibly destructive degenerative changes.

Years ago H.G. Wells was reported as having said, "The world is heavy with the promise of greater things." However, later in life he apparently became pessimistic and is quoted as saying:

> The writer sees the world as a jaded world devoid of recuperative powers. In the past he has liked to think that Man could pull out of his entanglements and start a new creative phase of human living. In the face of our universal inadequacy, that optimism has given place to a stoical cynicism .... Ordinary man is at the end of his tether. Only a small, highly adaptable minority of the species can possibly survive. The rest will not trouble about it, finding such opiates and consolations as they have a mind for. (Cited by Dale, 1967. Probably from Wells' book, *Mind at the End of its Tether*, 1945.)

The mind boggling advances of the last four and one-half decades have shown how wrong Wells' predictions were for the potential advances of mankind. Certainly man was not at the end of his tether back in the 1940's. Nor is it likely that we will be, at least for many years to come, unless we choose to persist in some of our destructive behavior toward our fellowmen and our environment. As Dale said in his article in 1967:

> Of key importance is the attitude of people regarding their ability to control the forces unleashed by modern inventiveness. Do most people feel that they can effectively cope with the future, or do they pessimistically conclude that the future is unmanageable, out of control?

> To ask people to take charge of their own lives is to assume a maturity that many either cannot or will not assume. Can we really start a new creative phase of human living?

What happens in the future is truly up to each of us and collectively up to all of us. The challenge is enormous, but the alternatives are frightening. We must each strive to be as much as we can be. We must work to stretch our imagination and our thinking capabilities beyond what we are inclined to think we possess. Can we contribute in some small way to move from "status quo" to something new? Can we muster the courage to fight through "eras of anti's"? One of the greatest challenges may be that of learning to work and live together, to work toward the good for the whole while at the same time gleaning the best for ourselves individually.

Dale (1967) has suggested that the future will look less foreboding when we learn how to reduce the gap between our potential and our achievements.

From the foregoing discussion it is obvious that creativity will be needed on every hand. We will need it, not only in dealing with science and technology, but in areas affecting learning, behavior and the social aspects of life. Can we devise ways of managing life so that we can be at peace even when dealing with great religious, economic, racial, educational, sexual, and other differences? Can being more creative help?

1-4 DEFINITION OF CREATIVITY

What do we mean when we say, "Be more creative"? Early definitions of creativity have ranged widely, from application to a process, to a product, or to certain abilities of a creative person.

Among a few are:

- New association of existing elements (Von Fange, 1959).
- Bringing something new into being (May, 1975).
- Making remote associations (Andrews, 1976).

Amabile (1983, 18-31) has discussed the definitions that have been used over time and in referring to creativity in several ways. Among these have been the ideas of something or some process that is original, novel, newly thought of, and in some cases as being useful.

The problem with "useful" is that at the time of initial discovery there often was no idea that there may one day be some usefulness. For example it is doubtful that anyone had any idea that some of the findings in early atomic physics were actually the principles that would lead to a wide array of practical uses of atomic energy (both constructively and destructively). Does that mean that elucidation of those principles was not creative? Obviously they were valuable and useful as new knowledge and in developing concepts of how things work in nature.

Morgan (1968, 22-32) indicated that people who perform good workmanship, have a knack or flair for doing something well, or who imitate or combine other's ideas are not necessarily creative. His view of creativity rested heavily on taking an unusual quality or attribute from one process or idea and applying it to something else. This shifting of attributes may then lead to a discovery or perception of something new, an innovation or novel way of doing something, synthesizing or making a different mixture of known elements into something new, or a mutation or alteration in the form or qualities of an existing concept or entity.

Throughout this book a broad definition of creativity is assumed to mean:

Having the ability to bring something new into being. Doing things that are original and/or are accomplished in the thinking and psychological processes by which novel products, concepts and understanding are fashioned.

This definition is meant to encompass both the thinking up of new things and the doing of new things. Some have used creative for the former and innovative for the latter (Levitt, cited by Peters and Waterman, 1982).

At times we may create without really thinking seriously about it for it may come from intuition. At other times the process may result from the accumulation of a series of small discoveries, innovations, syntheses or mutations which add up to something quite different. It may often come as a surprise.

1-5 WHO HAS CREATIVE ABILITIES?

We all have creative abilities, but in varying degrees depending upon many factors and experiences in our lives. Perhaps one of the most important aspects of who has creative capabilities is dependent on the encouragement or discouragement of the use of these abilities by others and the motivation and efforts exerted by the individuals themselves.

1-5.1 General Influencing Factors

Just about everything that affects what we are or have experienced while growing up, being educated and living in a society and an environment affects our creative abilities. Some things such as curiosity, imagination, perception, and intuition, as well as many other mental attributes no doubt play a role, but separating whether these are learned or inherent characteristics is extremely difficult. It has been clearly demonstrated that focusing on and being motivated to exercise these properties can help us be more creative.

1-5.2 IQ

In general, to be creative we need to have the ability to form concepts, make unusual associations, accurately recall previous experiences and to imagine and see where various new experiences and pieces fit into our thinking patterns. These things can be done by persons with a wide range of intelligence. Brilliant people are not always innovative (Herzberg, 1987, 183), and occasionally a person with a low IQ demonstrates unbelievable talents. Although a number of studies have shown there is little correlation between creativity and normal or higher levels of intelligence, at lower intelligence levels there generally seems to be a lower level of creative potential. Amabile (1983, 84) attributed at least a part of the reason for this to be the need for background study and experience in order to develop skills in many areas of endeavor. She indicated, however, that traditional intelligence tests do not adequately measure items essential for creativity such as "intrinsic motivation toward the task, and personality dispositions conducive to deep levels of concentration or uninhibited intellectual risk-taking."

1-5.3 Age

A study by Lehman (1953, 324-332) relating age to creative contributions (all subjects were deceased) strongly suggested that maximum creativity occurred before the age of 40 in science, medicine, music, art and literature. This kind of a generalization would not appear to be so completely true today. In fact Osborn (1963, 16-19), in one of the landmark books on creativity, *Applied Imagination*, cited a large number of individuals who made their mark in history well beyond the age of 50. Both came to the conclusion that age was not the major controlling factor, but that desire, effort and motivation were involved.

Factors which appear to make creative efforts more challenging with aging are:

a. Decline in physical vigor.
b. Reduced sensory and motor capacity.
c. Health problems.
d. Marriage, family and personal problems.
e. Concerns with promotion, success, and prestige.
f. Early achievement then resting on laurels (I personally witnessed a case where little was accomplished by a person in a 35-year career following a highly significant early-career contribution).
g. Deadening effects of not receiving recognition.
h. Being enticed to take on ever-widening responsibilities of leadership.
i. Lack of desire or energy present earlier.
j. Inability, fear, or giving up on keeping up with changes.
k. Allowing various diversions to sap our energies.

Amabile (1983, 84-85) indicated that a major reason why peak creative abilities seem to occur at different ages in different fields of endeavor is because "certain domain-relevant skills may be relatively less crucial in some domains than in others." It may take several years for a person in the natural sciences, for example, to gain the education and experience needed to contribute significantly. On the other hand musicians and other artists often produce outstandingly creative works at an early age. Their creativity apparently comes from their inherent traits and skills.

Cotman (1987, 2) reported that the brain is stimulated by use and continues to gather information over its lifetime. The nervous system is the bodily system slowest to decline in functional ability during aging and may still be functioning at 80 to 85 percent normal efficiency at age 85 (Fries and Crapo, 1981, 33).

1-5.4 Experience

One of the advantages of aging is that we accumulate more and more experiences to fuel our imagination and help us develop new concepts. This advantage is lost if we succumb to the various factors of aging and do not maintain the motivation and desire to keep creativity growing, even though the pace may be slowed. Osborn (1963, 19) said:

> Even if our native talent should not grow, our creative ability can keep growing year after year in pace with the effort we put into it.

A real danger of gaining experience is that we may become rigid and inflexible. We are apt to jump to the conclusion too quickly that the situation being presented is the same as a previous one. By doing so we are not taking all the facts into consideration, and are risking a devastating mistake. With aging and experience this tendency may become more a result of our over-confidence than of our growing old.

1-5.5 Sex

Women are often thought to be more intuitive than men. In fact Osborn (1963, 19-22) indicated that in over 1,000 "brainstorming" sessions women consistently came up with more ideas than men did. Yet if this is true, why are there so many more famous men than women? It may be due to the fact that only in this century have we given women a reasonable opportunity to show their creative abilities. Certainly, rearing customs may have some varying impacts on the creative tendencies of both men and women. Likewise, the effects of sex hormones may have differing influencing effects. We can safely predict that the differences between creative abilities of the two sexes would be much smaller than the variations found among individuals of the same sex. In this book both sexes are looked upon as having the same great potential for being creative and innovative.

1-5.6 Education

Education and early home life are two extremely important influences on the development of creativity. In general we are helped a lot by our rearing and educational systems if we are encouraged and granted freedom of thought and the use of imagination. Hopefully, we get to experience good role models and opportunities for practice. Standardization, conformity, and over-restriction can put lifetime dampers on our creative potential. These are discussed in greater detail in Chapter 10.

1-6 CREATIVE TRAITS

What traits must we possess to become maximally creative? One list of characteristics identified in highly creative persons contained 83 items. Many of these would also be found in other persons. Obviously, there were many items listed that are good synonyms for other items. Of course, no particular creative person would be outstanding in all the traits. An excellent short list of characteristics of creative adults compiled by Heinrich (1964, 8-9), but modified and abbreviated, is given in Table 1-1.

MacKinnon (1978, 123-135) listed seven main traits of creative persons. He included:

- intelligence;
- originality;
- independence;
- openness to experience;
- intuitiveness;
- strong theoretical and aesthetic interests; and
- a strong sense of destiny.

Creativity has been considered as a universal characteristic of self-actualizing persons (see Chapter 7-4 for Goble citing of Maslow's creativity-trait list). This list goes beyond defining creativity alone. However, Maslow has indicated that the concept of creativeness and the concept of the healthy, self-actualizing, fully human person seem to be coming closer and closer together, and may turn out to be the same thing. Terms used by Maslow to describe characteristics associated with creativity included flexibility, spontaneity, courage, willingness to make mistakes, openness, and humility.

We can expect that any creative individual will possess only a limited number of the characteristics suggested in the many lists. Thus it is apparent that creative individuals may reflect and fit literally hundreds of descriptions. We do not need match all these items to be creative persons.

1-7 FACTORS ENHANCING CREATIVITY

Amabile (1983, 65-77) suggested a set of component factors which she considered necessary for creative productivity in practically any field. She indicated that the three major categories were examples only and not necessarily a complete list. Her list included:

1. *Domain (field)-relevant skills* which include an individual's total knowledge set, such as factual knowledge, historical, principles, opinions, state-of-the-art, literature, experiences, other fields, etc.; specific field knowledge and technical skills; and innate cognitive abilities, and perceptual and motor skills.

2. *Creativity-relevant skills* which involve the capability of understanding complexities; skill in breaking out of old, traditional, and fixed sets and standards of performance; adept at generating novel ideas and making associations of seemingly unrelated ideas.

3. *Task motivation* which includes intense interest; giving undivided attention to the task; willing to respond to intuition; feeling self-reliant; and being especially resistant to pressure and control of distracting outside factors.

These major categories are addressed in several different ways in subsequent chapters.

With the above ideas of what creativity is and what some of the characteristics of creative individuals are, we should next examine what some of the factors that help promote and enhance creativity are. Repeatedly, over the years of attempting to teach something about creativity and encouraging others to be more creative in the classroom, on the job, and in their personal lives, I have asked participants to list things which increase their creativity. Some of the main categories indicated were:

- An encouraging and challenging atmosphere.
- Feeling good about myself.
- A feeling of self-confidence and relaxed.
- Liking what I am doing.
- Having an opportunity to improve myself and make advances.
- Freedom to manage my own time.
- Being surrounded by open, supportive, positive people.

Table 1-1
Some Characteristics of Creative Adults

1.	Flexible	- Goes beyond the obvious to the new, different, and unusual.
2.	Fluent	- Generates many ideas and comes up with several possible solutions to a problem.
3.	Elaborative	- Can expand and work out details for an idea or a solution.
4.	Tolerant of ambiguity	- Can hold conflicting ideas and values without undue tension.
5.	Original	- Can go beyond commonly accepted ideas to the unusual.
6.	Has broad interests	- Can see the "whole picture"; holds a wide range of interests.
7.	Sensitive	- Is aware of own inner feelings and feelings and thoughts of others.
8.	Curious	- Has the capacity for play, desire to know, and openness to new ideas and experiences.
9.	Independent	- Can think for one's self; make decisions; is self-reliant.
10.	Reflective	- Can consider, evaluate, and understand one's own ideas and the ideas of others.
11.	Action oriented	- Can put ideas into action and help shape that with which one is involved.
12.	Can concentrate	- Can work consistently with deep concentration.
13.	Persistent	- Proceeds with determination and does not give up easily.
14.	Commitment	- Becomes deeply involved and cares.
15.	Expresses a total personality	- Can express dual sides of nature (male & female, intellectual & emotional,etc.).
16.	Sense of humor	- Can use humor to maintain one's balance in life.

Constructed from text of Heinrich, 1964, 8-9. This list of characteristics makes a good creativity evaluation list if one simply rates one's self or others for each characteristic, using a scale of one (for low) to ten (for high).

- Having a considerate superior who involves and trusts me in decision-making and handling my responsibilities.
- Being a part of a progressive, people-oriented, communicative organization.

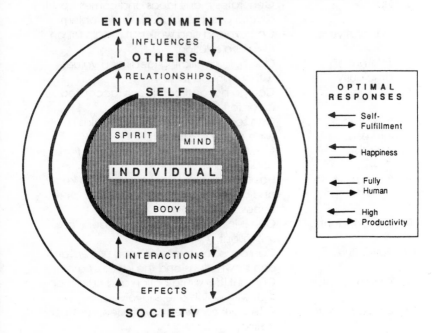

INDIVIDUAL CREATIVITY
Interactions and Responses

Fig.1-1 The Self as the Center of Creativity and the Anticipated Influences and Hoped for Responses

As we glance down this list, it is easy to add other items and other categories. Close examination shows that nearly everything we do and everything we interact with affects our creative abilities in some way. Some increase our creativity, others hinder it. In some instances an enhancing factor for one person may be an impeding factor for another person.

We can get a better notion of the complexity of creativity within the individual if we visualize the various influencing factors that come from the self, from others, and the things thrust upon us by society and the environment (see Figure 1-1).

Some potential interacting factors in each category are listed in Table 1-2. If these interact with each other in many different ways,

it is obvious that thousands of different interactions are possible. No
wonder we have trouble when we try to pinpoint ways to enhance our
own or others' creativity.

Table 1-2
**Potential Interacting Factors Affecting the
Creative Capabilities of the Individual**

SELF	OTHERS	SOCIETY AND ENVIRONMENT
Intellect	Trust	Upbringing
Memory	Respect	Culture
Recall	Acceptance	Nationality
Logic	Tolerance	Customs
Concentration	Dependability	Religion
Concepts	Responsibility	Affluence
Thinking patterns	Understanding	Poverty
Curiosity	Sensitivity	Comfort
Intuition	Compassion	Education
Imagination	Consideration	Community
Perception	Communications	Organizations
Creativity	Cooperation	Institutions
Self-esteem	Flexibility	Government
Self-worth	Honesty	Leadership
Attitudes	Caring	Minority
Emotions	Sharing	Distractions
Feelings	Support	Safety
Discipline	Loving	Climate
Awareness	Sense of humor	Time
Control	Domination	Regulations

1-8 BARRIERS TO CREATIVITY

All sorts of things can produce blocks and hindrances to our
creativity. Many we don't think of as being deterrents to our
capabilities until we examine how they affect us.

1-8.1 Barriers

Blocks, hindrances, impediments, inhibitions, locks or obstacles
to creativity have been classified in many ways by various authors.
Adams (1986) developed a list that he called "blocks." His list
included perceptual, emotional, cultural, environmental, intellectual
and expressive blocks. von Oech (1983) developed a list of 10 major
barriers which he called "mental locks." Morgan (1968) focused

especially on a number of personal emotional blocks or defenses that slow or stop creativity. Whatever way we wish to look at them, they can be considered as "internal" and "external" in origin, but are nearly always manifest by diminishing or blocking our efforts to be creative.

The remainder of this book is devoted to taking a closer look at how various factors affect us and ultimately our organizations and the creative output of both. Listed in Table 1-3 are some of the major kinds of barriers to our creativity that are purposely or unknowingly imposed on us.

Table 1-3
Various Factors that Affect Creativity

• Mental traits	
Capacity, thinking, distortions	(Chap. 2)
Curiosity, intuition, imagination,	
and perception	(Chap. 3)
Discipline, balance,	
and wisdom	(Chaps. 4 & 5)
• Attitudes and emotions	
General emotions	(Chap. 4)
Toward self	(Chaps. 4 & 7)
Toward others	(Chaps. 4 & 8)
• Problem-solving	(Chap. 6)
• Self	(Chaps. 7 & 11)
• Interpersonal relationships	(Chap. 8)
• In teams (groups)	(Chap. 9)
• Culture, education, and society	(Chap. 10)
• Environment	(Chap. 10)
• Management and leadership	(Chap. 12)
• Organizations	(Chap. 13)
• Putting it all together	(Chap. 14)

As we proceed we will first look at the barriers to creativity from the standpoint of those largely controlled by the self, then those that our interpersonal relationships are apt to cause, and finally go to those that develop from the influence on us of society, the environment, management and organizations.

1-8.2 What Can We Expect?

Keep in mind that barriers for some of us may actually be stimuli for others. Perhaps this indicates that a person's own state of mind may be the major controlling factor.

Workshop participants have come to some conclusions regarding what they see themselves facing and what they may have to do to become more creative. Some of their thoughts are recorded here in Table 1-4.

Table 1-4
Some Participants' Thoughts in Facing the Difficulties of Overcoming Blocks to Creativity

1. Must try to learn to deal with ambiguity.
2. Try to have patience with myself and learn to feel I don't have to do everything.
3. Learn to deal with the situation.
4. Realize that I can change some things but not others.
5. Realize that my perception of others may not be valid.
6. Try to increase aggressiveness in promoting creativity, my own, in school's efforts, etc.
7. Get over the feeling that one must necessarily score high all the time.
8. Realize that improvement will likely be mostly within ourselves.
9. Distinguish between professional role creativity and personal role creativity.
10. Must seek and carry out role of reinforcement.
11. Seek to develop more self-confidence.
12. Accept others where they are and help them grow too.

Items selected from lists recorded by workshop participants.

This list could go on and on. Perhaps at this stage we need to realize that becoming more creative is not an easy thing to do. We must recognize that it will take a continuing life-long effort if we are to continue to grow. Avoiding stalling out will be difficult unless we continue to become more creative.

We do have to exert considerable effort and take some risks to become more creative. Furthermore, we will likely have to pay a price if we are to stay creative in whatever endeavor we pursue. Summarized below are some of the aspects that Clark (1980, 53-55) discussed concerning the outlook (in terms of costs and benefits) for creative persons:

The costs of creativity:

1. Creative persons face new frustrations because of increased problem awareness.
2. Creative persons face new frustrations because of

increased opportunity awareness.
3. Creativity adds up to a lot of work.
4. Creativity adds new risks to life.
5. An idea can fail.

The benefits of creativity:

1. A person gets the thrill of making breakthroughs.
2. Persons get the thrill of building something bigger than themselves.
3. A person gets the satisfaction of making new friendships.
4. Creative persons increase their chances for financial reward.
5. Creative persons are much more apt to have broader and fuller lives.

These things suggest that for most people the benefits far outweigh the costs, if we wish a fuller and more rewarding life. Besides, there can be a great deal of fun for us from the challenge along the way.

1-9 HIGHLIGHTS OF CHAPTER ONE

1. Each of us possesses only an infinitesimal knowledge of the universe and what is happening within it. If we are satisfied to learn and practice only enough to survive, we will likely have little or nothing new coming into our lives.
2. Civilization and nature undergo constant and sometimes dramatic changes. To cope with changes we all must be creative.
3. Being creative means having the ability to bring something new into being, to do things that are original and/or are accomplished in the thinking and psychological processes by which new and better products, concepts and understanding are fashioned.
4. If we are creative we are much more apt to have broader, fuller, more challenging and interesting lives than if we are satisfied with "status quo" living.
5. We each have creative abilities and we do not have to be geniuses to be creative and contribute.
6. Blocks, barriers or deterrents to being creative exist everywhere. They are generated by us, ourselves, from the impact of others, and from the society and the environment in which we live.

7. We can avoid or overcome many barriers to creativity if we simply become aware of their impact on us and put forth the effort to resist, deal with or remove them.

1-10 AFTERGROWTH STIMULATORS

1. List the three most significant creative changes of any kind (in general or in your field) that you have witnessed in your lifetime.
2. Did these developments come as the result of contributions from one person? From a team or group? From one major contribution? From a series of small contributions?
3. What do you consider to be the most creative thing you have ever done?
4. What do you consider to be the most challenging problem or opportunity you are facing or have faced recently?
5. What is the greatest barrier to your creativity now?
6. What are you doing to avoid, remove or overcome your greatest creativity barrier?

CHAPTER 2

BRAIN POWER: THE BASE
- INTELLIGENCE

2- 1   Introduction
2- 2   The Importance of Intelligence
2- 3   Mental Powers
2- 4   Memory and Learning
2- 5   Thinking
2- 6   Concentration
2- 7   Mental Capabilities
2- 8   Free or Creative Thinking
         Versus Fixed Thinking
2- 9   Styles of Thinking
2-10   Mental Distortions As Blocks
2-11   Highlights of Chapter Two
2-12   Aftergrowth Stimulators

2-1 INTRODUCTION

For decades we have been attempting to understand how our intelligence and other mental capabilities function. We have been searching for clues as to how we think, learn and remember. We have wondered what our mental capacities are and what roles these capacities play in the process of memorization and our ability to make free associations. Understanding some of these functions should aid us in developing and enhancing our creative capabilities, as well as learning how to break through or avoid the hundreds of barriers to creativity that we encounter in everyday life.

2-2 THE IMPORTANCE OF INTELLIGENCE

Although many of our physiological and anatomical attributes are similar to those of many other mammals, our apparently greater intelligence, objective perception, realization of self-existence and the power of abstract reasoning are characteristics that set us apart from the animals. Great emphasis is placed on the importance of intelligence for people to survive and deal with the complexities of the world.

Dale (1964) pointed out in an article on "Who Has the Power?" that there are several kinds of power. He cited the power of knowledge, the power of thinking, and the power of heroic example. He asserts that those who stand out in these categories possess a deep concern for ordinary people, the power of creativeness, the determination not to follow precedents, and a devotion to the truth with a willingness to follow it where it leads.

The first of the above tends to focus on the intellectual side, and is discussed in this chapter. The second, thinking, also is dealt with from the intellectual aspect in this chapter; then more from the intuitive and feeling aspects in Chapters 3, and 4. The third, heroic example, involves concern for people and the impact of interpersonal relationships which are dealt with in Chapters 8, 9, and several other chapters in a number of different ways.

2-3 MENTAL POWERS

The brain is the message center and controlling organ of all voluntary and involuntary actions within the human body and mind. Many chemical reactions take place in the brain and throughout the body as the nervous system transmits its messages.

2-3.1 Brain Structure

The average human brain contains somewhere between 20 to 200 billion individual neurons or nerve cells. Each neuron can interact in many ways with 1,000 or more other neurons (Crick, 1979, 130). Thus the number of interactions possible within the human brain becomes astronomical (Buzan, 1974; Teyler, in Whittrock, 1977, 16-17). The brain has the capacity to take in, process and program more than 600 memories per second for 75 or more years. That is 36,000 per minute - 51,840,000 in 24 hours (Schultz, 1974).

2-3.2 How Much Brain Do We Really Need?

An interesting observation by a British neurologist, John Lorber, (reported on by Lewin, 1980) raised the question of the amount of brain tissue necessary for normal functioning. Lorber observed a young university student with very little brain tissue who had an IQ of 126 and had obtained a first class honors degree in mathematics and appeared to be socially normal.

The student was a hydrocephalic. A brain scan showed that he had a thin layer of brain tissue measuring a millimeter (0.04 inch) or so compared to our normal 4.5 centimeters (1.75 inches). This observation suggests that we must posses a tremendous amount of spare capacity in our brain. Further corroboration of this phenomena is shown by the fact that some hydrocephalics do not show one-sided paralysis. A surprising number of patients appear to escape functional impairment in spite of a grossly abnormal brain structure.

2-3.3 Suggested Structure of Intellect

In an attempt to describe and define the structure of intellect, Guilford (1967), and Guilford and Hoepfner (1971) developed a three-dimensional model of intellect. These dimensions included:

1. Operational. The functional parameters of our mental powers involving:

    a. Cognition - discovery, awareness, rediscovery, recognition of information, and understanding and comprehension;

    b. Memory - the ability to store information;

    c. Divergent production - development of variety, quantity, transfer, and creative potential;

d. Convergent production - using given information to generate new information, depending upon the given cue information; and

e. Evaluation - making judgments and reaching decisions, correctness, suitability, adequacy and desirability.

2. Contents. This dimension is divided into four major types of information including:

a. Figural - concrete forms or images;

b. Symbolic - signs or symbols with no significance in and of themselves, but denoting certain other things;

c. Semantic - denoting meanings to which words commonly become attached and may even be conveyed by meaningful pictures; and

d. Behavioral - usually essentially nonverbal interactions such as attitudes, needs, desires, moods, intentions, perceptions or thoughts of others as well as the individual involved.

3. Products. The results of processing information include six categories:

a. Units - individual items or things;

b. Classes - sets of items;

c. Relations - points of contact and connections;

d. Systems - organized or structured aggregates with complexes of interrelated or interacting parts;

e. Transformations - shifting existing information or changes in its functions; and

f. Implications - connections, extrapolation, expectancies, predictions, known or suspected antecedents, concomitant, or consequences.

2-4 MEMORY AND LEARNING

For many years attempts have been made to learn how the memory and learning functions of the brain actually work. These are still not well understood.

2-4.1 Memory Functions

There appears to be no evidence that there is a limit to the long-term memory capabilities nor on the number of distinguishable symbols that our brain can store. The informational processing system involved in memory consists of long-term memory, short-term memory, and external memory (Newell and Simon, 1972).

As we learn, certain stimuli from the various input channels cause the development of particular symbols which are recognizable. These recognizable stimulus patterns are called "chunks." It appears that the first step in the informational processing system is one of short-term memory (STM) which has a very small capacity. The short-term memory capacity in symbols or equivalent chunks seems to be limited to about five or seven symbols (think of the difficulty in remembering more than the ordinary seven digit telephone number). This restriction seems to be fairly consistent over a wide range of tasks. (A few notable exceptions indicate that perhaps as many as 70 items of recall, apparently associated with short-term memory, have been reported. Fincher, 1981, 81-89).

Information in our short-term memory decays rapidly or is overridden by interference among symbols. It thus must move fairly quickly from short-term memory into long-term memory or be lost. Some experiments suggest that it takes five to 10 seconds of processing time for us to store a symbolized stimulus in our long-term memory. Our recognition and retrieval processes in long-term memory apparently take from 0.5 second to a second or a little more.

Much of our difficulty in doing mathematical problems mentally results from the slow write times of our internal long-term memory and the small storage capacity of our short-term memory. Supplying an external memory (EM) can greatly enhance our problem-solving capabilities. External memory items consist of such things as paper, charts, chess boards, books, etc. It is not known precisely how the EM augments our STM, but the two seem to become a single functional unit in a problem-solving situation.

2-4.2 Remembering and Forgetting

The preceding brief account on short and long-term memory suggests some possible mechanisms on how our brain accumulates information. However, specifically how this occurs is still obscure. In some way our brain must receive messages via the several sensory perception routes (see Perception in Chapter 3), or through the intuitive route (see Intuition in Chapter 3). These are then processed and stored by our brain.

Although there is no known limit to the capacity of the human brain, despite many studies on the subject over the last century, it is still a puzzle how our recall of stored information is brought about. It is believed that our memory storage in some way involves chemical change, for an increase of RNA, ribonucleic acid, occurred in the brain cells of laboratory animals after learning had taken place (Fincher, 1981). This suggests that protein formation may be involved in some way.

Memory is our record of experiences. From this record we can recall, correct, add to, and realign and restore facts and concepts, thus learning the essentials needed for survival and growth. It is believed that many of our retrieval cues work unconsciously, following some triggering factor, such as occurs intuitively when we are asleep or not even concentrating on a particularly related thought during the day. Of course, we can trigger a deliberate stimulus as our minds pursue thoughts or seek to recall something.

We are fortunate that we can forget. Imagine what trouble we would have if all of the signals and perceptions we received each day remained stored in the forefront of our minds. There is an account of a Russian back in the 1920's who literally could not forget. It was shown upon a series of tests that his memory had no distinct limits. He could recall numbers or words in tables with as many as 70 items in them. Many years later when he was retested, he recalled the same tables - in the original order, backwards and diagonally (Fincher, 1981, 86). He had difficulties dealing with life and finally had to resort to showing off his unusual abilities to make a living.

How well do we remember after being presented with certain information? Much depends upon the rate at which it is presented. Sufficient time must be allowed and a definite effort must be made to get the information through our short-term memory and stored in our long-term memory. Buzan (1976, 56) presented a curve of our rate of loss of recall and the effects of review on our memory (see Fig. 2-1). Unfortunately, we forget 75 to 80 percent of the details within 24 hours if we make no review. With a review 10 minutes after the presentation of new material and reviews one day, one week, one month and six months afterward, we can recall most of what was recalled 10 minutes after it was received.

Buzan (1976, 52) also showed the effect of breaks every 20 to 40 minutes during a two hour learning period (as from a book, lecture, or mass media) on our ability to recall (see Fig. 2-2). Learning for a continuous period of more than two hours caused our recall ability to drop from a 75 to 80 percent starting level to 35

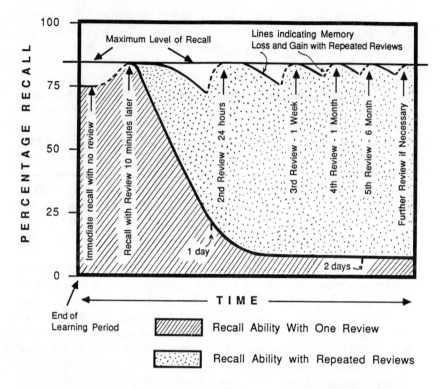

Fig. 2-1 Graphic Representation of Percentage of Recall with the Passage of Time with and without Reviews
(Adapted from Buzan, 1974, 56)

percent at the end. With a continuous two-hour period our recall was about 60 percent. With two hours broken every 20 to 40 minutes, our recall remained near the 75 to 80 percent level. Many kinds of change of pace, altered activity, discussion, humor, etc. can serve as a break.

2-5 THINKING

Although we still do not know just how the thinking process works, much attention has been given for many years to learning about some of the things that help and other things that tend to impair our thinking.

2-5.1 The Thinking Process

Branden (1969, 111-112) has characterized our ability to think

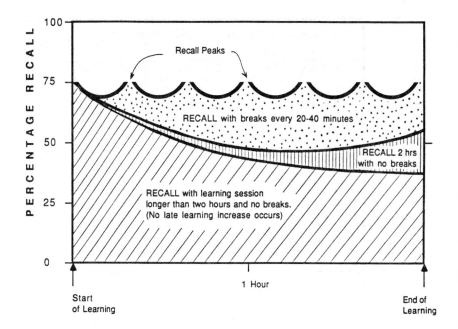

Fig. 2-2 Effect of Learning Period Breaks Every 20 to 40 Minutes on Recall and Understanding (Adapted from Buzan, 1974, 52)

and reason not only as a major factor differentiating us from animals, but also as our basic means of survival. He pointed out that thinking and reasoning are volitional. We can choose to initiate and sustain a sharp mental focus and try to understand at a high level of precision and clarity. Or, we can choose to remain in a state of passive, undiscriminating, goalless mental drifting. We can usually differentiate between knowledge and feelings and choose whether to let our judgment be guided by intellect or by emotions. Usually we can also decide what is right or wrong in most issues, or we can remain uncritically passive and accept the opinion of others without questioning.

Most dictionaries define thinking with several action verbs: to form in the mind, conceive, imagine, reason, cogitate, meditate, contemplate, or muse. Dale (1970) said:

> To think is to connect things up, to search for and discover hidden relationships, to judge, to evaluate, to generate hypotheses and follow them up.
>
> An educated person thinks in terms of cause and effect (and) reads not chiefly to remember but to reflect (and) thinks to

develop a form for formless experience, to establish connections for unorganized or disorganized experiences (and tries) to connect up his life experiences to find out where he has been, where he is now, and where he is going.

Thinking enhances our ability to analyze problems, see opportunities, make decisions, propose solutions, and determine what actions to take.

2-5.2 Concept or Construct Mapping

As indicated above, as we think and learn, bits and chunks of information are fed into our brains for processing and storage. Specific information is thought to be processed into concepts (referred to by some as constructs or maps) and stored, thus becoming a recorded experience. Our consciousness then consists of our own construct and record of the incoming information. As Ornstein (1972) said:

> Each person can change his consciousness simply by changing the way he constructs it.

Gowin's (1981, 29) definition was:

> A concept is a sign/symbol pointing toward regularities (patterns) in events, or to records of events. Concepts are usually words, terms, ingredients in sentences and propositions. They may be number concepts, of course, or concepts carried by other symbols (such as musical notations, etc.). But the key thing about concepts is their office of signifying regularities. Concepts are centrally important to us because people think with concepts.

If incoming information fits into, adds to, conflicts with, or differs entirely from a previously stored concept then we have to choose how to fit it into our concept map or personal construct. Gowin (1981, 96) said:

> Constructs are simply ideas that help to hold key concepts together.

Concept maps can be constructed to link a series of related things. Novak and Gowin (1984, 15) indicated that:

> Concept maps are intended to represent meaningful relationships between concepts in the form of propositions.

We can visualize such maps in our minds or use them as a good learning procedure by diagramming them. For example: Water is made of molecules (molecules are in motion), can change to different states (liquid, solid, or gas), is needed by living things (animals and plants), etc. Concept mapping frequently leads us to develop additional related concepts.

2-5.3 Right and Left-Brained Thinking

The two sides of the brain, the right hemisphere and left hemisphere, have come to be known to be involved differently in the thinking process. Left-brain thinking is usually associated with thinking that is logical, analytical, mathematical, technical, and with linear and sequential processing. It is usually referred to as controlled, conservative, planful, and administrative. Thus it has been traditionally linked with law, order, reason, logic, and mathematics. This type of thinking is usually associated in many ways with science, knowledge, and with organizing and planning. Tools, discipline and achievement have come to be symbolic of left-brain thinking individuals.

The right side of the brain dominates in our nonverbal ideation, intuition, holistic and synthesizing thinking, spacial, visual, and simultaneous processing. This type of thinking is considered to be conceptual, interpersonal, emotional, artistic, and symbolic. Terms such as beauty, sensitivity, playfulness, feeling, openness, and imagery are used in describing individuals dominated by right-brained thinking. This type of thinking results in art, music, expression, and seeing the whole picture.

A number of early considerations of creativity emphasized the need for right-brain thinking. This was likely because of the linkage with imagination and intuition. More recent studies have emphasized our need for whole-brain functioning for maximum creativity (Hermann, 1981). Both sides need to be working together and interacting to accomplish the several steps necessary in creative problem-solving. A consideration of the steps in creative problem-solving involving interest, preparation, incubation, illumination, verification, and exploitation make it obvious that the process has both left-brained and right-brained phases and that functioning of our brain as a whole is essential. Jerison (1977) quoted from work of Broadbent who had said that:

> The two hemispheres must be seen...as performing different parts of an integrated performance, rather than completely separate and parallel functions.

2-6 CONCENTRATION

Concentration means a focused kind of thinking or in some .

respects, convergent thinking as opposed to divergent or broad thinking. We attempt to fix, center, collect, and/or gather our thoughts on a particular issue. In essence it is a process in which we attempt to draw things together to find common events and determine the key aspects.

Learning to focus our minds is not an easy process, particularly if we have not been in the habit of doing so. If we push too hard to try to concentrate, we may actually impair rather than speed up the thinking process. Often focusing too narrowly can be produced by or associated with tension, competitiveness, repression, anxiety, inhibition, or over-active goal seeking. Thus we can learn to concentrate without over-concentrating only with experience and in an unhurried atmosphere. To be really effective we need to be free of our own distracting thoughts as well as free from extraneous distractions.

Efforts focused on "developing the concentration necessary for awakening intuition work best when they are combined with relaxation training," according to Vaughan (1979, 11). Gowin (1981, 136) said, "Students who are in the habit of seeking and using high-level concepts in their studies tend not to complain about an inability to concentrate."

2-7 MENTAL CAPABILITIES

Although research has shown that there is little correlation between IQ and creative capabilities, it almost goes without saying that in most instances creative persons need a large memory bank of experiences and knowledge from which new ideas can be synthesized. In addition to intellect, however, many other mental aspects have been shown to be highly contributory to creative capabilities. A willingness to use our mental capacity will often permit us (even if we have a lesser intelligence rating) to outperform an individual with a higher rating. Von Fange (1959) said:

It is not sufficient to merely accumulate and have on tap that knowledge and understanding to perform our job. We must continuously accumulate new knowledge and search for new ways of adapting it to our use.

Even if we have high intelligence, we may not always have a high level of curiosity. Likewise, we may be lacking in imagination or, as Hoagland (1968) pointed out, "putting imagination in action to result in creativity" may not flourish. Our ability to perceive and conceptualize situations or to associate the unusual may be lacking. At other times we may lack flexibility or may be too critical and judicious. Yet without being critical of ourselves, and without being judicious at some stage of the development, much time can be lost following an erroneous approach. Lack of discipline and an inability to concentrate may also be major factors in diminishing the use of our intelligence. As discussed in subsequent chapters, emotions are probably a very great factor in our ability to think.

Table 2-1
Some Generally Desirable Mental Capabilities of the Potentially Creative "Whole Person" Scientist (Individual)

Capabilities	
Intellectually sharp	A rapid learner
Capable of good recall	Able to concentrate
Willing to think	Able to associate the unusual
Perceptive	Imaginative
Creative	Curious
Intuitive	Flexible
Fluent	Critical
Mentally agile	Judicious

Constructed from text of VanDemark, 1979, 8.

Some important mental capabilities of a potentially creative "whole-person" scientist (VanDemark, 1979, 8), are presented in Table 2-1. These capabilities would seem to apply generally and equally well to creative individuals in most fields.

2-8 FREE OR CREATIVE THINKING VERSUS FIXED THINKING

The issue of how we can best teach individuals to think has long been debated. Is it necessary for us to have learning experiences in which we each learn to think in our own style, or should procedures and facts merely be memorized for future reference? More than just memorizing facts is needed if we are to be really creative and innovative.

2-8.1 Ideal Goals

American school systems have long had basic goals of developing rational powers and the ability to think. This has been combined with a dedication "to foster the development of individual capacities which will enable each human being to become the best person he is capable of becoming," (Education Policies Commission, 1961, 1). This Commission also declared, "Because the principal goal of the American society remains freedom, the requirements of freedom set the frame within which the school can discover the central focus of its own efforts." As laudable as these high ideals may be, there remains a constant struggle to achieve them. Freedom of the mind is something we each must develop for ourselves. Society needs to supply the environment and circumstances (and encouragement) in which we have the opportunity to attain "freedom of the mind." As indicated in a number of places in this book, educational systems, society and environment (Chapter 10), management (Chapter 12), and organizations and institutions (Chapter 13), impose many constraints upon those of us who are striving to exercise freedom of thought.

2-8.2 Freedom to Choose

Thinking is a matter of choice for us. It may be controlled largely by the individual or greatly influenced by others. Having control of our mental activities is essential to proper survival. However, this capability is not automatic nor insured by nature. We must choose to focus the mind and must try to understand. We must be aware, see things clearly and intelligibly if our ability to think about a specific issue or problem is to be maintained. Each of us has the choice of focusing or not focusing, thinking or not thinking, and in this sense, each of us is psychologically free (see Chapter 5-5).

To know what our mind is doing, and to be in full mental focus, to think, to judge the issues being confronted, we must make knowing what we are doing and the reasons why a natural process. Most of us know only too well what Vaughan (1979, 12) pointed out:

Tension and anxiety interfere with learning of any kind.

At any given moment, we may be so overcome by a violent emotion that it becomes impossible to think clearly. However, we usually know that by deferring action until our minds have cleared, thinking can begin again.

Reasoning consists of two basic functions, namely, cognition and evaluation. Cognition consists of discovering what things are, identifying the attributes and properties they have, and then determining their nature. Evaluation consists of discovering the relationship of things to one's self and deciding what is beneficial, what is harmful, what should be sought, and what should be avoided. Our emotions are the product of our rationality. Thus they cannot be understood without reference to the conceptual power of our consciousness. Unfortunately some fail to see the need. They think only as a last resort. If we fall into such a habit, we are apt to find that the opportunity for the best choice is gone. Thus, staying alert to what is happening around us needs to be taken as a high priority for survival and avoiding many troublesome and discouraging events. Black (1948, 232) wrote an excellent satirical article on "Principles of Really Sound Thinking" in which he emphasized the folly of thinking only as a last resort, and completely trusting our own feelings. Thus in making choices, in some instances, we need to learn all we can from others, and then trust thinking and logic and avoid being driven by emotions.

2-8.3 Directed or Conditioned Thinking

Some refer to directed learning as rote learning. Novak and Gowin (1984, 7) have described rote learning saying:

New knowledge may be acquired simply by verbatim memorization and arbitrarily incorporated into our knowledge structure without interacting with what is already there.

Directed thinking may be considered ordinary, fixed, memorization, mimicking, rote, or fact-stuffing. Many of these are associated with training or the practice to gain a skill or facility, to educate narrowly. Often, other persons try to direct exactly how we should think, which, of course, is not possible.

There is a great tendency in our attempt to teach and develop mental capabilities to push individuals through the directed-thinking route. As a result the educational process all too frequently becomes one of forced conformity, uniformity and standardization which squelches our individual desires to learn (see Chapter 10).

2-8.4 Creative or Free Thinking

Free thinking may be thought of as - extraordinary, creative, imaginative, innovative, associative, and problem-solving. It is divergent thinking, and leads us to think broadly. Novak and Gowin (1984, 7) refer to this type of thinking as leading to meaningful learning. It is learning in which:

Individuals must choose to relate new knowledge to relevant concepts and propositions they already know.

Is this not more educative than directed and conditioned thinking? Do we not learn to develop, cultivate, and discipline our minds more effectively? Note the comparative aspects pointed out by VanDemark (1979) in Table 2-2.

Table 2-2
Characteristic Results of Directed Versus Creative Thinking

Directed <————————— Thinking—————————> Creative

Directed	Creative
Status quo	Change
Conformity	Nonconformity
Nonflexibility	Flexibility
Immobility	Mobility
Locked in	Freedom
Set beliefs	New concepts
Fixed ideas	New theories
Limitations	No known limits
Habits	Dreams
Prejudices	Open-mindedness
Accepted opinions	New views
Dogmatism	Discovery
Application	Abstraction
80 to 90 percent <— SOCIETY —————>	20 to 10 percent
20 to 10 percent <— ARTS & SCIENCES —>	80 to 90 percent

Constructed from text of VanDemark, 1979, 11.

2-8.5 Results of Directed Versus Creative Thinking

To be balanced individuals we must use both directed and free thinking. We cannot become a biochemist who can solve biochemical problems and synthesize new medicines without a great deal of directed learning. There are basic aspects of chemistry and mathematics that must be mastered. However, just memorizing chemical formulas and knowing the principles of mathematics, etc. will not necessarily make us competent in the field.

As competent individuals in most fields (whether it be in the arts, sciences, skilled crafts, social sciences, etc.), we must be able to think creatively. We must be able to generate new ideas and have the ability to visualize what may be possible. We must be curious, energetic, questioning individuals, who can take ideas from widely different fields and perhaps come up with new concepts, breakthroughs, principles and new discoveries. We must be willing to constantly challenge the status quo, and must be ever critical of our own and other's theories, products, etc. The proportion of fixed learning and the amount of free and creative thinking and learning we need will vary a great deal in different fields. We can speculate that a much higher proportion of free and creative thinking is demanded in the arts, sciences, etc. However, in many fields we will need a host of basic facts from the experience of others. Practice may also play an extremely significant role.

Ordinary persons can probably exist in an everyday society with a lesser amount of creative thinking than would be essential if we want to be an artist or a scientist. However, even everyday living affords all kinds of opportunities for finding challenging, creative ways of living, learning, and developing better interpersonal relationships. New and easier ways of doing things are a constant challenge in society. Unfortunately, millions live in an atmosphere where the greatest challenge they face is just surviving with little opportunity of being creative.

2-9 STYLES OF THINKING.

Most of the time no two of us think exactly alike. Our perception of things, our past experiences and the concepts we have formed are bound to come into play affecting our thinking process and likely our thinking style.

2-9.1 General Thinking Styles

Harrison and Bramson (1982, 8-17) suggested that we follow one, or a combination of two (seldom more) general thinking styles. They offered five major categories:

1. Synthesist - persons who like to combine different things or ideas, be speculative, look for the best fit, link seemingly contradictory views, like change, become bored with status quo and routine, often disagree. Their favorite question is, "What if ....?"

2. Idealist - persons who like to take a broad view of things, pay attention to people's needs, are interested in social and ethical values, are future oriented, agree on goals, welcome a diversity of views, seen as helpful, open, supportive, trustworthy. Their common question is, "Where are we going and

why?"
3. Pragmatist - persons who like freedom from consistency, good at making do, approach problems piecemeal, do one thing at a time, look for shortcuts and quick payoffs, their approach may appear superficial, erratic and lacking in standards, want to be liked and accepted, are adaptive. Their motto is, "Whatever works."
4. Analyst - persons who approach problems carefully, logically methodically, collect information and plan carefully, analyze and judge things, have theories about nearly everything, prefer rationality, stability, and predictability, concentrate on objective data, procedure, and method, take pride in their competence. Their motto is essentially, "Find the best way."
5. Realist - persons who are almost complete opposites of the synthesist, are empiricists, believe what is real can be felt, smelled, touched, seen, heard, observed or experienced, believe people ought to agree, try to correct and make solutions to problems last, need to achieve, to move, to be in control, are often impatient. Their motto is, "Facts are facts."

The above illustrate well that individuals differ in the amount of attention that is given to a situation. Some focus on specific features, others tend to look at the whole general problem. Thus, for some the thinking processes are rather loose, in others they are quite precise.

2-9.2 Critical Versus Creative Thinking

Anderson (1980, 65-67) referred to our more precise thinking as "critical thinking or reasoning." He pointed out that critical thinking focuses on judging what is probable and what is improbable. He indicated that the central ingredient in close or critical thinking is doubt and a reluctance to believe. He said:

Doubt should express itself in at least two ways: a reluctance to believe that you have taken all the important elements of the problem into account and a reluctance to believe that you have understood correctly the way in which the elements are related to one another.

Often, especially in the midst of a problem, it may mean constant and thorough questioning. However, we must take care that this does not develop into worrying and holding back in the fear that we might make a mistake.

Creative thinking is more loose and associative than critical thinking. It is more concerned with generating ideas that are original or unusual. It may involve conceiving what may be possible, which Anderson describes as "getting our minds to work forward." It should include developing several possible approaches to seizing the opportunity or solving the problem. Then critical thinking should be used to decide on which approach is considered the best. We obviously use both critical and creative thinking in many of our endeavors.

2-10 MENTAL DISTORTIONS AS BLOCKS

Thinking, understanding, and knowing are all essential for us to be creative. If any of these processes are faulty or distorted, then our well-being and abilities are diminished or maybe even blocked. Burns (1980, 40-41) described a number of cognitive distortions that we may develop which then result in depression and suppressed abilities to think. Many of these distortions are the result of negative thinking and a lack of self-confidence and self-esteem (see Chapter 7-3 for further discussion of these). These distortions thus affect creativity. Some descriptions and interpretations of ten major categories from Burns' list are paraphrased in the following:

1. All-or Nothing Thinking: Things are viewed as extremes, if our performance is less than perfect, we consider ourselves absolute failures. We seem to be unable to realistically assess and evaluate situations in which we are involved.
2. Overgeneralization: We tend to view a single negative event as a pattern of never ending defeat.
3. Mental Filter: We tend to dwell on a single negative detail to the point where it blocks and blurs our vision of all reality. As a result, our entire spectrum is darkened and maybe even distorted.
4. Disqualifying the Positive: We discredit our positive experiences and insist that, for some reason or other, they don't count. We hold to a negative belief that negates our everyday experiences.
5. Jumping to Conclusions: We tend to immediately jump to negative conclusions without real evidence to support our conclusions.
   a. Mind Reading - Without any evidence we conclude that others are, or will, react against us. We don't bother to verify this.
   b. The Fortune Teller Error - We are always anticipating that things are going to turn out negatively, and we are convinced that our anticipation is already an established fact.
6. Magnification (Catastrophizing) or Minimization: We tend to over-estimate the importance of things (such as our mistakes

or someone else's accomplishments), or we minimize things until they appear tiny (our own good qualities or the faults of others). Burns refers to this as the "binocular trick" (looking through in reverse).

7. Emotional Reasoning: Because of our negative feelings, we assume that is the way things really are. Because we feel it, it must be true.

8. Should Statements: We think we have to constantly push and punish ourselves with should's and shouldn't's, in order to get anything done. (Musts and oughts are also offenders). As a result we constantly feel guilty. When we find it necessary to direct should statements toward others, we feel anger, frustration, and resentment.

9. Labeling and Misleading (extreme forms of overgeneralization): We tend to negatively label ourselves as "losers," instead of labeling and describing our mistakes. We also negatively label others when they rub us the wrong way, rather than describing their behavior. We are likely to mislabel an event by using language that is highly colored and emotionally loaded.

10. Personalization: We tend to blame ourselves as the cause of negative external events, even though we were in no way involved.

Further evidence, indicating that the way we think affects the way we feel, has been presented by Schmidt (1980, 38-62). He discussed how persons react if they have fixed patterns of thinking about themselves and the world around them. He cited such persons as those with paranoid, obsessive, or hysterical thinking patterns. These, obviously, greatly affect our abilities to think creatively. These are discussed more extensively in the chapter on Society and Environment, under the section dealing with "difficult people," (see Chapter 10-7.2).

2-11 HIGHLIGHTS OF CHAPTER TWO

1. Our creative ability is highly dependent upon our brain power, but more than just IQ is involved.

2. There appears to be no known limit to the long term storage capacity of the human brain.

3. It is estimated that, as average persons, we use no more than 10 to 15 percent of our brain capacity.

4. Usually we forget about 80 percent of the details of a learning situation in the first 24 hours after exposure unless we make

periodic reviews afterward.

5. Regular breaks during and frequent reviews after a learning exposure can greatly enhance our capacity to remember.
6. Our ability to think and reason is a major characteristic that differentiates us from animals.
7. Our ability to think is volitional; we can choose to focus the mind and try to understand, or we can remain passive and uncritical.
8. Both sides of our brain contribute to creative ability, but we need to exercise more of our intuitive and imaginative right side to help balance off the usually dominant logical left side.
9. We need to think laterally (think broadly) as well as vertically (think deeply) to be more creative.
10. A high proportion of our "school" learning is fixed or directed thinking and emphasizes memorization, rote, mimicking and fact-stuffing.
11. While fixed thinking is essential for us, intuition, imagination, and free-thinking are required for maximum creativity.
12. We vary greatly in our styles of thinking because we each tend to focus differently on various aspects of a situation.
13. Mental distortions and blocks are detrimental to our being creative.

2-12 AFTERGROWTH STIMULATORS

1. What percentage of your brain power would you estimate you have been using? Do you think you could increase that percentage? If you could double it, what might the results be?
2. Have you ever felt you were not smart enough to be creative? After reading this chapter, can you now see that intelligence may not be nearly as important for you as overcoming some other barriers?
3. Have you been relying too much on memorization and directed thinking rather than forming concepts and using free thinking of your own in solving problems, seizing opportunities, and being creative?
4. Have you tried to think carefully in defining and stating the challenging problem or opportunity you used in your response to question 4 at the end of Chapter 1? What has happened?
5. If you had the opportunity to work with a group of lower IQ persons, how would you go about getting them to think more, be more creative, be more self-reliant and more productive?

CHAPTER 3

BRAIN POWER: THE SPARKS
- CURIOSITY, INTUITION,
IMAGINATION AND PERCEPTION

3- 1   Introduction
3- 2   Curiosity
3- 3   Intuition
3- 4   Imagination
3- 5   Perception
3- 6   Serendipity
3- 7   Highlights of Chapter Three
3- 8   Aftergrowth Stimulators

3-1 INTRODUCTION

We all admire the "flash of genius," but usually seem to think that great accomplishments come only from those we refer to as geniuses. No doubt a great deal of intellect is usually possessed by those who do unusually creative things, but many outstanding feats have been the products of ordinary persons. We often say such persons are more perceptive. Is that true, or what attributes or knowledge do these people possess that allow them to exhibit such bursts of unusual thinking and imagination? Can we, as ordinary people, increase our curiosity, intuition, imagination and perception? Are we born with these traits? Are they learned? Do they increase if we cultivate and nurture them?

3-2 CURIOSITY

It is a long-known fact that the drive of curiosity is basic throughout the animal kingdom. We must be born with curiosity, for all normal newborn respond in ways verifying that they are curious soon after birth. Hoagland (1968) has said:

There is good evidence from well controlled experiments that the drive to explore for its own sake is a primary reason for learning and a foundation for creativity.

He went on to say that this drive is quite apart from seeking food rewards or escaping from painful situations. He also stated that:

A good case can be made for the view that man's concern with science, philosophy, political ideologies, and theologies is a reflection of a basic property of the nervous system integrating extensive environmental configurations in relation to the organism.

Curiosity, doubt and a healthy skepticism are, or become, key attributes if we as youngsters, and even as adults, are to continue to grow.

We should maintain a constant curiosity and doubt about things going on around us, if we desire to grow and be creative. This should include standard practices and procedures. Because something is printed, because some authority has said so, or because something is a long established standard practice, does not necessarily make it true, the best, the cheapest, the easiest or the preferred. Being curious and seeking proof of the truth is especially required of the scientist, as well as for most of the rest of us.

3-3 INTUITION

Over the years, I have often gone to sleep at night puzzling over how I should react or proceed in the face of a knotty problem, only to awaken the next morning with a clear "gut feeling" indicating what I should do to cope with the problem. To be sure I had given much thought to alternatives before going to sleep without any hint of what I ought to do, but the answer was there when I awakened. I do not know how or from where the answers came, but they often were mysteriously there and usually unquestionably good. I can only conclude that it must have been intuition.

The power of knowing or of attaining direct knowledge or cognition without rational thought and inference, direct perception of truths, and quick and ready insight are some of the definitions of intuition given us by dictionaries. The word is derived from the Latin *intueri*, which means to look at or contemplate from within. We often refer to this as being our "gut feeling." In many respects intuition is "The voice from within." Some consider and refer to it as "Divine guidance."

Intuition is something that most of us know about, but we often think of it as being possessed by others, especially by women, but not so strongly by men. Vaughan (1979, 3) indicated that intuition plays a vital role in our creativity, in our problem solving, and in our interpersonal relationships. But we often misunderstand, discount and mistrust it. She believed that everyone has intuition, but that it is more highly developed in some than in others. She also believed that intuition can be awakened and made more useful to us if we cultivate an awareness of the possibilities it offers and exercise our own intuitive abilities. For this to occur we must learn to listen and respond to the "voice from within," that is there for each of us.

Vaughan (1979), a psychologist, indicated that human intuitive experiences fall into four distinct levels of awareness: physical, mental, emotional and spiritual. Physical is associated with bodily sensations, mental with images and ideas, emotional with feelings, and spiritual with a knowledge of God.

Intuition originates spontaneously from within us. Thus as Vaughan (p. 10) said:

Awakening intuition is not about "getting more"; it is about "being more" who you really are.

She indicated that Carl Jung has characterized intuition as the function that explores the unknown, and senses possibilities and implications which may not be readily apparent. She stated that:

Intuition perceives what is hidden, and thus enables one to perceive obscure meanings in symbolic imagery, or subconscious motives in oneself and in others. It is also associated with insight, or the ability to understand the dynamics of a personality or situation (pp.47-48).

It is believed to be mainly a right brain function. Intuition helps us to draw on the vast storehouse of hidden knowledge which includes everything that we have learned consciously or subliminally. To tap this resource we must temporarily hold critical judgment in abeyance. This does not mean that we turn judgment off completely, for checking the validity of intuitive perceptions and evaluating the processes involved are still necessary.

We cannot force the process of intuition. Even our efforts to push too hard for intuitive answers may interfere with the whole process. However, even though we cannot force and make intuition happen, Vaughan suggested that there are several things that we can do to help allow it to happen. Among a number of items which she suggested are relaxation, meditation, open focus and imagination to a point where we lose attention and preoccupation with time. Also our receptivity to all kinds of experiences, a "noninterfering alert awareness maintained in the midst of the inner world of sensations, emotions and ideas," our receptivity to images, and the elimination of our desire for ego gratification are all important. She summarized these and others into three major steps:

1. Quieting the mind.
2. Learning to focus attention or concentrate on that aspect of reality that one chooses to contact at a particular time.
3. Cultivation of a receptive, nonjudgmental attitude that allows intuition to come into conscious awareness without interference (p. 34).

The first step we should initiate in taking advantage of possible intuitive revelations is to be receptive and utilize an expanding awareness of our feelings, hunches, or presentments. The second step is a critical one, and involves our reason and choice and the decision of whether or not to act on our feelings or hunches (p.27).

We then must recognize and act on choice. We also must believe in it. This is true for intuition as well. It will become real and work when we are consciously aware of it. At the unconscious level it functions for us like instinct. As we become more aware of it, we then are more capable of tuning in and acting on it. As we act on it, it becomes an effective factor in life. When reacting automatically, out of habit or conditioning, we do not feel free. Like choice, freedom becomes real only when we believe in it, and when we know we have it. To a great extent our lives as they are now are the result of choices we made in the past. The future will depend on the choices we are making now. Refer to 2-8.2 (Freedom to Choose), and 5-5 (Choice and Decision-Making) for more discussion of these topics. We need to be aware that making the choice to listen to intuition can have a dramatic effect on our personal life. Vaughan (p. 41) has said further:

> Making choices for your own growth, trusting your intuition, can become a habit. Each time you choose to take advantage of a new opportunity, trusting your intuitive sense of what is best for you, you are strengthening this habit, and the choices become easier and clearer. As your choices become increasingly self-determined and well-defined, you can have as much freedom as you choose to believe in.

Strangely enough, over the years, this too has worked repeatedly for me in relating to others as a teacher, scientist, administrator, and family member. I have rarely felt restricted or disappointed in my decisions that were derived under such circumstances.

Torrance (1979, 46) indicated that intuition often needs time to work most effectively for us. If we have been concentrating on some particular item and yet seem not to find clear thoughts or directions, allowing a period of rest with attention focused on something else can help. This kind of break in concentration has been referred to as an "incubation period." This technique of leaving a problem and doing something else seems to work primarily after a long and continuous period of conscious work. Often, during this time away from the problem, an answer will flash into our minds. This phenomenon is called "illumination." Intuition is believed to be a key element in triggering our imagination.

3-4 IMAGINATION

Imagination has been referred to as the key to creativity (Osborn, 1963). It is considered to be important for us in the "...process of recombining known elements to produce more valuable (satisfying) ideas than previously existed in the mind of the thinker" (Parnes, definition of creativity, *Creative Behavior Workbook*, 1967 Parnes et al. 1977, 161]). Imagining is our ability to envision, to picture in the mind, to form in the "mind's eye", to form a mental image of something not currently being transmitted by the senses. It has sometimes been referred to as our visual thinking. Creativity seems to be facilitated by "manipulatable visualizations."

Imagination is strongly fed by our visual imagery. Adams (1986, 89) refers to three kinds of visual imagery, cited by McKim (1972), as being essential for our visual thinking. The first of these is perceptual imagery, our sensory experience of the physical world, or what we see and record in our brains. The second, mental imagery, is made up in our brains and is constructed from stored information and perceptual images. He referred to the third type as graphic imagery, which is put on paper by drawing, sketching, doodling, or otherwise to communicate with others or to aid our own thinking. Adams pointed out that visual imaging is complex and depends both on our ability to form images and on our supply of pertinent stored information. He believed that by being motivated and putting effort into the process, we can control and improve our ability to strengthen imagination.

As a researcher attempting to understand certain natural events or sequences, I have frequently attempted to assemble the known parts of a scheme in as many different ways as I could think of. By imagining the events arranged in various ways, I was often able to spot logical and proven sequences, eliminate others because of proven contradictions, and often could identify what appeared to be possible missing links that I needed to investigate.

Although we may not fully understand the process of imagination, we know it does lead us to formulate mental images and concepts (Osborn 1963, 66). For almost any of us these imaginations can range from wild and futile to productive and creative. They may also run the gamut from highly creative and valuable to destructive and difficult to control.

The difficult-to-control non-creative kinds of imagination tend to run themselves and may include such severe things as: hallucinations, delusions of grandeur, persecution complexes, morbid self-pity, nightmares, and martyr complexes (Osborn, 1963, 28). Worry, fear, some dreams and daydreaming which lead to helter-skelter imagination without direction or design may be less severe for us, but can be considerable deterrents to our productive creativity.

We can usually control and enjoy creative forms of imagination. If allowed, our children seem to develop considerable imaginative capability. Unfortunately, we, as adults obsessed with an urgency to prepare children for the "real world" as quickly as possible, apply pressures that tend to slow or even extinguish some of our children's imaginative and creative potential. Bettelheim (1977, 123-135) pointed out how important fantasy and fairytales (imagination) are in aiding children in the transition from infancy to childhood.

One important form of imagination referred to by Osborn (1963, 31) is vicarious imagination, putting ourselves into another's place. We need to imagine what others are feeling and how they are likely to react to the actions we anticipate taking. As Osborn said:

The Golden Rule, do unto others, embodies the noblest use of vicarious imagination.

If we could manage to follow this practice, we would likely find more accord and less conflict in our everyday living.

Still another form of imagination is cited by Osborn as "anticipative imagination." When we guess or project what response may follow some action we are about to take, we are anticipating the answer or the outcome. All of us participate in this kind of imagination frequently. This is closely akin to "creative expectancy," which follows our attempt at something creative and, by working hard to make it come true, we may greatly enhance the chances for success.

In our efforts to be creative we repetitively disassemble and analyze component parts of an issue. As MacKinnon (1978, 49) said:

What is then needed, if there is to be a creative reorganization, is a compensating, free, spontaneous look at the whole situation, a naive and childlike apprehension of what is there. Such an attitude encourages the use of imagination in the form of analogies, similes, and metaphors which are so crucial in the insightful reorganization of any problem.

No amount of imagination will accomplish anything without follow up. We must evaluate, judge and act on the revelation before it will count. As Short (1965, 57) said:

Dreams based only on dreams, rather than on reality, will be as disastrous for the future as they are unsatisfying for the present.

However, we must take care not to prejudge and discard an item too soon. At first it may appear to be just like a past experience, and then turn out to be quite different. I have heard Schuller (1985), say it well:

See it, size it up (measure it), seize it, and then seal it with a decision to act.

Repetitive and routine activities tend to dull our imagination if an effort is not made to exercise this capability regularly throughout life.

We need to stay abreast of what is happening if this dulling is to be avoided as we grow older. However, we also must take care to distinguish reality from fantasy.

3-5 PERCEPTION

The dictionary indicates that to perceive is "to become aware of, know, or identify by means of the senses." The definition also includes "to apprehend, envision, or understand." The definition of perception goes further to indicate "apprehending by means of the mind and recognizing by intuition". Thus it appears that perception is the result of not only the five senses, but intelligence and a host of other aspects of the mind including attitudes, emotions and feelings all working in concert. We may see and recognize the reactions of others, sense that we ourselves are elated, tired, angry, happy, in love, or about to be attacked, or that things are not quite right, etc. ad infinitum. Thus we should not be surprised that aspects which disturb and inhibit not only our senses, but our over-all balance and well-being, play an especially important role in how creative we are apt to be.

Adams (1986, 13) suggested that without perception one can neither clearly understand and imagine a problem nor the information needed to solve it. Thus any perceptual obstacle or block that we are confronted with is going to greatly reduce our creativity and our problem solving capability.

Both Adams (1986, 13-37) and Morgan (1968, 100-111) have discussed several perceptual blocks to creativity. Table 3-1 is based on some of the suggested items listed in their separate discussions.

By being aware of the dangers of falling victim to some of these blocks to perception, we can make a conscious effort to counteract and avoid them. We must learn to use and respond to all our senses. We must take care in identifying, isolating and relating the problem to the situation at hand. We must be slow to jump to the conclusion that it is just like a previous experience without careful and detailed examination. Care must be taken to not let routine tasks lull us into complacency.

We are helped if we learn to tolerate ambiguity in developing solutions to problems even if the final solution must be specific. Continually trying to exercise flexibility in operations may help us, but care should be used not to become tied to a limited number of workable approaches. A good practice is to develop a questioning attitude toward all that we do. It is important to be cautious about believing that ours is the only good approach to a problem. However, it may pay us to be different sometimes, just for the sake of being different. Learning to be open and listening carefully to the views of others will often pay off. If we are constantly alert, the unexpected, surprising or serendipitous opportunity may suddenly become obvious.

Table 3-1
Some Causes of Perceptual Blocks to Creativity and Problem-Solving

1. Failure to utilize all sensory inputs.
2. Failure to relate the problem to the situation.
3. Difficulty in identifying and isolating the problem.
4. Failure to distinguish between cause and effect.
5. Delimiting the problem area too closely.
6. Inability to see the problem from various view points.
7. Stereotyping or drawing false conclusions from superficial likeness.
8. Difficulty in seeing remote relationships.
9. Inability to see small clues that solve big problems.
10. Reaching a state where one is saturated, over-whelmed, and/or over-worked.

Constructed from texts of Adams, 1986, 13-37, and Morgan, 1968, 100-111.

3-6 SERENDIPITY

Serendipty is still another phenomenon that may be connected to the whole intuitional process. This term is defined as finding something valuable or agreeable at a time when we are not looking for it. It may be making a discovery by accident. We often say such an occurrence is a surprise or luck. But serendipitous findings often occur to us when we have been concentrating on something for some time and are alert enough to recognize the surprising new and different aspect from what we had been looking for.

Dale (May, 1969) has emphasized that individuals who have learned how to learn often reap benefits that surprise them, gaining serendipitous results that were not being sought after at the time. If we are curious, imaginative, keenly aware and allow intuition to work for us, we are likely to profit from such discoveries.

3-7   HIGHLIGHTS OF CHAPTER THREE

1. Our curiosity is an inherent attribute and is especially notice-

able in early life, but seems to diminish greatly as we grow older, if we do not purposefully stimulate and exercise it.

2. Maintaining a high level of curiosity and developing a healthy degree of doubt and skepticism throughout our lives can contribute much to our creativity and personal growth.

3. Intuition, the power of knowing or attaining direct knowledge without rational thought and inference, is believed to come from our unconscious mind and helps us to tap our vast storehouse of hidden knowledge.

4. Many believe that looking for, listening for and exercising our potential intuitive power can help us to better utilize messages from the "voice from within."

5. Relaxation, meditation, and diverting attention away from an issue usually helps us to utilize intuitive power more effectively.

6. Intuition is thought to be a function of our right brain, and a major factor in triggering our imagination.

7. Imagination and the ability to recombine former experiences and knowledge to form new images seem to be essential components of our creativity.

8. Staying aware of the signals from all our senses, as well as utilizing images generated in our minds, helps us to be more perceptive.

9. Perceptual blocks often limit our creativity.

10. Serendipity, discovery of the unexpected by accident or good luck, often occurs if we are alert, creative persons.

3-8 AFTERGROWTH STIMULATORS

1. Would you say you were a curious person when you were younger? Are you as curious now as you were then?

2. What things do you do now to keep your curiosity alive?

3. Do you often, seldom, or never get intuitive messages from within? How do you respond to these "gut feelings"?

4. Where and when do such messages most often come to you? During sleep? When relaxing? When close to nature? Or, under what other circumstances?

5. Can you recall a time when you had an intuitive feeling that you should do a certain thing, and your responding proved it to be just the right thing to do?

6. Does it come easy for you to picture in your mind how you would like to see a particular situation develop and end up?

CHAPTER 4

ATTITUDES, EMOTIONS, AND FEELINGS

4- 1   Introduction
4- 2   General Mental Attitudes
4- 3   Attitudes Toward Self
4- 4   Impact of Emotions and
         Feelings on Creativity
4- 5   Attitudes and Emotions Involving Others
4- 6   Highlights of Chapter Four
4- 7   Aftergrowth Stimulators

4-1 INTRODUCTION

As biological creatures with complex minds, our creative capabilities are not governed by our intellect alone. Our emotions and attitudes together with our "frame of mind" largely control our feelings. These in turn play a significant role in the control of our intellectual responses, as well as our bodily responses, and these then are critical to our creative endeavors.

It is obvious that many of the qualities concerning mental capability and creativity are highly dependent upon our mental attitude, emotions and feelings. Some of the items involved have been brought together by VanDemark (1979, 8. See Table 4-1). These have been arranged with some classified as general attitudes, some as attitudes toward ourselves, and then a group called attitudes toward others.

Table 4-1
Some Generally Desirable Mental Attitudinal Qualities

General qualities	Toward self	Toward others
Motivated	Self-accepting	Respectful
Ambitious	Self-loving	Tolerant
Dedicated	Self-respecting	Trusting
Courageous	Self-developing	Communicative
Perseverant	Self-disciplined	Team spirited
Truth-seeking	Self-challenging	Cooperative
Freedom-loving	Self-confident	Competitive
Responsible	Insightful	Responsible
Honest	Self-assertive	Flexible
Aware	Self-reliant	Sensitive
Prompt	Self-sustaining	Considerate
Willing to risk	Self-renewing	Caring
Venturesome	Self-evaluative	Sharing
Humble	Self-starting	Loving
Optimistic	Self-responsibility	Kind
Fun-loving		Patient

Constructed from text of VanDemark, 1979, 8.

Some of the effects of these inner barriers and emotions that we generate are discussed later in this chapter. The latter part of the chapter is devoted to the impact of our attitudes toward others.

4-2 GENERAL MENTAL ATTITUDES

Certainly it is essential that, as creative persons, we be motivated, dedicated, industrious, and courageous in our efforts (see Table 4-1). None of these characteristics dares be short-lived, so we must also be perseverant. These characteristics serve to compel us to action, to do something. Without the ambition and commitment to exercise these traits we are likely to have difficulty in overcoming the ever-present inertia to do nothing.

We must have a compelling love for freedom and accept the responsibilities that accompany freedom, if loss of it is not to be a danger. We must also have a real drive toward seeking the truth and this requires complete honesty with ourselves and others. Sooner or later we will be discovered if dishonest acts are committed. Even if we are not caught, the acts will likely cause us anxiety which can be a severe emotionally distracting factor from our creative efforts. Time spent in worry or plotting to avoid having the dishonesty disclosed will be time lost from creative thoughts and activities.

If we are optimistic, fun-loving persons, we are apt to become so immersed in what we are doing that thoughts of failure either never occur to us or do not inhibit our drive to some venturesome act. As such persons we are usually aware of what is going on around us, and we often patiently continue our striving toward some goal to which we are dedicated. We are apt to be humble in our efforts. Blanchard and Peale (1988, 49) said, "People with humility don't think less of themselves, they just think about themselves less." Achievers often seem to be gifted with unusual will power, determination and ambition to succeed. They seem never to be easily discouraged, and hope seems ever present. Perhaps they succeed because they have an uncanny ability to maintain an optimism even in the presence of circumstances where the average person lets negative thoughts prevail.

4-3 ATTITUDES TOWARD SELF

Dale (May, 1969) quoted William Faulkner as having said:

I believe that man will not merely endure; he will prevail. He will prevail and we will prevail only ... if we're willing to put ourselves and what we believe on the line for whatever it may bring.

Dale (May, 1969) also said:

Everyone wants to be a somebody; nobody wants to be a

nobody. More people than we may realize have lost faith in their power to be somebody. They need mentors, guides, a helping hand over the rough spots. They certainly do not need punishment for their weaknesses - they have been punished enough already. They need to build a feeling of their own power, their ability to run their own lives.

If we are to develop self-esteem and a feeling of self-worth (see Chapter 7-3) and gain that feeling of power and control over our own lives, then we must put great effort into developing self-love and acceptance as well as a strong self-discipline. Most of the general qualities cited above can only be developed and retained when we will it and are determined to make those qualities a part of life. Such individuals are usually willing to suffer and strive in this endeavor. We must learn to be self-starting, self-renewing, self-sustaining individuals. Constant self-evaluation and self-implementation are essential. This kind of a self-disciplined effort is not easy for us to begin nor is it easy to maintain. However, once proper habits to achieve these goals are started, and the longer they are practiced, the easier adhering to them becomes.

All sorts of barriers to creativity are generated within us. Some of those involving emotions and feelings are discussed below, others are dealt with in later chapters.

4-4 IMPACT OF EMOTIONS AND FEELINGS ON CREATIVITY

It is well recognized that our emotions and feelings affect our performance, sometimes positively and sometimes negatively. Gaylin (1979, 1) defined "emotions" as the general term used to describe the "feeling tone, the biophysiological and chemical changes" that cause the changing sensations that we feel. The term "feelings" describes our awareness of the emotional states we are experiencing.

Even the Bible refers to the immense powers the emotions have over doing what we intellectually know is right and desireable, but cannot manage emotionally.

I don't understand myself at all, for I really want to do what is right, but I can't. I do what I don't want to - what I hate. I know perfectly well that what I am doing is wrong, and my bad conscience proves that I agree with these laws I am breaking. But I can't help myself, because I'm no longer doing it. It seems to be a fact of life that when I want to do what is right, I inevitably do what is wrong. (Romans 7:15-17, 21. Living Bible 1971.)

Adams (1986, 42) indicated that we create for reasons of inner drives which may result from an attempt to bring about conflict resolution, or from self-fulfillment, or a combination of the two. We also may create for a number of other reasons, one of which may be for money. Emotions play a role in creativity because it appears certain that at least a part of our creativity occurs as a result of intuition or at least activities of the mind which are below the conscious level. It appears that our conscious mind or ego is the control valve on creativity.

Emotions may play a role also because, as creative persons, we may experience anxieties. Anxieties may come from being different, from being questioned, or from believing in something unusual. It is important that we keep our lives as trouble free as possible if we are to be creative individuals. As Medawar (1979, 40), a Nobel Laureate, said:

> To be creative, scientists need libraries and laboratories and the company of other scientists; certainly a quiet and un-troubled life is a help. A scientist's work is in no way deepened or made more cogent by privation, anxiety, dis-tress, or emotional harassment.

Almost immediately upon being threatened by fear, danger, or anger, chemicals (hormones) are released that trigger us to "fight or flight." Emotions, signalling well-being, trigger the release of other chemicals that give us good body feelings like pleasure, relaxation and euphoria.

4-4.1 Fear and Anxiety

Fear and anxiety probably affect our well-being and creativity as much as or more than any of our other emotions. Even as far back as Biblical days people were encouraged to keep fear from control-ling their lives:

> For God has not given us the spirit of fear; but of power, and of love, and of a sound mind. (II Timothy 1:7, King James Version.)

We usually think of fear as being a deterrent to creativity, and in most instances that is true. Fear of the new, fear of authority, fear to risk, fear and doubts about our own ability, can result in a serious diminution of our creative ventures. However, some fear is a needed stimulant to our creative efforts. If we did not experience some fear and anxiety, we might not get out of bed and go to a job every morning.

It has been suggested that a certain amount of anxiety brings improved performance. Without it we would likely not be pushed to change. Thus growth, psychologically and spiritually, would not be as great if we did not have some degree of anxiety. Further, we would likely not be stimulated to understand ourselves and others without the push that anxiety gives us. Another positive way of looking at being afraid can be to be so afraid of missing the really good things of life that nothing holds us back from trying for them.

Fear is the anticipation of a painful experience, physical or psychological. Anything that is painful for us is almost always expected to be survival-threatening, and therefore we usually avoid it if at all possible. Fear ranges from mild to severe, "from trepidation to terror, from dismay to dread, from perturbation to panic, from anxiety to alarm" (Gaylin, 1979, 19). Fear is the life-saving emotion which enables animals, and early man especially, to survive by fighting or fleeing. Today many of our fears result in anxiety which is unfounded. Much about which we generate anxiety is imagined and without basis-in-fact.

In my early years of college teaching and research, I saw a graduate student who feared appearing before a group to make a presentation. This student managed to overcome the fear enough to get all the way to the final exam and defense of the dissertation. At that point, much to my chagrin, panic took over and he could not bring himself to get help in overcoming the fear and consequently was never able to complete the degree.

Filled with anxiety we worry a lot. Osborne (1967, 37) suggested that nearly all of us expend at least 50 percent of our psychic energy keeping repressed memories below the level of consciousness. He said psychologists agree in general that all of our actions are efforts to avoid anxiety. He also firmly believed that anxiety is creative and necessary up to a point, but beyond that it becomes destructive. He listed four usual sources of anxiety as:

1. attempting to pursue incompatible goals;
2. guilt areas, recent or of long-standing; actual or false;
3. early childhood conditioning; and
4. failure to achieve some goal.

Although Osborne repeatedly emphasized that there is nothing wrong with non-destructive anxiety, he indicated that there are four ineffective ways of dealing with anxiety. These are to:

1. deny the existence of it;

2. avoid it (seek to avoid the feelings, situations or thoughts which arouse it);
3. rationalize it; and
4. narcotize it (drugs, alcohol, over-busyness, and many other ways).

He suggested that a fifth, and the only effective way for us to deal with an all-pervasive and destructive anxiety, is to seek out and remove the source of it.

Anxieties cause us to worry. Oftentimes, all too many of our worries are things over which we have no control. Thus it is fruitless to worry over things which we can not change or do anything about. An excellent book, *Stress And How To Live With It*, (Robinson, 1982, 47), offers several suggestions for managing worries. The following are based in part on those suggestions:

1. Develop a worry list - if it's worth worrying about it's worth listing. Be specific about what causes you to worry.
2. Sort the problems into two groups; problems over which you have some control, and problems over which you have no control.
3. Set the ones over which you have no control aside. Trust yourself, others, God to help you live with these or respond to when some action besides worry would help.
4. Taking them one at a time, plan a strategy for attacking those over which you have some control. What resources do I need (have) to solve each one? How can I get resources? Who can help me? When? What can I do today? Discuss it with a friend or helper.
5. Start with those that can be handled quickly and easily and build a backlog of success. Delay the difficult only long enough to be confident that your plan is the right one.
6. Follow your plan of action. Listen to what others have to say. Plan for success. Failure leads to failure. Review each success with pride.
7. Do all you can, then let go and trust.

Fear is a basic element in a number of categories of emotional blocks to creativity. Fear of the unknown, fear of failure, fear of making a mistake, and fear of taking a risk are just a few that involve the elements of fear and anxiety.

Morgan (1968, 55-56) said that:

Emotional blocks or defense mechanisms constitute the most serious inhibitors to creative functioning.

He listed these principal groups:

1. need for superficial security;
2. personal feelings of insecurity;
3. inability to use the unconscious freely;
4. inability to use the conscious mind effectively;
5. work-oriented barriers; and
6. environmental barriers.

4-4.2 Superficial Security - False Security from Tradition, Habit and the Familiar

We all face and struggle with the tendency to be satisfied with "status quo." We are apt to think we are holding our own when we stick to tradition, habits and the familiar. In truth, however, we are likely standing still while the rest of the world moves on. We find comfort in the familiar. Doing what our parents and forbearers did becomes habit. It comes easily, for that is what we learned in our early years. Breaking with tradition means breaking from our teachers and our parents. It implies that what they taught us was not adequate. Thus we are challenging them. To challenge our predecessors is risky and may be frightening. This kind of insecurity stems from our fear of change, and a wariness of the new and unknown. As a result we have a great tenacity for the traditional and a need for the familiar.

This kind of superficial security is often accompanied by our need for excessive order and integration. Disorder and ambiguity are not easily tolerated. If we are inflexible and resistant to change and the new, then we will also likely be afraid of risk and speculation. We find stability and security in being in the familiar and we become attached to our way of doing things. Inertia and habit take over. We become conservative and get into a rut. Laziness and advancing age can contribute to the malady. It can readily be seen that if we feel we must hold on to the familiar and are bothered by newness and change, we will be greatly restricted in our creative abilities.

Such fears will likely cause us to take few risks in making changes and we are apt to thwart the efforts of those who are prone to trying new things. We will be intolerant of ambiguity and disorderliness in others. In all likelihood, if we feel that way, we will make poor team leaders, but we may be good at routine, and repetitive tasks. What should we do about the problem? My personal suggestions (based in part on Morgan, 1986, 66-76) are:

1. We need to be aware of the danger of becoming too comfortable with our usual procedures. We can help ourselves by taking a new route to work. Listen to a different type of music or program, etc. Make it a habit to constantly question the way we or others are doing things.
2. Don't be afraid to break our habit patterns from time to time.
3. Purposefully overcome our inertia. Is there really good reason why we have taken no action to make changes?
4. Make sure we find a place in our hardened categories to fit in a new approach to the patterns we have fallen into.
5. Try being a little less orderly.
6. Instead of just being lazy, try dreaming and thinking of new ways to do things.
7. Be sure we don't develop a conservative defensiveness and reject every new idea or bit of information that comes our way.

Above all keep in mind the quote I coined a few years ago (at least I don't recall having ever seen it before):

Let tradition guide you, but don't let it blind you or bind you.

4-4.3 Personal Feelings of Insecurity

Our feelings of insecurity can be great deterrents to creativity. Such feelings are apt to show up as a lack of self-confidence and anxiety about self-esteem. Feelings involving not only the individual but interpersonal relationships include such emotional items as:

1. fear of authority and related dependency feelings;
2. anger;
3. fear of criticism; and
4. fear of failure (see 4-5, attitudes toward others).

Lack of self-confidence usually results in our not exerting ourselves to the fullest. We may be afraid of being wrong, being challenged, or we may even fear to learn that our best may seem none too good. But to be creative we must reach beyond where others have reached before. We cannot achieve new things without stretching beyond where they have been before.

Morgan (1968, 58-59) suggested some steps to help increase self-confidence. The following are modifications of his list:

1. Get experience - keep trying, for creativity depends on building a storehouse of knowledge and experience.
2. Watch out for dead-end jobs - they stifle our creative potential.

3. Push yourself to act enthusiastic - enthusiasm almost always helps us to be creative.
4. Put failures in proper perspective - creative people experience failures too. They try more things and take more chances, so the odds of coming up with something new are increased.
5. Recognize your weaknesses - either strengthen them or work to offset them.
6. Be courageous - a bold and persistent approach may be just what it takes to get you there.
7. Watch your health - you need all that your body and brain can give you. So take care of them.
8. Be optimistic and give your best.

Probably most important, but most difficult of all, is as a line credited to Eleanor Roosevelt who suggested: "No one can make you feel inferior without your permission."

Anxiety about self-esteem is frequently found if we have low self-esteem. We can easily get caught in what has been referred to as the vicious circle of feelings of inferiority. We usually are constantly comparing ourselves with others. We tend to overestimate the other's state of affairs, don't recognize the difficulties, troubles and failures that our idols are experiencing, and then further underestimate our own value. We may reach a point of systematic self-denigration. Tournier (1965) said:

Very few people judge themselves fairly. Some are too sure of themselves, a rather disagreeable trait which marks them out as a mediocre personality. But others - more sensitive, more adult and more agreeable - easily fall into a sort of prejudice against themselves.

If they do fall into this pattern, they are apt to recognize their own shortcomings and then exaggerate them. He went on to say that it is very difficult to bring such persons to a more objective point of view. If we suffer from a lack of self-esteem, then developing self-confidence may be extremely difficult. We need some successes and the acknowledgment of our accomplishments by others to begin to feel that we have something to offer the world. We need to remember that nearly everyone likely has moments when they have anxiety about themselves. Using the suggestions above to help control anxieties and in combatting a lack of self-confidence can help us. Also implementing the suggestions given later for combatting fears of criticism and failure may prove to be helpful for us. Recognizing that such anxieties occur commonly, even in the most creative persons, helps us to put the anxieties in proper perspective and thus reduce their damaging effect on our creative effort.

4-4.4 Feeling Bad

When we feel bad, whatever the cause - physical, psychological, or otherwise, we are likely to have our creative capabilities impaired. A wide array of feeling terms such as upset, agitated, mixed-up, disturbed, stirred-up, depressed, beside-ourselves, irritated, confused, interrupted, out-of-control, are used to describe these signals that things are not going right and we feel bad. Often these feelings are indicators that we are not getting enough sleep, proper nutrition, relaxation, or that we are about to be struck with a sickness. Or they may be warning signals that things are not holding well for us psychologically. Usually if bad feelings persist or recur often, we should try to determine the cause, even if professional help is required. The major concern is to avoid a prolonged period of feeling bad.

4-4.5 Feeling Good

Gaylin (1979) said:

In one sense, feeling good is the opposite of despair; in another sense it is the opposite of feeling upset. The major ingredients of feeling good are the antithesis and antidotes of those negative feelings. To feel good is to have a sense of hope, mastery, self-confidence, and self-esteem.

We often equate the term "feeling good" with pleasure. Gaylin indicated that he believed the common ingredient of various sources and forms of pleasure is that "all seem to contribute to an enhanced sense of self." Over and over we find that an enlargement of the sense of self seems to be an important ingredient for the creative person.

In his analysis of pleasure and feeling good, beyond the pleasures of our senses, Gaylin pointed out several items. First he cited discovery as an important element. There is something in the learning experience that gives us joy and satisfaction. Through discovery we enlarge the intellect, which in itself is an enlargement of the self. Next he cited expansion and mastery. They too contribute to growth of the self. He considered creativity as an extension of mastery. Still another item he considered important was the matter of becoming so immersed in something as to lose the sense of time, perception, and even the sense of self. All of these are joyous experiences for us.

Obviously we feel good when we are relieved of pain and escape from distress, depression and despair. We feel good to have reassurance, to have hope, and to fuse with nature and other people. All these can contribute to the good feeling of being lifted out of ourselves, allowing us an "attachment beyond groups, things, people, world." As Gaylin said, "We are reminded that we are a part of something even larger than the course and activities of our life." When this happens, simply being alive can make us feel good.

Perhaps the important aspect of feeling good is that we then feel that we are in a physical and mental condition to make the most of our capabilities in facing life. It is then that we have the courage to take life one day at a time. It is then that we find happiness in our striving, even if there are troubles and pain to face. When we feel that way we are free to be creative in whatever we do.

4-5 ATTITUDES AND EMOTIONS INVOLVING OTHERS

In order for us to live in today's society, a healthy attitude toward others is highly important. Without respect and tolerance, living in close proximity to one another can become extremely difficult. Without being sensitive and trusting, it is not likely that we, our communications or our communities will flourish. Without these there is little chance for team efforts to succeed in solving problems (see Table 4-1, attitudes toward others). Thus, being cooperative, responsible, and flexible in relationships with others would seem to be highly desirable traits for us as creative persons, especially if our creative efforts require a partnership or team approach.

If we work and live close to others, we may experience many kinds of opportunities for good and bad emotional responses that can affect our creative abilities. These can vary over a wide range from hurt, jealousy, anger, fear of authority and dependency, fear of risk and speculation, fear of criticism, fear of failure, fear of rejection and compulsion to conform, to a spirit of cooperation, encouragement, inspiration, joy, adulation, loyalty and love.

4-5.1 Feeling Hurt and Jealous

Although they may seem minor because they appear to be mild and don't often result in violent response unless they trigger anger, we probably experience these negative emotional responses more often than most other feelings toward others. They generally occur as a result of our feeling slighted, left out, or not getting the material or psychological rewards that we thought we deserved or someone else got instead of us.

Usually if we feel hurt or jealous we think that we were just as, or even more deserving than the persons who did get the rewards or recognitions. Our feelings seem to inhibit our ability to think rationally about our qualifications or performance as compared to other persons. This inability, just as with many other inhibiting factors, causes us to waste much energy and put excessive thought into the injustices which we feel have been committed rather than being able to concentrate on creative thoughts. Of course injustices do frequently occur. However, brooding over the issue actually does not change things and only takes energy away from our performance that might qualify us for similar or other rewards. Brooding may also cause us to show undesirable and degrading personality traits which may diminish our chances for later recognition.

Incidents and conditions which produce hurt and jealousy are likely to produce anger and resentment. These then will also contribute to the diversion of thought, concentration, and intuition which are so essential for making the most of our creative abilities.

4-5.2 Feeling Angry

Anger is an emotion that frequently causes us to react aggressively. Anger, indignation and upset feelings occur when we think our rights are being violated. We become angry when we perceive that someone or something is encroaching on or threatening our geographical or psychological territory. Since anger, all too often, comes out in negative, destructful and hurtful ways, many of us have been taught that anger must be suppressed. We should not say or do something if it will hurt someone. Our anger must be kept within. However, that approach does not solve anything. If not dealt with in some way, anger may come out as sarcasm, sly innuendos, put-downs or humor that hurts. If dealt with in this way, anger is usually harmful both to us as the perpetrator and the recipient of the outburst.

Many have thought that the most effective way of dealing with our anger is to let it out, or ventilate it as some say. But more recently Tavris (1982, 25-35) has suggested that ventilating anger only serves in many cases to rehearse the event that caused us the anger and as a result worsens the feelings of the parties involved. She indicated that anger occurs in combination with other emotions and talking about the anger alone excludes the other feelings. She said, "If you want to 'let go' of anger, you have to rearrange your thinking, not just lower your pulse rate." This corresponds to the long-held advice to count to ten before letting go.

The difficult aspect of dealing with our anger is learning to handle it constructively. When we become angry considerable energy is generated. It becomes difficult to keep our composure and direct our energy toward a positive response rather than through negative and destructive aggression. Often a calm, low-key but assertive, response can help to avoid putting the other person on the defensive. If we can obtain results that way, our own anger subsides and others are not threatened and provoked to anger in return.

We aren't likely to be very creative when angry. Thinking energies are blocked and tend to be irrational under the stress of anger. Anger that is repressed continues to control our thinking and block creative thought. Thus a careful but assertive effort to deal with the causative issue immediately, or at least as soon as possible, should be sought to clear the disagreement or altercation.

4-5.3 Over-Dependency and Fear of Authority

Although we generally think that establishing good communicative and close relationships to be helpful and encouraging to creativity, becoming so close that a deep dependence is formed can actually be destructive. There is considerable danger of losing our autonomy in such a situation. This dependency can also degenerate into a fear of authority. With the fear of authority we are in danger of falling into a fear of risking and speculating. Our fears can easily broaden into fears of criticism and failure. Taken all together these fears spell disaster and devastation for our feelings of self. Further considerations of the self in creativity are discussed in Chapter 7.

4-5.4 Fear of Risking and Speculating

Any feelings that are destructive of our self-esteem and the courage to be ourselves, affect our individual creativity. Repeatedly in our up-bringing, in much of our formal education (see Chapter 10-3 and 10-4), and in our everyday jobs we are admonished to be careful, to play it safe, and seek security, all of which cause us to become afraid of taking risks. We hesitate to speculate, for we might be wrong and we have been conditioned to believe that great honor, praise, and acceptance come from being right. This hesitancy of risking and speculating ties in with the fears of failure and criticism.

Risking and speculating open us up, and sometimes make us vulnerable, to challenge, criticism, betrayal, being misunderstood, increased stress, being accused of weak leadership, etc. But there are real values to be gained through risking and speculation, for example: increased trust, improved communications, better cooperation, constructive criticism, reduced stress, increased sensitivity, improved morale and productivity, increased flow of ideas, development of creative efforts, etc. Some suggestions to overcome the risk and speculation barriers to creativity include:

1. Remember the rewards of risk-taking.
2. If you take risks and open up, others are more apt to do so too.
3. Remember it takes time to build trust.
4. Realize that you can't win them all, but the odds are great that you will win more than you lose.
5. Have back-up ideas to supplant the failures.
6. Don't dwell on your losses.
7. Remember, the more ideas you come up with, the greater the chances of coming up with good ones.

4-5.5 Fear of Criticism

It is important to keep in mind that creative ideas are challenging, threatening to replace, and sometimes destroying established and accepted principles, concepts, and/or materialistic products. Thus we are suggesting that the "old" and "established" are antiquated, of lesser quality, or perhaps just not good. Suggesting change or replacement may come as a shock to those who have originated or held to the old for perhaps a long time. Our new idea may even pose a threat to the reputation, future financial or job security of others.

The more unique and original our ideas, the more we can count on being challenged and likely criticized for them. We may even be ridiculed, disapproved, or maybe even censored. In fact, as creative persons, we are likely to find that we are called on to prove our point over and over again.

Constructive criticism can be exceptionally valuable. Others are likely to view things from a different perspective. Their experience may allow them to see aspects of the new idea that have evaded us or others. Without constructive criticism we may make a really big mistake, so it is valuable to have others scrutinize and tell us openly and frankly what their opinion of our idea is. All too often we withhold criticism because we think it will hurt the feelings of others. To withhold constructive criticism actually may be a disservice to others. Criticism given with objectivity and out of love and concern for other persons will almost always be helpful to them, if they are willing to accept it with an open mind.

Unfortunately, we tend to fear criticism because our first reaction to it is that it is an attack on us personally. We don't like to think we have done something stupid. We expect that others are reacting negatively to us when their reaction may be an honest reaction to nothing more than the idea we have disclosed. It isn't always easy to determine which is the case. If we become overly worried about being criticized we are apt to greatly impair our creative abilities. We then are using our thinking energy for worrying instead of applying it to creative thinking.

How can we handle criticism? The following are based on the suggestions that Burns (1980, 264-265) has made:

1. Remember that others' negative criticisms of you may be due to their irrational thinking.
2. If the criticisms have some correct bases to them, take steps to correct them. If you are human, you are bound to make mistakes. You can learn from correcting them.
3. If you goofed, it does not mean you are a born loser. Think of all the things you have done right.
4. Others cannot judge your worth as a human being, they can only judge what you do or say.
5. Everyone will likely judge you differently, no matter how well or poorly you do. One rejection does not mean there will be a continuing series of disapprovals.
6. Criticism and disapproval are uncomfortable but will pass. They will upset you only to the extent that you "buy into" the accusations made against you. Get into something that you have enjoyed in the past and get on with life.
7. Disapproval of your ideas doesn't necessarily mean disapproval of you as a person. Your disagreement with other persons doesn't make them all bad. Arguments are a part of living; discussion can usually clear the differences.
8. Be self-critical. Be skeptical of conventional answers. Refuse to take anything for granted.

Further suggestions are made in Chapter 11-7.1 (Willingness to Accept Criticism).

4-5.6 Fear of Failure

Fear of failure is usually an extreme form of the fear of criticism. We imagine that we will make a miscalculation or mistake, be it for some reason of our own doing or otherwise. Then, certain persons or the community for whom we care a great deal will ridicule or reject us. Or perhaps we feel our own or the family reputation will be tarnished. The fears may range all the way from a flat-out flub to a fear of success which would put unusual demands upon our capabilities. In between those extremes, a fear of inadequacy of background, training, or certain talents, or a problem with self-confidence as a cause for failing may be involved.

Sometimes our desires for successes are so great that we put forth over-zealous efforts that almost guarantee failures. We try to force things that need to be allowed to progress at a slower rate. Sometimes timing is bad. The economy is declining, the community was not ready for it, too few preparations were made before starting, etc. may have caused us to fail, but we ignored or lacked the savvy to detect these critical circumstances. We may like to constantly blame others for things for which we ourselves were or should have been responsible.

Thus it is obvious that there will be a wide array of barriers or blocks to creativity that accompany the fear of failure. Many of these are internal with the individual, and there are many that hinge on external blocks.

Morgan (1968, 61-62) suggested several ways to overcome the fear of failure:

1. Accept the possibility of failure.
2. Learn from failure, if it occurs.
3. Take on smaller tasks within your ability to establish success.
4. Move then to more difficult tasks.
5. Advance by succeeding in a challenging project.
6. Take risks, within reason.
7. Show courage; it underlies all creativity.

It is amazing how much feeling loved, accepted, moved to action (touched), sensitive, in relationship and part of community will help enhance our creativity and insure our successes.

4-6 HIGHLIGHTS OF CHAPTER FOUR

1. Motivation, courage, perseverance, willingness to risk, etc. are general mental characteristics that we need to have to be creative persons.
2. As creative persons we are likely to have a high respect and acceptance of ourselves and show these by being insightful, responsible, self-challenging, self-disciplined and self-starting individuals.
3. Many barriers to our creativity are generated from within us (internal barriers).

4. Our attitudes, emotions and feelings, as well as our intellect, play a major role in enhancing and/or inhibiting our creative capabilities.
5. Our attitudes, emotions and our "frame of mind" largely govern how we feel. Our feelings in turn are highly influential on our bodily and mental performance.
6. Our fears, anxieties and our personal feelings of insecurity are usually major emotional deterrents to our creativity.
7. Feeling enough anxiety to constantly self-evaluate and then act in making changes to improve ourselves is a must for persons who are striving to be more creative.
8. Positive attitudes such as respect, tolerance, trust, love and sensitivity toward others generally increase our creative output.
9. We need to be aware and cautious in submitting to the many pressures to conform that come from others.
10. Constructive criticism can be especially valuable in helping us avoid making mistakes and improving our creative productivity.

4-7 AFTERGROWTH STIMULATORS

1. Do you have trouble breaking out of, or away from, certain long held habits, traditions, or familiar practices? Are these real barriers to your creativity? When was the last time you took a new route to work? Stopped to explore a new shopping center? Did something new for the fun of it?
2. Do thoughts of being ridiculed, laughed at, or scorned prevent you from trying something new or breaking away from common practices?
3. Do you let fear of failure or of not measuring up stop you from trying new things?
4. Do you often let anger, hurt or jealousy interfere with your thinking and/or stop you from taking an appropriate action?
5. Do you find it difficult to give or accept criticism? Do you often feel criticism is more of an attack on you personally than on your ideas or how you are doing something? Do you let these feelings guide you in criticizing others?
6. What do you do that is a real boost to your emotions and feelings? Does it make you feel happy? Are your spirits raised? Does it relax you? Does it help you feel more creative and in control of your life?

CHAPTER 5

BALANCE, DISCIPLINE AND WISDOM

5- 1   Introduction
5- 2   Probabilities of Being a Half-Person
5- 3   Self-Discipline
5- 4   Learning to Learn
5- 5   Choice and Decision-Making
5- 6   Freedom and Responsibility
5- 7   Excellence and Perfection
5- 8   Positive Thinking
5- 9   Wisdom and Common Sense
5-10   Balanced Whole-Person
5-11   Problem-Solving Capabilities
5-12   Highlights of Chapter Five
5-13   Aftergrowth Stimulators

5-1 INTRODUCTION

If we accept the premise that balance and becoming a "whole person" is essential, if we are to come nearer to reaching our creative potential and a level of excellence, then we must pay attention to all aspects of ourselves. We must learn to discipline ourselves and become more proficient in making choices and decisions.

Seriously, we must ask, "Are we so materialistically oriented, so success oriented, so production oriented, so selfish in our drives that we are missing many of the aspects that will enable us to be more fully human? If we focus only on our intellectual side, are we giving ourselves the opportunity to develop a "radiance all our own? "

It would seem that we need to focus on rearing, educating, and being "whole persons."

5-2 PROBABILITIES OF BEING A HALF-PERSON

Over and over in today's world we emphasize the importance of an education. Learning to use our intellect is of prime importance. But from the previous discussions (and further clarified later) there seem to be two major considerations when we think in terms of the making of creative persons. Both our intellectual and emotional sides must be developed. There is a great chance that our intellect will be under-utilized if we are non-schooled persons. By the same token there is great chance that our emotional (altruistic, feelings of love, empathy, awareness, and fantasy) and intuitive aspects will be neglected if we are only intellectually-educated persons. Lyon (1971, 13) pointed out that the latter is the case in our schools of today on most levels. He referred to this as teaching (training, educating) half a person. All too frequently, as parents and teachers, we get so caught up in our attempt to develop the intellectual side of our young people that we largely ignore the "other half." Many of us believe that this is why a great deal of our teaching today seems to be ineffective (see Chapter 10-4).

If we take a look at the world we live in, at the neighborhoods we live in, even the households we live in, it is obvious that we are going to need the best possible thinking available if we are to survive the future. The people who contribute most, the people who we will be most dependent upon, will be those with power. Dale (1964) pointed out that, in addition to the power of knowledge and thinking, there is power in interacting with people (see Chapter 2-2). Certainly our future must be concerned more and more with people as populations

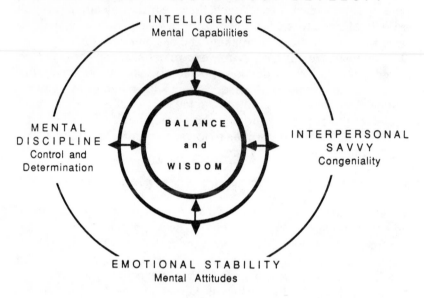

Fig. 5-1   Requirements for a Balanced Creative Individual

grow, and greater and greater interdependencies develop. (A discussion of power in interpersonal relationships is dealt with in Chapter 8-5 and 8-6). Thus we most certainly must be concerned with greater and greater focus on becoming "whole persons."

As concerned individuals, who want to have fulfilling lives and have our contributions count, we will likely want to be as well educated and balanced as possible, and in tune with our emotions, attributes and intelligence. A number of the possible needed mental capabilities (see Chapter 2), general attitudes, attitudes toward ourselves, and attitudes toward others (see Chapters 3 & 4), as well as contributions of our emotions (see Chapter 4), were presented earlier (VanDemark, 1979). Altogether, if we are to be creative individuals, we would seem to need, in addition to intellect, a high degree of emotional stability, mental discipline, and interpersonal relational savvy, in balance and mixed with a goodly portion of wisdom (see Figure 5-1).

Discussions concerning attaining portions of these and a number of other contributing factors are considered in this and subsequent chapters.

5-3 SELF-DISCIPLINE

In the first section of his book, *The Road Less Traveled*, Peck (1978, 18-69) presented some excellent materials on discipline (This book is highly recommended for further reading). He defined discipline as a:

... basic set of tools we require to solve life's problems.

Since life consists of a series of problems which make life difficult at best, we all must develop the discipline to cope, or we fail to solve those issues. Often solving the problems of life is not only difficult, but painful. This means that we are often provoked to frustration, grief, sadness, loneliness, guilt, regret, anger, fear, anxiety, anguish, despair, or other emotionally discomforting disturbances.

Peck indicated that:

Fearing the pain involved, almost all of us, to a greater or lesser degree, attempt to avoid problems. We procrastinate, hoping that they will go away. We ignore them, forget them, pretend they do not exist. We even take drugs to assist us in ignoring them.

The anxiety over problems and the emotional upsets involved are believed to be the primary cause of much of the illness we suffer. Yet he pointed out that "Problems are the cutting edge that distinguishes between success and failure. Problems call forth our courage and our wisdom; indeed, they create our courage and our wisdom."

The "tools" Peck suggested for dealing constructively with our pains and the almost certain suffering involved in life's problems include:

- delaying gratification;
- acceptance of responsibility;
- dedication to truth; and
- balancing.

He referred to these as simple tools, the application of which is troublesome because of the will needed to use them. None of them comes easy and all require the investment of a lot of time on the part of parents, teachers and the individuals who are receiving or attempting to strengthen their own self-discipline.

In order for us to sense the value and develop the ability to *delay gratification*, we need to have good role models to pattern our lives after. Much of this must come from self-disciplined parents and teachers. Through them and from them we learn a sense of self-worth and a degree of trust that life can be safe and rewarding. With guidance and determination we learn that pain can be expected, and careful scheduling of our actions so that getting the pain over with first enhances our pleasure later.

We cannot solve a problem unless we are willing to *accept the responsibility* that "this is our problem and it's up to us to solve it." In other words, for us individually, "If it is to be, it is up to me." We all have a great tendency to fall into the trap of blaming our condition on other people, society, circumstances beyond our control, or just plain bad luck. We then sit back and wait for others or society to solve the problem. In the meantime we go on suffering, while nothing is done to correct the situation. The solution usually means that a personal effort or change is required. Or perhaps we may need to be the spark that stimulates a leader or a group to action to implement change.

One of the dangers, that often is not realized when we attempt to place the responsibility for our behavior on someone else or on society, is that we may be unwittingly forfeiting our freedom and control to some other person, group or organization. As Peck said:

> In attempting to avoid the pain of responsibility, millions and even billions daily attempt to escape freedom.

Dedication to the truth is Peck's third suggested disciplinary tool for dealing with the pain of problem-solving. The poorer our concept of the truth (reality) of the world, the more confused and misguided we are. Consequently, we are then less capable of making wise decisions and charting correct courses of action. Peck pointed out that, unfortunately, all too often we get hung up in perceiving and responding to the world because of a set of ways which were developed early in our lives. To avoid this he suggested that we subscribe to:

> ...a life of total dedication to the truth.

To do so requires:

> ...a life of continuous and never-ending stringent self-examination.

It also means a willingness to be personally challenged. His final point was that it requires a life of total honesty. It seems that it all boils down to our being constant truth seekers, which in turn comes down to striving constantly to learn whatever, wherever, and whenever it is possible for us to learn.

5-4 LEARNING TO LEARN

All too often we let biases, prejudices, traditions, previous habits, laziness, lack of and misguided imaginations, lack of concentration and perseverance, etc. force us into abandoning the learning that could lead us to finding the truth. Dale (May, 1969) emphasized the critical role that learning plays in growing and preparing for the future. He pointed out that the most important aspect of learning is "learning how to learn and develop a taste for learning." He went on to emphasize that there is a multiplier effect. Knowledge learned in one field becomes usable in other fields. Little ideas put together from different fields often result in generating new and bigger ideas. The knowledge gained becomes catalytic and speeds up and enhances our thinking in new and different channels. If we are wise and balanced persons, we soon learn to capitalize on such procedures and often benefit from serendipities that are triggered by such efforts.

Rogers (1983, 120), in discussing the future of education, said:

> We are ... faced with an entirely new situation in education where the goal of education, if we are to survive, is the facilitation of change and learning. The only man who is educated is the man who has learned how to learn; the man who has learned how to adapt and change; the man who has realized that no knowledge is secure, that only the process of seeking knowledge gives a basis for security.

Learning to learn would thus seem to be the great challenge for us if we are to be balanced whole persons of the future. More on the role of education in creativity is discussed in Chapter 10-4.

Novak and Gowin (1984, 11) said:

> We know that individual persons can learn about learning, can become consciously aware of their power to take charge of their own experience in ways that transform their lives.

They suggest that in meaningful learning "...individuals must choose to relate new knowledge to relevant concepts and propositions they already know." The older concept of learning was looked upon as primarily bringing about changing behavior, which can be the result of training. Novak and Gowin go beyond that and state:

Educational programs should provide learners with the basis for understanding why and how new knowledge is related to what they already know and give them the affective assurance that they have the capability to use this new knowledge in new contexts.

The Novak and Gowin procedure for more effective, meaningful learning suggests that we should work at, and practice at becoming proficient at, identifying and understanding the nature and role of concepts as they exist in the written and spoken word. Then we should attempt to relate the concepts "out there" to those present in our own minds. They suggested that concept mapping (see Chapter 2-5.2) usually is an especially helpful way of establishing hierarchial relationships among and between our own and other concepts.

As balanced whole persons we are likely to be enthusiastic and get joy and satisfaction from learning. When the learning efforts have helped in developing new coherent concepts that have brought us closer to what is believed to be the truth, we experience great feelings of accomplishment and pride. We are then much better prepared to make choices and decisions.

5-5 CHOICE AND DECISION-MAKING

Choices and decisions are made by all of us many times a day. We make many of them almost automatically, without any great amount of thought. But in making most choices we have to be aware of the alternatives and act on them. Otherwise, if we are not aware that we have choices, no action will be taken. In responding out of habit or conditioning we do not feel free because there is little or no awareness that we can react one way or another.

In many places (especially in the U.S. and many parts of the western world) the idea of freedom for the individual is considered a privileged benefit. It is considered that we all have the freedom and right to choose as we see fit to a great extent. Even though we tend to think this way, are we all really free to choose? For example Fromm (1964, 160) said:

Can one really claim that a man who has grown up in material and spiritual poverty, who has never experienced love or concern for anybody, whose body has been conditioned to drinking by years of alcoholic abuse, who has had no possibility of changing his circumstances - can one claim that he is "free" to make his choice?

Fromm (p. 162) believed that we cannot talk about the freedom of choice for people in general, but can only refer to freedom of choice for a specific individual. He said this because one person may be free to choose and another may have lost that freedom as indicated above. He also indicated that the argument for the view that we have no freedom to choose is usually based only on the last decision made in a chain of events.

According to Fromm the decisive factor for us in choosing is awareness. This means we need to be aware of the facts, consider the alternatives and their appropriateness to the situation, recognize our own desires, see the consequences of our choices, and accept the necessity of personal actions required by the decision.

Vaughan (1979, 40) indicated that choices are made even concerning our level of awareness. She said:

What you choose to believe shapes your reality. To a great extent your life as it is now is the result of choices you made in the past, and that your future will evolve according to the choices you are making now.

Fromm (1964, 167) said that:

Freedom is nothing other than the capacity to follow the voice of reason, of health, of well-being, of conscience, against the voices of irrational passions.

Both Fromm and Vaughan have emphasized that the more we get in the habit of making courageous choices that we believe are right, good and desirable, the easier and clearer the choices become. On the other hand, the more we surrender to wrong-doing, coping-out, laziness, procrastination, etc., the easier it becomes for us to be lured into further undesirable actions and eventually our freedom to choose is lost.

Decision-making is often impaired because of our poor planning and preparation for the situation being dealt with. Without the facts at hand, making decisions is not only difficult for us but may easily lead to bad decisions. Kepner and Tregoe (1979, 165) have suggested seven major items that can be helpful in decision-making. These are:

1. Setting objectives against which to choose.
2. Classifying objectives as to importance.
3. Developing alternatives from which to choose.
4. Evaluating alternatives against the objectives to make a choice.

5. Choosing the best alternative as a tentative decision.
6. Assessing adverse consequences from the choice.
7. Controlling effects of the final decision.

While these suggestions can be helpful for us, Engstrom and MacKenzie (1967, 125) have suggested several don't's in making decisions. These are:

1. Don't make decisions under stress.
2. Don't make snap decisions.
3. Don't drag your feet.
4. Don't fail to consult other people.
5. Don't try to anticipate everything.
6. Don't be afraid of making a wrong decision.
7. Once a decision is made, don't delay but go on to something else.

In an article in *Executive Digest* (April, 1975) entitled "Be a Decision-Maker," four ways to make a bad decision were suggested. These were:

1. Making your decision solely on the basis of someone else's opinion.
2. Assuming that what worked in the past will work as well today.
3. Basing your decision on a hunch rather than on facts.
4. Delaying making a decision in hopes the problem will go away or solve itself.

One costly fault in decision-making, that we all too often make, is failing to envision the consequences of the decision. We need to relate the decision to the here and now, but also should not fail to consider the relationship to the past and the impact of the decision on us in the future.

One of the most costly ways to lose time in decision-making is for us to worry about items which cannot be changed. Marshak of the US Department of Agriculture suggested a concept of a response grid which illustrates this point clearly (see Figure 5-2).

If things are not going well and if we have no flexibility in dealing with the situation, then making the decision not to worry and waste time in that area or on those items is extremely important for us. Not unless or until some change suggesting the possibility of flexibility, which we can influence, should items in this disaster area take up our time in thought or action. We need to remember that every decision has its consequences; even if we choose not to decide, it is a decision. Furthermore as Dale (1970) said:

Everything matters. Nothing is insignificant. We are all constructing a world or destroying it by action or inaction.

Robert Ranftl (1978) conducted a study on productivity over a five-year period from 1973 through 1978. The study involved some 59 major organizations from industry, government, and education. Suggestions on solving problems and making decisions made by the study participants included (see Ranftl p. 64):

1. Anticipate problems - be alert for symptoms - whenever possible, head off problems with preventive action before they fully materialize.
2. Get into the habit of solving problems and making decisions - avoid indecision, vacillation, procrastination, and rationalization. (One important note: don't handle problems or make decisions when tired, preoccupied, or irritated.)
3. Give problems/decisions priority in accordance with their importance.
4. Define the problem - strip it of all unnecessary elements - distill it down to its simplest terms.
5. Subdivide particularly difficult problems, when appropriate, into related segments. (Often by solving one segment, the other segments more readily lend themselves to solution.)
6. Get all the facts - discard irrelevant material - eliminate biases - challenge assumptions - correlate all relevant material.
7. Analyze material carefully - draw affected people into the decision process. (People who share in a decision, even an unpopular one, are more likely to be committed to its success than if they had no part in it.)
8. Formulate possible solutions.
9. Assess risks and consequences.
10. Incubate - set a time limit - decide as promptly as possible but avoid premature decisions. (Remember that frequently more than one choice will work equally well).
11. Plan implementing action clearly and effectively - consider the need for contingency plans and develop them as appropriate.
12. Take timely action - follow up, taking corrective action as necessary.

THE RESPONSE GRID

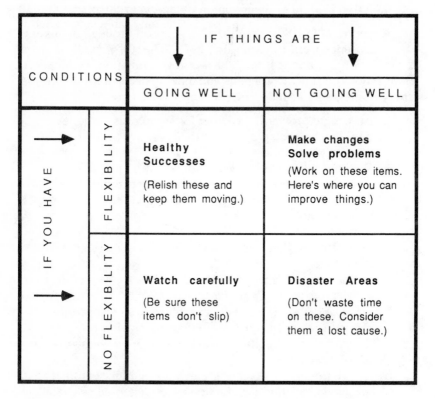

CONDITIONS	IF THINGS ARE	
	GOING WELL	NOT GOING WELL
IF YOU HAVE FLEXIBILITY	**Healthy Successes** (Relish these and keep them moving.)	**Make changes Solve problems** (Work on these items. Here's where you can improve things.)
IF YOU HAVE NO FLEXIBILITY	**Watch carefully** (Be sure these items don't slip)	**Disaster Areas** (Don't waste time on these. Consider them a lost cause.)

Fig. 5-2   Conditions Affecting Our Ability to Respond in Making Decisions for Change (Adapted from Marshak, 1981)

13. Accept responsibility for each decision and its consequences.

5-6 FREEDOM AND RESPONSIBILITY

Freedom and responsibility go together. As Dale (1967) has said with regard to the fantastic mechanical improvements in our ability to communicate:

Increased power to communicate wisdom also means increased power to communicate stupidity.

This is the point where individual decision and responsibility come into play.

Like it or not, in some way every day we are affecting someone, even if we attempt to withdraw. As is sometimes said by people with a Christian religious bent, "You may be the only Bible some youngster ever gets to see." Every day decisions must be made that will affect our own and other's lives. Hopefully, these decisions will affect people in a positive way. Peck (1978, 76) said:

> The best decision-makers are those who are willing to suffer the most over their decisions but still retain their ability to be decisive.

Such persons realize that they are affecting others' lives as well as their own and then take responsibility for their decisions.

Because of the complexity of the world today, many of us do not wish to get involved. We are apt to want to let someone else deal with the problems. Because of laziness and not wanting to take responsibility, we would rather be followers than leaders in groups. That way we feel there is no need for us to agonize over complex decisions, plan ahead, risk popularity, exercise initiative, exert courage, or be responsible for the group's performance. I saw this a number of times while in the armed services during WWII. Intelligent and capable individuals in lower ranks often attempted to avoid the responsibilities that moving up in the ranks would entail. They often did less and attempted to hide their capabilities because they did not want to take on greater responsibilities.

When we avoid taking on responsibilities, we turn our freedom and responsibility over to others. We thus regress and become more immature as we join a group. Peck (1983, 223) suggested that groups are frequently at a level that is more primitive and immature than might be expected. All too often individuals in a group are happy to "pass the buck" and thus refuse to take a fair share of the responsibility for the group's actions.

But, someone must mind the store. Someone must take responsibility for perpetuating the truth. If we are balanced persons we realize that we too must carry a fair share of the load and responsibility for the way things are and especially for the direction the future takes. We dare not "pass" or "sit out" every event. Often we underestimate our potential and the possible influence that we, as individuals, may be able to have on getting changes made.

All too often we fall into irresponsible practices without thinking and because "everyone is doing it." This may be especially true with unethical practices (see Chapter 7-3.6). Irresponsible behavior can have a devastating and destructive effect on our self-esteem. Excessive and repetitive unethical practices by us are likely to lead to loss of trust and respect by others. This, in turn, can result in isolation for us and loss of friends, job, business, etc., and even imprisonment. The result is loss of freedom, not only for us as violators, but also often for innocent persons because new laws and regulations are imposed on everybody. In addition there can be real harm because the perpetrators are setting patterns for others, who may have unwisely (or innocently) picked them as models or mentors.

Too often we lead young people to believe they are not capable of accepting responsibility. Dale (1970) indicated that he felt young people do not take responsibility because they are not given it and expected to show it. He said, "Social responsibility comes with the opportunity and the ability to respond in depth to the critical questions of the day." He especially emphasized that young people want their education to be relevant and tied to important issues and needs, and we should put more responsibility on young individuals to educate themselves. He said one reason why we don't let young people have more responsibility in school and college is because we don't know how.

5-7 EXCELLENCE AND PERFECTION

Excellence is frequently used to describe our performance by a comparison against other individuals for some measure of mental or physical skill or accomplishing a task more creatively, more rapidly, or more effectively. Another way of measuring excellence is by comparing one of our performances with another as we compete with ourselves to become more proficient or improved.

Some kinds of excellence involve doing something; others may depend upon being a certain kind of person. We usually narrow the definition when we are testing, training or selecting for some specific trait or task. Usually in specific items, certain standards have been developed, or have evolved, which are used in determining the degree of excellence.

For the most part, we profess that we would like to have all individuals reach a level of perfection and excellence commensurate with their capabilities. Yet we still, as Gardner (1961, 27) said, have two major forces which mitigate against that goal. In the first we are granted status on the basis of our hereditary privilege. That is, not by our capabilities, but by membership in a family, class or community. Membership then, not ability, determines our status, power, prestige, rights and privileges. We still see much of this type of force in the world and it is even still present in the U.S. to a lesser degree. In some cases we see sons and daughters forced to carry on the profession or craft followed by their parents. They are confined to a caste, an economic level (poverty), a culture, or a national level of development which completely blocks any opportunity for changing things for the better for them. Thus those individuals have little or no opportunity to follow a career that might fit their abilities far better than what the father or mother has been doing. Or perhaps they are forced into a situation for which they lack the capability and skills needed to succeed.

We also see a kind of hereditary privilege (but not blood related as the name implies) that is widespread and quite destructive to us if we have been striving for and have attained a creditable degree of excellence and perfection. This is political favoritism. If we, as persons with outstanding abilities, are bypassed and persons with lesser abilities are rewarded with such items as a position on a team, a promotion, an award, or a significant salary increase, etc., based solely on being one of the crowd, on "cronyism" or the "good buddy" or "good old boy" system, we suffer much harm to our pride and to our initiative. I could cite all kinds of examples of this in academia, communities, churches, and in families.

Gardner (1961, 15) also focused on a second force, equalitarianism. This too can thwart our ambition, aptitude and reaching higher levels of performance and perfection. In its worst and extreme forms it tends to reduce us to mediocrity. It tends to deny that there are differences in our capacities. Although we are well aware that people are not equal in their mental and physical gifts nor in their motivation to achieve, some would still like to reward everyone the same. Such a practice ignores and attempts to hide our differences and removes a strong motivational force for us to strive for excellence and perfection.

We are all (even our nation as a whole) faced with an extremely challenging situation in our need and attempt to preserve freedom for the individual to achieve and excel. Gardner (1961, 115) stated it well, "How can we provide opportunities and rewards for individuals of every degree of ability so that individuals at every level will realize their full potentialities, perform at their best and harbor no resentment toward any other level?"

Dale (1967) said:

Providing access to excellence is only the beginning to

wisdom, not the end. Access to excellence must be accompanied by mastering the ability to receive and to use messages. To use the available best, one must be able to communicate well by reading and writing, listening and speaking, visualizing and observing.

He went on to point out:

In creating the future we must decide whether we wish to develop an inclusive society or an exclusive one. Do we want to shut others off from access to excellence or do we want to include them as participants in the world's bounties? Instead of providing rich experiences for all, we spend too much of our first-rate energy holding other people down.

As admirable as the drive to excel usually is, it is not without some dangers. An over-emphasis on excelling can lead us to overpowering cases of perfectionism. In such cases we become so obsessed with the desire to excel that we feel everything has to be done perfectly. As perfectionists we set standards for ourselves that become unrealistic. Such afflicted persons are never satisfied with their performances or products. They always feel that they should have done better. Weisinger and Lobsenz (1981, 235) pointed out:

This need to be perfect also stems from childhood experience of parental criticism. To bolster their own self-esteem, parents often expect a child to achieve results beyond the youngster's desires or abilities.

As a result the person involved can become "endlessly preoccupied with physical, intellectual or social accomplishment" (Missildine, 1963, cover).

Missildine and Galton (1974, 148-155) said:

The driving force for the perfectionist is not a need to win over competition; rather it is a never-ending need to try to escape the awful feeling within that he or she could "do better."

They have suggested that we can strive for perfection without being a perfectionist if we like turning out top quality work and enjoy striving for that goal without feeling that the outcome is a "do-or-die" situation and is being done to prove our worth. They warn that we need to be wary of feeling superior to others who may be less driven. There is also danger in feeling that ordinary standards do not apply to us because we wish to excel. We need to learn that the leisure, relaxation and the less harried pace that others enjoy can also be rewarding for us. More will be discussed about factors that cause us to develop excessive perfectionist tendencies in Chapter 10. There is no question that the drive to excel can bring us great rewards if we control that urge and apply it wisely. We may need to excel in the art of relaxing and staying loose so that the many other physiological and mental functions can stay in top form. Here again "balance" may be the key to greater achievement and personal satisfaction for us.

5-8 POSITIVE THINKING

Is positive thinking an attitude, a feeling, a discipline, or mainly a process of the intelligence? It appears to me to be a mixture of some, and maybe portions, of all of these. Whatever it might be classed as, Peale (1959, 9), an early and strong proponent of the power of positive thinking, has said that positive thinking is tough-mindedness. It is refusing to accept defeat as a totally negative experience. It is finding something positive in a situation; no matter how bad it is. It is making do; no matter how little one has to do with. It is refusing to get locked into the negative aspects of a situation.

Unfortunately when things are not going well, we tend to react negatively. If we are positive thinkers, we do not refuse to acknowledge the negative, we simply refuse to dwell on it. We must train ourselves to shut out negative thoughts and focus on the positive by exerting our energies looking for solutions, alternatives, or opportunities instead of using untold energy blaming someone or something for the disastrous situation. Believing enough in our abilities and the help that can be obtained from various sources, no matter what comes along, can help us use our energies constructively, rather than fruitlessly, in dealing with problems.

How do we manage problems using positive thinking? Schuller (1983, 72-90) suggested some general principles:

1. Don't underestimate the problem or your ability to deal with it. We tend to underestimate serious problems.
2. Don't exaggerate the problem. At first we often think smaller problems are bigger than they really are.
3. Don't procrastinate. The problem is yours, don't expect someone else to take the initiative in dealing with it.
4. Take care not to aggravate it with self-pity, jealousy, cynicism, hatred, anger, or lack of positive faith in the future.
5. Clarify in your own mind what the problem really is.
6. List and consider all the positive actions you could take.

7. Select the most promising actions you might take.
8. Be persistent. New possibilities may appear each day.
9. Believe that every adversity holds within it the seeds of an undeveloped possibility.
10. Give it all you've got.
11. Remember there may be others who can help.
12. Avoid negative forces and negative personalities.

Many of us react to ideas in a negative fashion almost immediately upon hearing them. For several years Robert Schuller has been a strong advocate of positive thinking. He has used the term "possibility thinking" widely in his sermons and workshops. He has suggested several guidelines for possibility thinkers to counter the tendency to be negative about ideas. He says never reject an idea because:

1. You see something wrong with it.
2. You won't get the credit.
3. It's impossible.
4. Your mind is made up.
5. It's illegal (maybe the law can be changed).
6. You don't have the money, manpower, muscle, or months to achieve it.
7. It will create conflict.
8. It's not your way of doing things.
9. It might fail.
10. It's sure to succeed (it's against their religion to be anything but humble).

It is amazing how quickly the down feeling of an undesirable situation will disappear when we take the positive thinking path. If we seek alternatives and opportunities that the occurrence may have presented instead of dwelling on its imagined negative aspects, we will often find there is an opportunity present. If we are in the habit of taking the negative route, considerable effort will likely be needed to change to thinking positively. However, just as self-discipline becomes easier with continued effort, taking the positive route becomes easier with practice. This approach is one that can greatly improve our problem-solving abilities.

5-9 WISDOM AND COMMON SENSE

What then do we need to pull together all the several items discussed in this, preceding and succeeding chapters to make a practical, effective, working philosophy for a creative individual? The word philosophy itself is kind of a key. It is derived from the Greek words *philos*, meaning loving, and *sophia*, meaning wisdom, thus the love of wisdom. In addition to being able to utilize intelligence, tap our intuition and imagination, discipline and control our emotions, and integrate all factors into a creative output, we must possess wisdom, common sense and enthusiasm.

The dictionary definition of wisdom is that it is the quality or state of being wise and having knowledge of what is true or right coupled with good judgement. Wise is having the power of discretion and discerning and judging properly as to what is true and right.

Common sense is defined as sound practical judgment that is independent of specialized knowledge, training, or the like. It is normal native intelligence - plain practical horse sense.

Wisdom and common sense have been recognized as valuable personal assets since Old Testament days:

Wisdom gives: a long, good life, riches, honor, pleasure, peace. Wisdom is a tree of life to those who eat her fruit; happy is the man who keeps on eating it.(Proverbs 3:16-18. Living Bible)

Have two goals: wisdom - that is, knowing and doing right - and common sense. Don't let them slip away, for they fill you with living energy and are a feather in your cap. They keep you safe from defeat and disaster and from stumbling off the trail. (Proverbs 3:21-23. LB)

Learn to be wise and develop good judgment and common sense! I cannot overemphasize this point. Cling to wisdom - she will protect you. Love her - she will guard you. (Proverbs 4:5-6. LB)

Even though we don't know just where the driving force lies within or outside us (Is it the spirit, the supernatural?), nor do we know where and how all the factors involved are brought together and controlled by the human brain, it has long been known that if wisdom and common sense are lacking, we will likely suffer chaos.

Like many other aspects which we have discussed, there is no easy way of telling another how to develop wisdom and common sense. Much is learned and absorbed during childhood from good examples set by those rearing and teaching us. We can also learn throughout life by developing our knowledge and making the most of our experiences (both successes and failures). We can learn from living examples who surround us and demonstrate daily, both good and bad judgment, wise and stupid decisions, as well as creditable and foolish actions. Over time, depending on how observant we are, what kind of background experiences we have had, and how much personal effort we are willing to put into evaluating daily occurrences, we can grow in wisdom and continue to develop and utilize common sense.

5-10 BALANCED WHOLE-PERSON.

Thus far in this book we have focused on the need for the creative person to possess a number of inherent and learned characteristics such as intelligence, curiosity, intuition, imagination, perception, as well as having developed helpful attitudes toward self and others. In this chapter we have looked at other factors including discipline, making choices, handling freedom and responsibility, striving for excellence, thinking positively and developing wisdom and common sense.

What still needs a careful look is how to find a happy balance among these many factors, as well as several that will be discussed in the remaining chapters of this book. How do we decide how much effort should be placed on each item? What if we feel we are lacking in a particular area? Does that mean there is no chance of our being creative? Certainly not. We are each a special mix of these items. None of us could possibly have all of these items well developed. What we need is our own special mix and balance that will work for us individually. We each must strive to search out, find, develop and constantly update the proper balance for our needs. Peck (1978, 64, 73) said this can only be done by balancing and bracketing.

Balancing is Peck's fourth suggested disciplinary tool. It is the type of discipline required to discipline discipline. It often requires us to develop a personal flexibility, which is needed in order to respond to different situations in different manners, depending on the circumstances involved. Peck said (1978, 66):

> Mature mental health demands an extraordinary capacity to flexibly strike and continually restrike a delicate balance between conflicting needs, goals, duties, directions, responsibilities, et cetera.

He used the term "bracketing" to describe the balancing of need for stability and assertion of the self in order to take in new knowledge and develop better understanding. This can require us to temporarily set ourselves aside in order to take in and assimilate new aspects into our makeup. In essence this means letting (giving up) old ways die to let new ways come into being. It essentially becomes a discipline of being willing "to give up." We will frequently be required to give up well established patterns of behavior, ideologies, personality traits, and maybe even whole life styles. Peck (1978, 66-67) said further:

> Balancing is a discipline precisely because the act of giving something up is painful. In its major forms, giving up is the most painful of human experiences.

As creative persons, as well as for all others too, then we can expect a constant series of painful experiences if growth is to occur; and new and original things are to be brought into being and take the place of the old. Thus the more capable we are of balancing, and the better balanced we become, the greater the likelihood that we can handle a diversity of situations and bring new ideas into play in our creative endeavors.

5-11 PROBLEM-SOLVING CAPABILITIES

Because problems and even opportunities frequently are painful and threatening, we all would usually like to avoid them. We do in fact often ignore them, forget them, procrastinate in facing them, hoping they will go away, solve themselves or have someone solve them for us. We even go to great lengths by taking drugs, going to excesses in eating, sleeping or busying ourselves with other things to help us ignore or deaden our pain because of their presence. For the most part many of us are not willing to delay gratification, accept responsibility, or accept the truth of the situation and face the problems.

The sooner we learn to discipline ourselves to accept the fact that there will likely be difficulty, pain, or disappointment in facing problems, the sooner we learn what relief there is in finding a resolution, even if the outcome is not what we might have hoped for. A balanced "whole-person" should have at his/her disposal more of what it takes to face and solve problems. Knowledge, attitudes, and discipline combined with wisdom and common sense usually will provide us with the essentials for dealing with problems and opportunities in a less painful way than is the case if the problems are not faced head-on as soon as we recognize them.

5-12 HIGHLIGHTS OF CHAPTER FIVE

1. If we over-emphasize the development of only our intellectual

side and neglect our emotional side, we may become what has been called "an intellectual half-person."

2. We must give attention to developing our emotional, as well as our intellectual aspects, if we are to achieve balance and find our greatest creative, "whole-person" potential.

3. Developing the discipline to discipline our discipline is usually one of the hardest tasks we face.

4. If we learn how to learn and use discipline to practice learning throughout life, the probabilities of our continuing to grow and improve are high.

5. Careful planning, gathering the facts, considering the alternatives, and envisioning the consequences of the choices we make can help us to make better decisions.

6. Even though many of us tend to think that complete freedom would be ideal, freedom without responsibility and consideration for others can be disastrous.

7. Striving for excellence in all that we do is a fine idealistic goal, but perfection in everything that we do is impossible and trying too hard can be debilitating and destructive.

8. Maintaining a positive frame of mind and avoiding negative thinking not only makes us more acceptable to be around, but gives us a head start on converting problems into opportunities.

9. Using wisdom, common sense and balancing all the various factors involved in making ourselves "whole persons" are ultimate challenges for all of us.

10. With balance and wisdom in bringing all our capabilities to bear in problem-solving, we can become more proficient at finding solutions and recognizing opportunities.

5-13 AFTERGROWTH STIMULATORS

1. How do you feel about the balance you have had between the intellectual and the emotional aspects of your background and education? From your parents? From your schooling? From your own doing?

2. What have you done to discipline yourself to delay gratification? Take responsibility? Seek the truth?

3. Has your education and upbringing given you good fundamental training for learning to learn? For making choices and decisions?

4. Do you think freedom and responsibility can co-exist in our society today? How free are you today? How responsible?
5. How do you go about avoiding negative thinking? Does it help you in thinking more positively?
6. Do you think wisdom and common sense can be taught? How can we best go about developing these traits? In youngsters? In ourselves?

CHAPTER 6

PROBLEM-SOLVING:
IDENTIFYING AND FINDING SOLUTIONS

6- 1　Introduction
6- 2　The Need for Problem-Solving
　　　　and/or Opportunity Assessment
6- 3　Problems Come in Many Forms
6- 4　General Problem-Solving Capabilities
6- 5　Some Basic Approaches to
　　　　Problem-Solving
6- 6　Frequent Sources and Types of Errors
6- 7　Becoming Aware of the Problem
　　　　or Opportunity
6- 8　Defining and Stating the Problem
6- 9　Developing Ideas, Brainstorming,
　　　　and Coming Up with a Hypothesis
6-10　Seeking a Solution
6-11　Transforming the Solution into Action
6-12　Problem-Solving in Scientific Research
6-13　Highlights of Chapter Six
6-14　Aftergrowth Stimulators

6-1 INTRODUCTION

For probably as long as people have existed they have been confronted with solving problems, seizing opportunities, and the need to contribute new knowledge and understanding of themselves and the universe. For centuries little attention was given to anything but the major concern of survival. Throughout history, and even today, a large percentage of the people of the world are content to just survive and live on the past facts and practices that have been contributed to humanity's "Stream of Knowledge" (see Figure 6-1).

But an inherent human curiosity apparently drives some of us to face and even attack the "Mountains of Deterrents" (that seem insurmountable to most of the population), and seek to discover and harness new knowledge from the "Dark Pool of the Unknown" to add to the "Stream of Knowledge."

Throughout the advance of knowledge and civilization, many have apparently, repeatedly thought that all that was to be learned and known had already been discovered, only to be astonished to learn later that "We hadn't seen anything yet." We have problems and opportunities on every hand. They range from simple every-day problems related to our finding enough to eat and a place to sleep to complex problems of science, the world, and even our attempts to understand the universe. However, we can solve problems as complicated and complex as understanding the universe and solving international relationships only by breaking them down into smaller bits. We must find component solutions and then integrate the numerous solutions of smaller parts into the whole. Over the years many attempts with various approaches have been made to develop more certain and effective procedures for solving problems, seizing opportunities and discovering new facts.

The whole process can be more effective if we follow some established practices and systematic approaches. Here, we are going to concern ourselves primarily with problem-solving, opportunity seizing, and establishing facts by individuals and small working groups.

6-2 THE NEED FOR PROBLEM-SOLVING AND/OR OPPORTUNITY ASSESSMENT

We all, at any age and in almost any situation, are faced with problems and opportunities. In fact, a large proportion of life's problems must be solved by individuals. Only individuals can feel

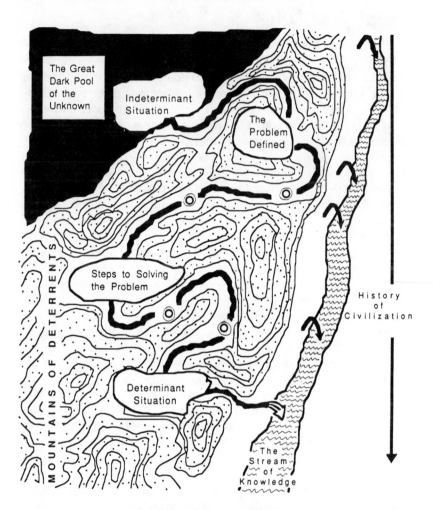

Fig. 6-1 Conceptualization of Solving Problems and Contributing to Man's Stream of Knowledge

and enjoy, or feel regret, and suffer in the solution or failure to solve problems or seize or miss opportunities. Others around us can play a major role in influencing (helping or hurting) the process and the speed with which it is accomplished.

We may be in a situation which we do not like and want to change it. There may be a discrepancy between where we are and where we would like to be. There may be aspects of nature or the world around us about which we are curious and don't understand, but would like to understand or change. Thus these differences between an initial state (the given or situational facts) and the desired final state (goals) call for us to develop ideas, responses, or actions (operations, solutions) to close the gap and bring about a resolution of the discrepancies or differences. These needs call for problem-solving and opportunity seizing.

6-3 PROBLEMS COME IN MANY FORMS

Problems and opportunities occur in many, and often hard to distinguish, forms. Being aware of some of the forms that occur can often aid us in recognizing and defining problems.

6-3.1 "Mind Benders"

Anderson (1980, 2-3), pointed out and labeled one kind of problem "mind benders." These problems are generated because we lack ideas and thus are required to resort to creative thinking:

1. Problems of invention - We have locked ourselves out of the house. How can we get in?
2. Problems of anticipation - What will the opportunities of space travel offer me? How will I perform when I am out of the grips of gravity?

6-3.2 "Mind Bogglers"

This is the kind of problem that presents a profusion of ideas and requires us to think critically to eliminate those of lesser value:

1. Problems of prediction - How long will it be before every large business will be required to supply child care facilities?
2. Problems of explanation - I have not been feeling well lately. Is it because I have not been getting enough rest, not eating well, not sleeping well, not exercising enough? Have I been experiencing more stress than usual? Could I be coming down with some kind of mental or physical ailment?
3. Problems of choice - What make and model should we select for a new audio-video system for our apartment?
4. Hidden problems - problems of awareness. A widely used pesticide, originally considered safe, has been found to be slowly polluting the water supply. We were not aware that

the problem existed (personality problems also often fit this category).
5. Complex problems - Many of life's difficulties are complex and thus may include several of the above kinds of problems.

6-3.3 The Search Process

Researchers believe that problem-solving consists of a highly selective search process through what they call large problem spaces in which we compare present situations with ultimate goals, recognize one or more differences in them and recover from our stored memory, items that may be helpful in reducing the differences. Developing keen selective capabilities is necessary if we are to complete the search in a reasonable amount of time. Our background and experience can be extremely important in this aspect. The problem-solving process consists of a sequence of actions triggered by the recognition of some clue suggesting the relevance of the item to the current situation. Thus efficiency is important for us in acquiring, generating, and using information in the strategies involved in problem-solving.

6-4 GENERAL PROBLEM-SOLVING CAPABILITIES

We can develop various capabilities which will help us in dealing with the multitude of problems of various kinds in everyday life and in certain scientific and other specific situations.

6-4.1 Attitudes

The fact that problems are a part of everyday life is one of the first things that we must accept and face up to. Some of us, usually the poorer problem-solvers, tend to try to avoid problems because we find them unpleasant and threatening. Usually, if we are this type of person, we try to shift the responsibility for solving the problem to someone else or even put off working on it and pretend that there is no problem, hoping the problem will go away. A constant awareness of conditions around us is necessary to be aware of problems and to find solutions for them. If we are to be good problem-solvers we must be adept at detecting problems and even actively seek them out. We also are likely to be quicker in recognizing opportunities if we remain aware of things around us.

To deal with problems, we should think positively about them, seek to identify them, and actively pursue solutions. We need to be doubters. We need to look for imperfections and trouble in order to avoid the discomforts and undesirable situations which problems will bring us if we do not deal with them.

In addition to thinking positively about problems, we need to develop an attitude of thinking positively about our ability to solve problems. If we know our strengths, are aware of pending problems, and are willing to face up to them, we usually can become competent problem-solvers. Accomplishing this capability, however, requires that we learn to think systematically and take positive action in dealing with problems. This usually requires that we:

1. develop the ability to recognize that we have a problem or opportunity;
2. can define and state the problem;
3. are able to assemble the established facts concerning the situation;
4. focus on these facts in generating ideas for a solution;
5. choose the best probable solution; and
6. act on that probable best solution to bring about change.

The Creative Education Foundation (Osborn, 1963) has described these steps as fact-finding (the situation), problem- finding, idea-finding, solution-finding, and acceptance-finding (plan of action).

6-4.2 Basic Skills

To become adept at problem-solving, we must develop certain skills which help in recognizing the problem, seeing beyond the surface of the problem, looking at the situation from many angles, recognizing similarities and differences and, in many cases, developing an ability to place ourselves in the position of another. Even when solving puzzles or other simple problems, skills are sharpened that help develop keen observation, insightfulness, curiosity, persistence, mental agility and adroitness. We also develop perceptive and associative outlooks that can be helpful to us. (Try the following exercise (you may be surprised at the results):

Try naming 25 birds in 3 minutes. Do this with someone using a stop watch and reporting the time to you after the first one and one-half minutes, at 2 minutes, and then every 15 seconds until the 3 minutes are up. What about your ability to think under the pressure of time?

Now take a bird book and see just how many of the birds named in the book are familiar to you. Or just relax and see how many more names of birds you can add to your list when you are not under the pressure of time. Why is it there are so many that you know but did not think of in attempting your original list of 25? Can it be that we know a lot more than we usually think we know? Recall may be our big problem.

6-4.3 Overcoming Blocks

The environment in which we operate, as well as our own inner feelings, plays an extremely important role in developing problem-solving abilities. Fear, laziness, procrastination, and the inability to break habits or pay attention to details are detrimental to our problem-solving capabilities. Paying attention to our physical senses, gut feelings, intuition, and becoming adept at transition and the use of imagery are tools that help facilitate problem-solving. Learning to look beyond the surface of a problem is especially important for us.

6-5 SOME BASIC APPROACHES TO PROBLEM-SOLVING

Before turning to the more major breakdown in problem-solving of looking at the situation, defining the problem, etc., it may be well to look at some of the basic approaches as suggested by Wickelgren (1974). Problems illustrative of each of these steps are also suggested. Most of the problems have been borrowed from Wickelgren.

6-5.1 Drawing Inferences

Making transformations of the goals or the givens is probably the first problem-solving method we should employ in attempting to solve a problem. In this approach we are essentially expanding the goal or the givens by bringing to bear all of the knowledge available from our memories, and/or the literature or experiences of others. Now try solving Problems 1, 2, and 3:

1. **Cube Sawing Problem: Based on Givens**

You are working with a power saw and wish to cut a wooden cube, three inches on a side, into 27 one inch cubes. You can do this by making six cuts through the cube, keeping the pieces together in the cube shape. Can you reduce the number of necessary cuts by rearranging the pieces after each cut? (From Wickelgren, 1974, 32)

2. Heavy Coin Problem: Based on Operations

You have a pile of 24 coins. Twenty-three of these coins have the same weight, and one is heavier than the others. Your task is to determine which coin is heavier and to do so in the minimum number of weighings. You are given a beam balance (scale), which will compare the weights of any two sets of coins out of the total set of 24 coins. (From Wickelgren, 1974, 34)

3. 63-Link Chain Problem: Based on Goals

Wanda the witch agrees to trade one of her magic broomsticks to Gaspar the ghost in exchange for one of his gold chains. Gaspar is somewhat skeptical that the broomstick is in working order and insists on a guarantee equal in days to the number of links in his gold chain. To facilitate enforcement of the quarantee, he insists on paying by the installment plan, one gold link per day until the end of the 63-day period, with the balance to be forfeited if the broomstick malfunctions during the guarantee period. Wanda agrees to this request, but insists that the installment payment be effected by cutting no more than three links in the gold chain. Can this be done, and, if so, what links in the chain should be cut? The chain initially consists of 63 gold links arranged in a simple linear order (not closed into a circle). (From Wickelgren, 1974, 43-44)

6-5.2 Trial and Error

When confronted with a problem, most of us start applying allowable operations. To avoid going around in circles, we need to try to remember what sequences of actions we have taken. It is better still if we develop a systematic approach using different approaches. Now give Problem 4 a try, keeping tabs on the actions you take:

4. Six Arrow Problem: Requires a Systematic Approach

You are given six arrows (arranged) in a row; the left three pointing up, and the right three pointing down. The goal is to transform these arrows into an alternating sequence such that the left-most arrow points up, the next arrow to it points down, the next up, then down, then up, then down. The actions allowed are to simultaneously invert (turn upside down) any two adjacent arrows. Note that you cannot invert one arrow at a time but must invert two arrows at a time, and the two arrows must be adjacent. Achieve the solution using the minimum number of actions (inversions of adjacent pairs). (from Wickelgren, 1974, 49)

Getting out of a loop - An excellent first step in getting out of a loop (going around in circles) and doing something different is to analyze the action sequences of what we have been doing.

Often it may help to use the incubation technique - Put the problem aside for several minutes, hours, or days and work on something else or get a good night's sleep before coming back to the problem (we may have been fatigued and we will come back fresher). There may be intellectual fatigue or interference as a result of a large number of incorrect actions. Our memories will likely be altered by a new set of things on our mind. Our minds may go on working unconsciously on the problem during the incubation period. See Chapter 3-3 and Vaughan (1979).

6-5.3 Hill Climbing

In this approach we try an action that will bring us a step closer to the goal. Sometimes a detour or a reversal may be required. Now try Problems 5 and 6, using a step by step approach:

5. Bus Driver Reversal Problem: Step by Step Action Needed

Because the boys from a junior-high school were causing problems by pestering the girls, the driver of one of the small buses decided to separate the boys and girls. The boys quickly opted for the rear of the bus. Instead of pestering the girls the boys then began fighting among themselves. The driver decided to make a game of reversing the situation and making the boys sit in the front, and the girls in the rear. With all but the front row of seats of the seven rows filled (back three rows with boys, the next three with girls), he instructed them to reverse the seating, boys in front and girls in the rear, with one row at a time making the move. Moves could be made by going one, two or three rows forward or backward to a vacated row of seats.

The driver said he didn't care where the vacant row of seats was left after the reversal had been made. What would the minimum number of moves be to accomplish the reversal?

6. Wilderness Dweller Dilemma: Detour and Reversal May Help

A north country wilderness dweller has acquired a pet fox, a goose, and a bag of corn in his visit to the nearest village. On his route back to his cabin he suddenly remembers he has to cross a lake in his kayak that he left at the lake on his way to the village. He only has room for himself and one of the items he has acquired on each trip in the kayak, thus he will have to make three or more trips. How can he get all of these across without the pet fox eating the goose or the goose eating the corn. He obviously does not dare leave the fox and the goose, nor the goose and the corn together alone. Can he do it?

6-5.4 Subgoals

Breaking a problem into parts is often a helpful procedure (see Problems 3 and 7). First refer back to the 63-link chain problem (Problem 3). Then give Problem 7 a try:

7. **Ordering Letters in a 2x3 Rectangle Divided into Squares**

A 2x3 rectangle is divided into six squares. The two left and the upper middle squares are labelled A. The lower middle square is left open. The upper right square is labelled C, the lower right B. Letters from any square can be moved up, down, right or left to an adjacent vacant square within the rectangle. The problem is to make moves which will rearrange the sequence so that the A's are in their original position, but B is in the upper right and C in the lower right squares. (Modified from Wickelgren, 1974, 101)

6-5.5 Contradiction

As amateur problem-solvers we often do not pay enough attention to the goal or the set of possible goals as part of the problem. We frequently do not consider applying operations to possible goals in order to get to the givens or to meet the givens halfway. Give Problems 8 and 9 a try, but be alert for contradictions:

8. **Smith, Jones, Robinson Problem: Make Use of Contradictions**

Smith, Jones, and Robinson are the brakeman, fireman, and engineer of a train, not necessarily respectively. Today only three passengers are riding this train, and, by an extraordinary coincidence, their last names are the same as the last names of the brakeman, fireman, and engineer. To distinguish the passengers from the trainmen, let us refer to the passengers with the title Mr. - Mr. Smith, Mr. Jones and Mr. Robinson. Here is some other relevant information:

    a. Mr. Robinson lives in Detroit.
    b. The brakeman lives halfway between Chicago and Detroit.
    c. The passenger who lives in Chicago has the same name as the

brakeman.

d. The brakeman's next-door neighbor, one of the passengers, earns exactly three times as much as the brakeman.

e. Mr. Jones earns exactly $ 2,000 a year (and collects a lot of food stamps and welfare payments).

f. Smith beat the fireman at billiards. Who is the engineer? (From Wickelgren, 1974, 121)

9. **Donald, Gerald, Robert Problem: Use Contradictions to Help**

```
    D  O  N  A  L  D
 +  G  E  R  A  L  D
    R  O  B  E  R  T
```

This problem is to be treated as an exercise in simple addition. All that is known is the following: (a) D=5, (b) every number from 0 to 9 has its corresponding letter, (c) each letter must be assigned a number different from that given for any other letter. The goal is to find a number for each letter, stating the steps of the process and their order. (From Wickelgren, 1974, 128)

6-5.6 Working Backwards

Sometimes one can find the answer by working backwards (now try Problem 10):

10. **Doubling-Game Problem: Don't Forget to Work Backwards**

Three people play a game in which one person loses and two people win each game. The one who loses must double the amount of money that each of the other two players has at that time. The three players agree to play three games. At the end of the three games, each player has lost one game and each person has $ 8. What was the original stake of each player? (From Wickelgren, 1974, 141)

6-6 FREQUENT SOURCES AND TYPES OF ERRORS

Whimbey and Lochhead (1982, 18-20) developed a checklist of sources and types of errors which we frequently make in solving problems. Most of our difficulties occur as a result of inaccuracies in reading; inaccuracies in thinking; weakness in problem analysis; lack of perseverance; or failure to think aloud. Too often there is a tendency to read material without concentrating on its meaning. Often we skip parts that are not well understood. This can lead to errors later. Reading too rapidly can also lead to a lack of comprehension. Sometimes one or more words may be critical and if we do not read carefully we will err. The same is true if a fact or an idea is missed. We need to reread difficult sections to be sure they are clearly understood. These all apply (as do others that follow) just as importantly in paying careful attention when we are dealing with an everyday problem or opportunity.

Carelessness in thinking can also lead us to errors. A high premium needs to be placed on accuracy. Often, under pressures of time, we sacrifice accuracy for speed. Care must be taken in performing operations so that we do not miss certain aspects or fail to think them through. Oftentimes, we can quickly and readily pick up an error by simply checking the answer obtained. Working too rapidly, inaccuracy in visualizing a description or relationship, or jumping to a conclusion in the middle of a problem without sufficient thought can also be causes for error.

Often, with a complex problem, we fail to break the problem into pieces which causes us to get stalled. Taking such a problem step-by-step, making sure that we do not miss an important step can help us in reaching a solution. It is amazing how often we ignore or fail to utilize prior knowledge and experience, thus capitalizing on what we know but may have missed because we did not think we knew. Constructing patterns or tables, or simply recording ideas on paper can help in understanding problems.

All too frequently we make too little effort to solve a problem through reasoning (think back to the cube sawing problem, where reasoning quickly tells you there is no way of sawing six sides of the center cube in less than six cuts), or because we feel that we are not capable of dealing with this type of problem. We may have been confused because the situation presented was different than any we had previously encountered. Tackling a problem with only a superficial consideration, or a guess as to what the solution might be, or pursuing the problem with reason part way through then giving up and jumping to a conclusion can lead us to erroneous conclusions. Throughout problem-solving, we should be thinking about what is being pursued and not lapse into a mechanical manner of operation without thought. Sometimes it helps to vocalize our thinking in sufficient detail to realize what has been performed and to think through what is yet to come.

Careful attention to most of the items above can help us become better problem-solvers. It is important to look beyond the surface, beyond the usual single interpretation. For example, what do you see and think of when you look at the face of a clock? What are your primary thoughts (first thoughts)? What secondary thoughts or images are triggered by your first thoughts of the clock face? Do you come up with 10, 20, 40 or more combined primary and secondary thoughts or images? (Some have reported over 50.)

Assess what kinds of difficulties you encounter in trying to work out problems and puzzles:

- Do you have trouble visualizing a problem or an opportunity?
- Does habit cause you to limit your thinking?
- Are you able to work backwards from the ultimate goal?
- Do you remember to break the problem down into sub-problems?
- Are you able to eliminate possible answers because of contradiction?

Further experience for puzzle enthusiasts can be found in books such as *101 Brain Puzzlers*, Emmet, 1970; *The Lady or the Tiger*, Smyllyan, 1982; *Super Strategies for Puzzles and Games*, Levmore and Cook, 1981; and many others.

6-7 BECOMING AWARE OF THE PROBLEM OR OPPORTUNITY

Olson (1980) suggested that problems arise from needs, aggravations, goals, opportunities, voids, trouble-shooting, trouble prevention, improving whatever exists, and looking into the future. We may just be curious about how some natural event comes about. A problem or opportunity usually results from a situation or difference between that which exists and what we would like to have exist. In some cases, we are presented with a problem or challenge. Sometimes a problem that has occurred before occurs again, and although there is a known solution, we are not aware of it. In this situation finding the solution becomes the challenge. In other cases, we may not even know that a problem or challenge exists. Then we discover that there may be an opportunity to change something that is not to our liking.

Often the most difficult step in problem-solving is recognizing that problems exist. Einstein is credited with having said:

The mere formulation of a problem is far more often essential than its solution, which may be merely a matter of mathematical or experimental skill. To raise new questions, new possibilities, to regard old problems from a new angle requires creative imagination and marks real advances in science." (cited by Parnes et al. 1977, 180)

6-7.1 Recognizing the Problem

Often the closeness to the mess or the gradual development of the situation prevents us from seeing that we have a problem or opportunity. Gradually, we may become aware that we have a challenge, but we recognize that things are not as we would like them to be.

Being alert to what is going on around us and developing an awareness to changes taking place can help us recognize problems and opportunities. We need to become constant observers (not to excess) and constant, gentle, challengers to those things occurring around us. If we do so, we are much more likely to become aware of the development of problems and recognize them before they reach a level of severity or become a missed opportunity.

We also need to be aware that not all problems are bad. In fact, if we can look at problems as challenges and opportunities, life can be much more enjoyable and problem-solving can become fun. It takes constant practice to learn to recognize and become aware of problems and to learn to identify and define what the real problem involves. We usually get a great deal more practice in solving problems than we get in learning to recognize problems as they are developing. Recognizing our personal problems may be even more difficult than recognizing problems around us. This occurs because we tend to block out those things that appear threatening and knowingly or unknowingly we hope that they will disappear; but they usually do not.

6-7.2 What Are the Facts in the Situation

Once we are aware that a problem or a challenging situation exists, it is important to determine just what is occurring or has not occurred. Fact-finding involves learning as much as possible about the background of the situation, who are the people involved, or what kinds of facts relative to people, things, or situations can be identified. Doing this should help us bring a picture of the situation into focus. As much data as possible should be collected so that we can better understand what is going on. We need to look at the situation from as many points of view as possible. We need to ask - What do I know about this situation? What can I learn from others about it (from the literature, from discussing it with others)? Has it happened before? Why is this a problem? Why is it important now? Soon with fact-finding, we begin to get a clearer picture of precisely what the problem is. We can then begin to define it.

6-8 DEFINING AND STATING THE PROBLEM

All too often problem definition is done too hastily. Without careful problem definition, we have little opportunity of understanding exactly what the situation is that is being faced. Years ago, John Dewey said that a problem is half solved if it is properly stated. We cannot state a problem unless we can clearly define it.

To define the problem, we must concentrate and focus our energies on the specific aspects. To accomplish this, we need to focus on why the problem exists, and then try to identify the broader focus of the problem. This in turn may lead us to the need to subdivide the problem so that individual aspects can be focused on one at a time. Determining why the problem exists can frequently lead us to a broader problem statement, perhaps even more appropriate than the problem we initially thought we faced. Then we should focus on separate components. Problems can often be subdivided. There are usually functional aspects; the people involved, the timing elements, the improvements needed, etc., which need to be considered separately as sub-problems. By this process, we can begin to determine the important components and elements which must be considered.

Next we need to define the opportunity or problem in specific terms. Usually we should define and redefine the problem several times in order to narrow it down and focus on the really important aspects.

When we have sufficient clarification of the situation, adequate facts gathered, and the problem or opportunity defined, we should be able to clearly state the problem. Usually this process, too, needs to be repeated several times. What are the important issues, elements, components that need to be considered? How can we state the problem so that many approaches will be taken in looking for solutions? Not "How can we...", which often can be given one answer, but rather "In what ways might we...," or "In how many ways might we...," which should prompt the development of several approaches. We need to write and rewrite the problem statements. Recombine words and phrases until we get a problem statement that clearly says what the problem is.

6-9 DEVELOPING IDEAS, BRAINSTORMING, AND COMING UP WITH A HYPOTHESIS

Once the situation has been clarified to the point where the problem has been defined and a careful problem statement has been developed, we are ready to begin the search for approaches to solutions to the problem. This stage is often referred to as the idea-finding stage.

The major focus in the idea-finding stage is one of developing many alternative ideas for solving the problem. We need to find ways to get our creative wheels rolling.

6-9.1 Stimulating the Idea-Generation Process

Ideas come from individual minds. Therefore the initial step in developing ideas rests with the individual. One way of stimulating ideas individually is to use a self-interrogation procedure. Osborn (1963) developed a series of self-questioning ideas to help with generating numbers of possible solutions. His list is reproduced in Table 6-1. These questions help us to manipulate the stated problem by looking at it from different angles, rearranging the order of the issues, expanding or contracting the ideas, and maybe even developing combinations of separate, originally undreamed of associations.

Just as deliberate efforts to generate ideas must be used, deliberate efforts must also be used to avoid premature judgment. Time spent on judgment is time not spent on generating ideas. We also run the risk of closing off the route to the best idea, or problem solution. All paths must be left open to insure our chances of success. More will be said about deferred judgment on the following pages. In the meantime we must digest two basic principles of idea-generation.

1. Defer judgment; This will help us maximize the number of ideas we can think of in a given period of time. It also increases the number of ideas by leaving all options open.

2. Think of as many ideas as possible; The more ideas we generate, the more likely we are to come up with good ideas.

6-9.2 Brainstorming

This is a particular process in which we seek to generate quantities of ideas, or solutions to a problem or opportunity. As a process it differs little from idea-generation except that brainstorm-

Table 6-1
Osborn's Suggestions for Self-Interrogation to Stimulate Coming up with Ideas

- Put to other uses? New ways to use as is? Other uses if modified?
- Adapt? What else is like this? What other idea does this suggest? Does past offer parallel? What could I copy? Whom could I emulate?
- Modify? New twist? Change meaning, color, motion, sound, odor, form, shape? Other changes?
- Magnify? What to add? More time? Greater frequency? Stronger? Higher? Longer? Thicker? Extra value? Plus ingredient? Duplicate? Multiply? Exaggerate?
- Minify? What to subtract? Smaller? Condensed? Miniature? Lower? Shorter? Lighter? Omit? Streamline? Split up? Understate?
- Substitute? Who else instead? What else instead? Other ingredient? Other material? Other process? Other power? Other place? Other approach? Other tone of voice?
- Rearrange? Interchange components? Other pattern? Other layout? Other sequence? Transpose cause and effect? Change pace? Change schedule?
- Reverse? Transpose positive and negative? How about opposites? Turn it upside down? Reverse roles? Change shoes? Turn tables? Turn other cheek?
- Combine? How about a blend, an alloy, an assortment, an ensemble? Combine units? Combine purposes? Combine appeals? Combine ideas?

Constructed from text of Osborn, 1963, 286-287.

ing is often thought of as an intense, concerted effort at generating ideas. In addition, it is often a planned activity, attended by two or more invited people, usually several. These factors probably led to coining of the term "brainstorming session."

Research has shown that we often come up with more ideas if we work in a group. Hearing other people voice their thoughts can cause us to think of more ideas than we might have without their input. We can "hitchhike" on their ideas to form new ones. The effect is similar to a chain reaction with ideas coming out of ideas coming out of ideas.

Deferred judgement is even more crucial in a group than it is on an individual basis. Besides using the time for ideas only, psychological factors are involved. To be successful a brainstorming session must be free of inhibitions. There should be a "free-wheeling" atmosphere where people are invited not to be reluctant in expressing their ideas. Even the wildest, silliest, and most outlandish ideas should be noted. Shooting down ideas tends to inhibit the less expressive, but perhaps just as creative, members of the group. Criticism cuts off the free flow of ideas. In a group it is unlikely that everyone has the same level of psychological security. By suspending judgment the "playing field" can be levelled to make everyone an equal player. In organizational situations, such as business, industry or education, where brainstorming groups might meet regularly, even the most "timid" souls can feel free to express themselves. Their basic insecurity may not diminish, but they may feel more inclined to express their ideas (Matthews, article in Parnes and Harding, 1962). The whole point is to have everyone participate as fully and freely as possible. This furthers the creative possibilities by providing the opportunity for another process to begin.

Creating as many little or big ideas as possible is extremely important because in most cases connections can eventually be made. Two, or more, ideas can often be combined, and recombined to form a larger, more encompassing idea or solution. This process is sometimes referred to as being synergistic, because the end result may far exceed the simple sum of the separate ideas.

6-9.3 "Mind Prompting" Brainstorming

Often unusual ideas can lead to really creative approaches. Olson (1980) called the initial step in this process "mind prompting." This occurs in brainstorming where ideas suggested by one person trigger new ideas in the mind of another. The process is a deliberate effort to get ideas from others. This can occur also on our part through seeking advice, reading, or otherwise expanding our own horizons. Often contacts with persons in completely different fields other than our own can help trigger new ideas.

Olson referred to a second aspect of this process as "mind surprise". In this procedure we intentionally and deliberately try to generate crazy, foolish and wild ideas. Such an effort stimulates us to catalyze new, fresh, and good ideas and insights. Maintaining a playful or sometimes even silly approach can help us release useful ideas.

The third stage Olson called "mind freeing." In this process a deliberate effort is made to examine the similarities to something else. Choosing a physical object, picture, plant or animal, or other item remote from the problem and listing the characteristics of that item, then following with forced associations between the problem at hand and the attributes of the item chosen can bring out new and different thoughts often triggering extremely creative ideas. In the final stage we combine and synthesize. Olson called this stage "mind synthesize." The objective is to synthesize diverse ideas and make combinations and recombinations where the whole of the new item results in more than the separate parts of the idea.

6-9.4 Coming Up with a Hypothesis

In the next stage of dealing with a problem or an opportunity we attempt to formulate several hypotheses. The word hypothesis implies insufficiency of presently attainable evidence and therefore a tentative explanation. Each hypothesis is a tentative assumption that is made in order to draw out and test the logical or empirical consequences of the problem or some segment of the problem. Beveridge (1957) indicated that the hypothesis is the most important mental technique for us in the investigation. Its main function is to help us with new ideas and suggest new experiments or new observations.

In idea-development we go through a process of speculating on what is involved in a problem and thus attempt to design an experiment or data gathering procedure which will result in gathering evidence to clear up the problem. We need to state the hypothesis so we can make comparisons within the structure of the experiment or the approach to the problem. We usually state the hypothesis in the negative and call it a null hypothesis. Usually the results of an experiment are expressed as the difference between two sets of collected data. Since it is highly unlikely that we can show that the two sets of data are exactly the same, it is common practice to state the hypothesis in the negative and by the use of statistics, to attempt to prove that the two sets of data are or are not different. In other words, it may be possible to prove that the magnitude of the differences is large enough that those differences are not occurring due to chance. Once the null hypothesis is drawn up and well stated, we are ready to start to find the solution.

6-10 SEEKING A SOLUTION

After we come up with a number of possible approaches or ideas for solution to a problem, our next step becomes one of evaluating and selecting the approach to be taken. In this step we design (designing the experiment) and prepare to implement the procedures needed to gather the necessary data. We then must be prepared to collect and process the data so that we may draw conclusions.

6-10.1 Identify the Best Approach

In deciding on what approach we think will be most promising, we must exercise our best judgment, anticipate and respond to criticism, and then decide on whether or not to proceed. The following steps will help:

1. *Use best judgment* - In this step we are concerned with determining the most valuable and workable idea(s) which promise(s) to lead us to a solution. Olson (1980) suggested what he called "mind integration" to help with this process. This step supplies the catalyst to help improve the selection of the best idea. It emphasizes that we should not only draw on our conscious minds but also on our intuitive thoughts. At this stage we should eliminate the nonsensical, ridiculous, or too difficult or impossible suggestions for solutions. We should also take heed of the advice from others and make an intelligent evaluation of all the facts we have gathered.
2. *Anticipate and respond to criticism* - This process, which Olson calls "mind strengthening," is designed to help us strengthen our minds against our own tendency to avoid self-criticism and criticism from others. We must see the negative aspects, then try to transform these drawbacks into positive strengths by modifying our ideas to satisfy valid criticisms.
3. *Decide on "go" or "no go"* - In this final decision step, which Olson calls "mind energize," we attempt to increase our capacity to exert the energy to implement our ideas or to clear our minds of doubts about the idea being too risky or not worth our time and effort. This is the point of "go" or "no go" for the solution of the problem. Action must be decisive so we can make maximum effort to follow through, or the idea should be dropped.

6-10.2 Develop Evaluative Criteria

When we have decided on the probable best way of attempting to solve a problem, but before we launch into the effort, we should make a decision regarding what evidence will convince us that we have achieved the best answer. What "yardsticks" are we going to use to test the effectiveness of our procedures? We need to approach the problem from every conceivable point of view, try to anticipate all the various effects, consequences, outcomes, and/or repercussions that might occur.

We need to think of one, or maybe several, "if-then" propositions that may result and decide what basis will be used for accepting or refuting the hypothesis as it has been stated. What if the differences are small enough to fail to be statistically significant? Then, are we willing to accept that as the final answer? Or, has our sampling been too small to be representative of the situation, or generally applicable. Are we attempting to measure a minute difference (grams or milligrams) with a large capacity (several ton capacity) scale? If our means of measuring are not appropriate, we may need to rethink our approach. Thinking of several "if-then" propositions can help us come up with the appropriate experimental design to more accurately assess the solution to our problem, opportunity, or fact search.

6-10.3 Set Up an Experimental Design

It is important to set up our plan (design) for conducting the problem-solving stage prior to expending a lot of energy in getting underway. We should establish methods so that the results can be appropriately evaluated. Frequently, in the excitement and enthusiasm of solving a problem, we have a tendency to proceed without carefully designing the approach so that valid, statistically sound comparisons and evaluations can be made.

If statistics are needed to help us determine whether or not the results could have occurred due to chance, the design should be chosen before data are collected so that appropriate test and control data are obtained. It is also essential that adequate (not too small and not excessive) sampling (numbers) of an unbiased nature be an integral part of the design. If we are going to use statistical applications, it is wise to involve the statistical experts (if we can't handle that part ourselves) in setting up the plan for data or information collection.

6-10.4 Collect and Process the Evidence

When we have taken the previous steps, data collection may become routine. However, it is wise in nearly every situation for us to pay close attention to the early evidence that is collected, for it may not be revealing what was anticipated at the planning stages. The design or methods may need to be modified in order to obtain the kinds of evidence desired. It is better that we notice this early rather than after much time and effort have been spent collecting valueless data.

If we have properly designed our experiment for statistical analysis, processing the data may be routine and completed rapidly.

6-10.5 Draw Conclusions

The final step in the "solution" phase of problem-solving comes with interpreting the results we have obtained. Does the evidence indicate a clear resolution of the dilemma, mess, opportunity, puzzle, problem or situation which prompted the search for a solution? If clear-cut valid evidence has been obtained, then hopefully the problem has been solved. If not, we may need to start all over again.

6-10.6 Persist Until the Problem is Solved

Olson (1980) has said:

> The creative process does not end with a good solution to a problem - it begins with one. We often have inspirational ideas, but for most of us our creative genius is lost because our creative ideas fall like leaves around us and rot.

Persistence, withstanding the resistance from others, overcoming our own self-doubts, and continuing the flexibility to modify our plan, taking advantage of more optimal routes, and finally following through are all important in finally transforming the problem or opportunity that was defined into a final solution.

6-11 TRANSFORMING THE SOLUTION INTO ACTION

No problem-solving process is complete without the final stage of applying, implementing, recording, or putting the solution to use, or in the records for posterity. All too frequently we have a tendency to consider the task completed as soon as we have seen the evidence collected and interpreted in the solution phase of problem-solving. Some find the final state of transforming the solution into action difficult and even distasteful.

In each case of solving a problem, capitalizing on an opportunity, or clarifying a mess, someone must know that a resolution has been found, and be satisfied that the conclusion is reasonable and valid, at least for the time being.

In exploring this, perhaps the most critical phase of the problem-solving process, we need to think of each of the who? what? when?

where? why? and how? aspects in order to transform the solution into action and/or use.

6-11.1 Who Needs to Know?

Convince ourselves. If we explore the issue of "who needs to be convinced?", we quickly arrive at the conclusion that first and most important is having evidence that firmly convinces us as the problem-'solvers. Unfortunately, we sometimes fail to appreciate the importance of this aspect, and an attempt to fool ourselves and others is made with padded, concocted, or falsified data. The seriousness of such a move, of being dishonest with ourselves, is often not recognized as the "forever-to-be-lived-with, self-destructive-ness" that it brings. The aura of "never-to-be-trusted-again" may remain for the rest of our lives and may become a ghost that will appear and reappear over and over again making the all important aspect of convincing someone else virtually impossible.

Inform and convince others at the early stages. Most of the time it is highly advisable and many times nearly imperative for us to alert and involve at least the leaders of those who will be affected by the outcome of the problem. The persons involved like to feel they have been in on (or at least have helped) in solving the problem or seizing the opportunity. Failure to include important parties can often lead to alienation, causing them to "oppose" when otherwise they might have become strong "advocates." Bringing them into the early planning can also serve to help in clearly defining the situation and in avoiding errors and pitfalls which otherwise may be overlooked. However, we must take care not to make the planning group too large, for then it may become difficult to reach an agreement on how the problem should be approached. Each situation is likely to indicate the need for a different set and different numbers of key individuals. This is suggested by Ranftl (1978) in his "Suggestions for Solving Problems and Making Decisions" (see Chapter 5-5), as well as in the early planning and all the way through the implementation stage. Usually it is not necessary to inform others if they will not be affected by the outcome of the problem.

Inform others of the final result. The conclusions reached in problem solving usually call for us to issue some kind of visual record or written report even though oral reports or other preliminary non-official revealing of results may have been made. Our written reports may vary from notes to ourselves as a matter of record, to a more sophisticated published report in an edited journal, book or official report. We need to carefully decide on who will make up our audience and should have access to the information in order for us to choose the most effective means of reaching that particular audience. Critical for us in the decision concerning whom to inform is the issue of reaching key persons who may help in implementing the action needed to put the solution into use. Usually it helps to keep these individuals apprised from the beginning and as progress is being made in solving the problem or seizing the opportunity.

6-11.2 Communicating Results - Who? What? When? Where? Why? and How?

Each of our problems or opportunities usually calls for a specific set of answers to these interrogatives, depending on what is being considered. However, we should be certain that each of these is answered for the problem or opportunity being reported upon. The extent of the detail for each depends greatly upon the audience being addressed.

Several suggestions for writing reports, making presentations at meetings, using visual aids and other means of communicating results have been presented earlier in this book. Further help can be found in: Doyle and Straus 1976; Day, R.A. 1979; Garfield 1977; Stock 1985; and Woodford 1981.

6-12 PROBLEM-SOLVING IN SCIENTIFIC RESEARCH

Various problem-solving procedures are suggested in the litera-ture. Some 18 of these have been summarized by McPherson in the Journal of Creative Behavior (2:2, 1968), and reprinted in Parnes et al. *Guide to Creative Action* (1977, 146-151). There are many similarities and some dramatic differences among these methods. Some have been put together for general problem solving, some to meet industry needs, others to serve military purposes and some designed for other purposes. None is quite the same as the suggested pattern for scientific research that appeared in unpub-lished materials of G. W. Salisbury (1951, 1-10) that are discussed here.

6-12.1 The Salisbury Pattern for Research Compared to the Creative Education Foundation Approach.

Some of the similarities and differences in these two methods are shown in Table 6-2.

Table 6-2
Comparison of the Problem-Solving Approach of Osborn and Parnes (Parnes et al. 1977), and the Salisbury (1951) Pattern for Scientific Research

Osborn & Parnes approach	Salisbury pattern
The mess, fuzzy problem, fact-finding, (the situation)	The indeterminate situation
Problem-finding	Statement of the problem
Idea-finding	The hypothesis
	The proposition for testing the hypothesis
	The experimental design
Solution-finding	The collection of data
	The colligation of evidence
	The processing of data
	Developing warranted assertions
Acceptance-finding	Getting the results into the continuum of inquiry
	The use principle.

6-12.2 A Pattern for Productive Scientific Research

Salisbury (1951) developed a pattern for scientific research which he called, *An Approach to the Scientific Solution of Problems in Applied Biology.* This pattern consisted of 10 major steps that are presented here in abbreviated form. Since its inception, the pattern has proven to be highly effective for a host of experienced investigators and graduate students. It outlines some of the procedures that are especially important in scientific investigations, but many of the procedures work well in many kinds of problem-solving. Here are the 10 steps:

1. *The indeterminant situation* - Many of us (especially experienced investigators) do not often find ourselves in an indeterminant situation. However, we (especially if we are inexperienced investigators) may find ourselves in a situation in which we are not sure where to turn. If so, we must begin to analyze where we are in dealing with a problem or an

opportunity. The situation must be broken down into its component parts, classified, and the evidence sifted, and an endeavor made to simplify the situation.

2. *Statement of the problem* - If we can clarify the indeterminant situation sufficiently, a point should be reached where the specific problem and a suggested solution can be stated. Unfortunately, all too frequently we start collecting data before we have clearly defined the problem upon which we should gather evidence or facts.

3. *The hypothesis* - We need to state the hypothesis so there is opportunity for comparisons to be made within the structure of the experiment itself. Usually this means the basic hypothesis to be used is the null hypothesis. Usually this would be "There are no real differences between two or more groups of observations." In other words, it may be possible to prove that the magnitude of the differences between or among groups is large enough that those differences are not occurring due to chance.

4. *The propositions for testing the hypothesis* - After we have stated the hypothesis, it is essential to decide what basis will be employed for accepting or refuting the hypothesis as stated. Probably at least one and maybe several "if-then" propositions may be involved. If the difference observed between two groups of things reached a certain magnitude, then the null hypothesis did not hold. (Conditional probabilities, Anderson, 1980, pp. 72-73, are if-then statements.)

5. *The experimental design* - The word design means that our experiment will be so planned and so conducted that when the data are available they may be brought together, described, and studied statistically. The use of an acceptable design is no guarantee against poor science, poor logic, or mental bias.

6. *The collection of data* - Once we have established the operational design for conducting the experiment, the collection of the data may become routine. We need to keep records so that they can easily be deciphered later by us or by others.

7. *The colligation of evidence and processing the data* - Once the data are brought together, most investigators then make use of statistics in reducing their data to an understandable set of figures. Usually the statistical procedure applied is used to determine the percentage of probability that the observed differences between sets of data could have occurred by

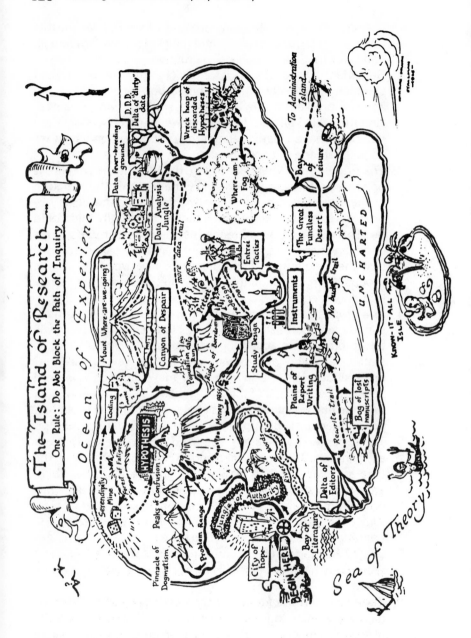

Fig. 6-2   Conceptualization of Problem-Solving Pitfalls and Diversions in Science (From Harbury 1966, 470, by permission)

chance. (For example, a 5% probability that they could have occurred by chance or a 95% probability that such differences as those observed could not have occurred by chance.)

8. *Developing warranted assertions* - If we have properly stated the problem in the first place and made a correct working null hypothesis, properly designed the experiment and carried it out to test the hypothesis, it can be asserted that the differences observed could have or could not have occurred by chance more often than a certain proportion of that number of times had the experiment been repeated on the same population that often. Such conclusions are warranted.

9. *Getting the results into the continuum of inquiry* - It is our responsibility, as experimenters, not only to accumulate and verify certain knowledge, but we must make that knowledge available to all. Thus some form of publication or announcement is essential.

10. *The use principle* - As investigators we have the responsibility for making the results available for application, getting those facts into the thinking of others, evolving new ideas from the facts, and making the ideas and the facts available to others for use.

Whatever the procedure used in solving problems, the route, especially if we are beginners, is usually strewn with evidence of the pitfalls to which we have fallen victim. Harbury (1966, 470) illustrated well some of the disruptions often encountered in the endeavor to solve problems in scientific research (see Fig. 6-2).

Comments: I was privileged to have Glenn W. Salisbury as my Ph. D. faculty adviser and mentor and then associate for over 20 years. He was an early applicator of statistical methods to biological research, which kept him on course in making many, many valuable contributions to the field of biology of animal reproduction. I profited enormously from his guidance and friendship. The above research guidelines helped me and literally hundreds of other first, then second and now third generation of students following in his paths of wisdom.

6-13 HIGHLIGHTS OF CHAPTER SIX

1. In many situations, if we are alert to what is happening and sensitive to people's feelings and the things that are going on around us, the development of problems can be avoided and

can often be turned into opportunities.

2. We need to learn to anticipate problems; recognize opportunities; see the need for new facts; and plan for appropriate, timely action in order to be most effective.

3. Systematic efforts can help us in recognizing the situation, defining the problem, coming up with ideas for the solution, selecting what is considered the best solution for solving the problem, and then getting the best solution implemented.

4. We often have troubles in solving problems because we fail to utilize our prior knowledge, are careless in our reading and thinking, fail to view the problem from all angles, jump to conclusions, and try to work too rapidly.

5. Positive approaches to problems and opportunities are almost always more fruitful for us and encourage more enthusiastic participation in finding solutions than are negative approaches.

6. We need to develop several ideas as possible approaches to solving each problem or seizing each opportunity, then select the most promising approach to try.

7. Solution finding in problem-solving involves careful listening and evaluating ideas and proposed solutions as they are developed.

8. Working with others in a cooperative spirit can enhance our problem-solving capabilities.

9. Coming up with a solution to a problem or an opportunity is of little or no value unless we get the results recorded for the use of others and can convince decision-makers and/or those affected in the situation to take action in implementing and using the suggested solution.

6-14 AFTERGROWTH STIMULATORS

1. What is one of the most recent problems you have faced? Was it easily defined?   How long have you known that it was becoming a problem? How have you been dealing with it?

2. Are you systematic or haphazard in your approach to solving problems?   Do you seek to identify more than one possible way of tackling problems?

3. Do you face problems head-on and deal with them as soon as you can, or do you put off facing them and hope they will go away?

4. What is your own greatest problem-solving fault, difficulty or barrier?
5. Have you developed ways of looking at problems as potential opportunities? Give some examples of where you have, or where you perhaps could have, done so.
6. Do you find yourself getting part way through solving a problem, but then having trouble finishing? By delaying making decisions? Because of your dislikes for writing, telephoning, discussing the issue with other parties, etc.?

CHAPTER 7

THE SELF IN CREATIVITY

7- 1   Introduction
7- 2   Individual Needs
7- 3   Self-Esteem
7- 4   Self-Actualization and Self-Fulfillment
7- 5   Motivation
7- 6   Motivational Theories of Creativity
7- 7   Self-Controlled Barriers
7- 8   Self-Development
7- 9   Highlights of Chapter Seven
7- 10 Aftergrowth Stimulators

7-1 INTRODUCTION

To be successful we must be satisfied, ambitious, productive, feel valued, and be happy with ourselves. New ideas for solving problems come from our individual, creative minds. Satisfaction for us comes from knowing that what we have contributed is valued. What is the future going to be like for us as individuals? Are we willing to look inward as well as outward? Can we build confidence in ourselves and build toward perfection? Or does the term "perfection" itself frighten us? As Dale (1967) has said:

Many of our good words such as truth, faith, responsibility, courage, and discipline have been dulled by careless use. But if we are not perfectible, what ideal do we hold for ourselves?

The self is at the center of potential creative abilities for each of us. Little or no change or gain can occur for us if we do not wish it and will it.

From Biblical days to more recent times we have been admonished to be courageous and willing to be ourselves. To be different, to be individuals:

Don't copy the behavior and customs of this world, but be a new and different person with a fresh newness in all you do and think. (Romans 12:2. Living Bible)

Life...is a game played once. Everyone has an intuitive sense of the tremendous gamble of life: that every move, every choice, every personal decision, every initiative we take, every adventure to which we commit ourselves is going to determine the rest of the game and will have its repercussions on the outcome. (Tournier 1965a, 43-44)

To find deeper meaning (in life), one must become able to transcend the narrow confines of a self-centered existence and believe that one will make a significant contribution to life - if not right now, then at some future time. This feeling is necessary if a person is to be satisfied with himself and what he is doing. In order not to be at the mercy of the vagaries of life, one must develop one's inner resources, so that one's emotions, imagination, and intellect mutually support and enrich one another. Our positive feelings give us the strength to develop our rationality; only hope for the future can sustain us in the adversities we unavoidably

The CENTRAL ROLE of SELF in CREATIVITY

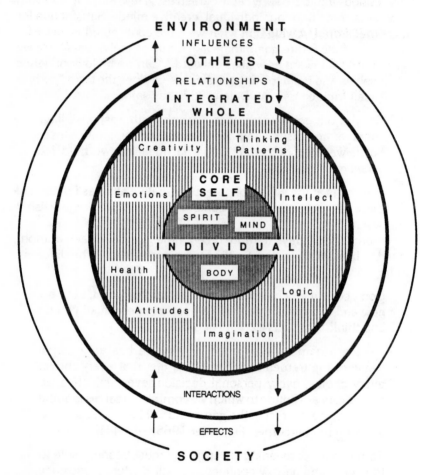

Fig. 7-1 Factors within the Self in Its Central Role in Creativity

encounter.(Bettelheim, (1977, 3-4)

Even though there are many external factors affecting our creativity (see Table 1-2), the self is central to our ability to be creative, to be productive, to find self-actualization, to becoming fully human, and to enjoy happiness and self-fulfillment (see Fig. 7-1).

The many other factors, including the relationships with others and the influences of society and environment that play an influential role, ultimately act through the self to enhance or inhibit the expression of our creative capabilities.

7-2 INDIVIDUAL NEEDS

Maslow's (1970, 35-51) hierarchy of needs (see Fig. 7-2) can help us to better understand the forces that drive us. Maslow's theory of human motivation can be applied to many aspects of life. Our whole person is motivated, not just a part of us.

HIERARCHY of HUMAN NEEDS

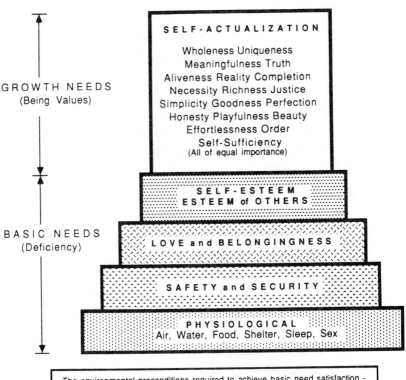

Fig. 7-2 The Hiearchy of Human Needs as Perceived by Maslow
(Adapted from Goble, 1970, 37-52)

7-2.1 Basic Needs

The basic needs are species wide, apparently unchanging and of genetic or instinctual origin. The first four are considered as basic needs and may not appear in the order listed. They have been referred to as "deficiency" needs because they manifest themselves primarily when they are absent or unfulfilled. Some characteristics of these needs are as follows:

1. *Physiological needs:* These are basic and probably the most powerful of all of a our needs for survival. These include our need for food and liquid, oxygen, shelter, sex, and sleep. If these and our other basic needs are not being met, we will risk everything, including our lives, in attempting to satisfy them. Until these needs are being met, little attention can be paid to fulfilling our growth needs.

2. *Safety needs:* Along with our physiological needs, or separately, comes concern for our safety and security. Safety needs are usually met if we are healthy, normal adults in today's world, so long as we do not live in an environment where others are attempting to overpower one another. If we are insecure we have a compulsive need for order and stability and go to great lengths to avoid the strange and unexpected. Even when we are healthy, we seek these same needs for order and stability.

3. *Social needs:* The belongingness and love needs - along with the preceding basic needs come our needs for belonging and association and being loved. We seek affectionate relations with people, particularly within our own group. We strive with great intensity to find this love. Maslow (1970, 181-202) and Rogers (1977, 42-68) defined love as "being deeply understood and deeply accepted." Maslow indicated that love "involves a healthy loving relationship between two people, which includes mutual trust. In the proper relationship, there is a lack of fear, a dropping of defenses."

4. *Ego and self-esteem needs:* These needs are described as falling into two categories. The first, self-respect or self-esteem, includes such items as our desire for competence, mastery, adequacy, achievement, independence, and freedom. In essence, it involves becoming everything that we are capable of becoming. The second aspect is that of gaining high esteem and respect from others. This includes such items as our gaining prestige, recognition, acceptance, atten-

tion, status, reputation, and appreciation.

7-2.2 Growth or Being Needs

The fifth category of our needs is called self-actualization or self-fulfillment needs. Contrasted with the basic or deficiency needs, which only become evident when they are missing, these peak needs consist primarily of our need and desire to become more and more of what we really are. Thus these are frequently referred to as our growth needs or being values. As creative persons we must be free to attempt to fulfill these needs.

Items in this fifth group are called "growth" or "being" needs because they come into play as real motivators for and in response to our needs for self-fulfillment. Self-actualization and self-esteem are especially important for us as creative individuals.

7-3 SELF-ESTEEM

Since self-esteem is so essential for us as creative persons, a closer look at self-esteem is especially important. Moustakas (1956, 8) said:

Maintenance of the real self is of primary significance for the individual. It is the most stable, consistent value in his life. The real self is the central core within each individual which is the deep source of growth. To operate in terms of the persons we are is natural, comforting, and satisfying. It permits us to be creative, to utilize our capacities.

7-3.1 The Nature and Source of Self-Esteem

Branden (1969, 109) has indicated that there is no value judgement more important to us than the evaluation we place on ourselves. This feeling is so emotionally a part of our total being that it is impossible to separate it from our other feelings. It takes on almost a life and death importance for us because it is an integral part of the sense of personal efficiency and the sense of personal worth. It indicates to us that we are competent to live and are worthy of living. It is our basic means of surviving.

7-3.2 The Need to Be Right

It is of our own volition that we choose to live, and to live we must feel that what we are doing is right. The conviction that we have chosen what is right is basic to our survival. We can choose to activate and sustain a sharp mental focus and seek understanding or we can choose to block out the thinking and thus will drift. We can choose to let intellect direct our actions or relinquish the direction to emotions. Making these choices and feeling good about them are essential in living. We must be confident that we are able to think, that our minds are propelling us in a proper direction, and that the commitment to be in contact with reality is of our own choosing.

We must feel good about ourselves and if we fail to satisfy the standard we desire, then our personal worth and our self-respect suffer. Our self-esteem, self-confidence, and self-respect are inseparable in governing our actions.

7-3.3 The Need to Understand

To achieve and maintain self-esteem, we must have an indomitable will to understand. This is essential for our mental health and for our intellectual growth. As long as we continue to work at this issue and do not give up the will to understand, we will keep our minds and desires for efficacy intact. A policy of thinking in principles and conceptualizing is a basic characteristic of psychological maturity for us. We must preserve the will to understand.

7-3.4 The Need to Feel Good

As indicated in Chapter 4-4.5 (Feeling Good), pleasure enhances our sense of self. Gaylin (1979, 207), indicated that this is a common ingredient that gives us a sense of hope, mastery, self-confidence, and self-esteem. These then help us with discovery, the concept of expansion and mastery, creativity, immersion, fusion with people, and transcending and feeling lifted out of ourselves. Also, being alleviated from distress, being reassured, being removed from pain, being revived in hope, and feeling good simply because we are alive, all contribute to our feelings of pleasure and self-esteem.

Even tears can help us feel good. Hunt (1955) summarized a number of aspects regarding feeling good and tears:

> So there is genuine wisdom in tears: in tears of grief, of remembrance, of sympathy, of aesthetic pleasure, of appreciation of grandeur, of poignant joy. They all express deep-seated needs - the need to love and be loved, the need to cast out anger and hate, the need to wash away trouble and

tension. In permitting ourselves to weep instead of manfully repressing the impulse, we help ourselves to health and wisdom. For in the state of physical release which tears bring, our thoughts can flow freely, and bring insight and understanding we never knew were within our grasp.

7-3.5 The Need for Self-Worth

Our deepest pride results from achieving self-esteem, of being proud of our attainments, of feeling worthy. A sense of measuring up to the challenges of life, of being competent, enhances our feeling of self-worth. Our self-esteem should not be dependent upon our particular successes or failures. All too often we make the mistake of placing impossible or unrealistic demands on ourselves and thus judge ourselves by a mistaken or irrational standard of perfection. Learning what is realistic for us is an important aspect of keeping this issue in balance. Achieving is crucial not only for a feeling of self worth, but also for our self-esteem and self-fulfillment.

7-3.6 Self-Esteem and Ethical Behavior

Blanchard and Peale (1988, 48) have pointed out that self-esteem is a major factor in helping us to be able to resist the temptation to do unethical things. They believed:

> People who feel good about themselves have what it takes to withstand outside pressure and to do what is right rather than do what is merely expedient, popular, or lucrative.

They also emphasized that, "There is no right way to do wrong things." Yet many of us rationalize and do wrongs, for we have trouble resisting the temptation because we feel we must go along with the crowd. We are apt to feel that it's O.K. because "Everyone is doing it." We tend to ignore many good sets of guidelines.

Rotary International suggests a Four-Way Test of the appropriateness of the things we think, say and do:

1. Is it the TRUTH?
2. Is it FAIR to all concerned?
3. Will it build GOODWILL and BETTER FRIENDSHIPS?
4. Will it be BENEFICIAL to all concerned?

Blanchard and Peale (p. 27) suggested three "ethics check" questions to help guide us in deciding whether an issue or an act is ethically right or wrong:

1. Is it legal? Will I be violating civil law or company policy?
2. Is it balanced? Is it fair to all concerned in the short term as well as the long term? Does it promote win-win relationships?
3. How will it make me feel about myself? Will it make me proud? Would I feel good if my decision was published in the newspaper? Would I feel good if my family knew about it?

They also have listed five principles of ethical power which are meant to help us in making decisions about the ethics of certain situations or acts. Their principles are given in Table 7-1.

Table 7-1
The Five Principles of Ethical Power for Individuals

---

1. **Purpose:** I see myself as being an ethically sound person. I let my conscience be my guide. No matter what happens, I am always able to face the mirror, look myself straight in the eye, and feel good about myself.
2. **Pride:** I feel good about myself. I don't need the acceptance of other people to feel important. A balanced self-esteem keeps my ego and my desire to be accepted from influencing my decisions.
3. **Patience:** I believe that things will eventually work out well. I don't need everything to happen right now. I am at peace with what comes my way!
4. **Persistence:** I stick to my purpose, especially when it seems inconvenient to do so! My behavior is consistent with my intentions. As Churchill said, "Never! Never! Never! Give up."
5. **Perspective:** I take time to enter each day quietly in a mood of reflection. This helps me to get myself focused and allows me to listen to my inner self and to see things more clearly.

Taken from Blanchard and Peale, 1988, 80 (by permission)

The important aspect of all this is to feel good about what we have done or are doing. If we feel guilty and uncomfortable because we know that our actions have been ethically wrong then our ability to think and be creative will be greatly impaired. Blanchard and Peale (1988, 46) reproduced a poem, written by Dale Wimbrow, which speaks clearly to this point. Here it is:

The Man in the Glass

When you get what you want in your struggle for self
And the world makes you king for a day,

Just go to a mirror and look at yourself
And see what THAT man has to say.
For it isn't your father or mother or wife
Whose judgment upon you must pass;
The fellow whose verdict counts most in your life
Is the one staring back from the glass.
Some people may think you a straight-shootin' chum
And call you a wonderful guy,
But the man in the glass says you're only a bum
If you can't look him straight in the eye.
He's the fellow to please, never mind all the rest,
For he's with you clear up to the end.
And you've passed your most dangerous, difficult test
If the man in the glass is your friend.
You may fool the whole world down the pathway of life
And get pats on your back as you pass,
But your final reward will be heartaches and tears
If you've cheated the man in the glass.

Blanchard and Peale emphasized in their discussion that an unethical act will severely erode our self-esteem. They presented an excellent saying that highlights it all: "There is no pillow as soft as a clear conscience." We must behave ethically all the time, not just when it is convenient and popular to do so. In fact it may often be especially important when it is inconvenient and unpopular to do so. If we are to maintain self-esteem, it is absolutely essential for us to be completely honest with ourselves and with others (see Chapter 8-9.1 and White, 1979).

7-4 SELF-ACTUALIZATION AND SELF-FULFILLMENT

Realizing self-actualization, self-fulfillment or fully human needs appear to be the peak of our human attainment. As indicated above, Maslow has referred to these as "growth" or "being-values." Goble (1970, 25-36) has presented a 12 page compilation and summarization of Maslow's research descriptions and discussions of these "fully human" characteristics. His research showed that "self-actualizing" people usually possess several common characteristics. However, no one individual possessed all these characteristics, nor were they exhibited to the same extent when they were present. The following consists of a digest and excerpts from Goble's lengthy compilation of:

Characteristics of Self-Actualizing Persons

1. The most universal and common aspect was their ability to see life clearly, as it is, rather than as they wished it to be. They did not allow their hopes and wishes to distort their observations.

2. Superior perception - they were more decisive and had a clearer notion of what was right and wrong. They were more accurate in their prediction of future events.

3. They possessed a kind of humility, and ability to listen carefully to others, to admit that they didn't know everything and that other people can teach them something. This superior perception resulted from and in a better understanding of self.

4. Their perception was less distorted by desires, anxieties, fears, hopes, false optimism, or pessimism.

5. They were dedicated to some work, task, duty, or vocation which they considered important. For them work was exciting and pleasurable. It was not enough to have an important job - the self-actualizing person had to be doing it well. Their involvement often meant hard work, discipline, training, and often postponement of pleasure.

6. Creativity was a universal characteristic of all the self-actualizing people that Maslow studied. This characteristic was almost always accompanied by flexibility, spontaneity, courage, willingness to make mistakes, openness, and humility.

7. There was a low degree of self conflict. These persons were not at war with themselves; their personality was integrated. Trust, goodness and beauty were well correlated with each other, so much so that for all practical purposes they may be said to fuse in a unity. These people wasted little time or energy protecting themselves from themselves. There was little confusion about what was right or wrong, good or bad, and there was little trouble operating on the perception of right behavior.

8. They had a healthy attitude toward work and play. They enjoyed play; they enjoyed work; work became play; vocation and avocation became the same. The research indicated that healthy people were most integrated when facing a great creative challenge, some worthwhile goal, or a serious threat or emergency. As they became more unified as individuals they saw more unity, and the possibility for unity in the world.

9. Mature persons had a healthy respect for themselves, a

respect based upon the knowledge that they were confident and adequate.

10. The psychologically healthy individual was highly independent, yet at the same time enjoyed people.

11. Self-actualizers were able to make their own decisions even in the face of contrary popular opinion. They resisted their culture when it did not agree with their own point of view. They were not generally unconventional about things which they did not consider important: language, clothes, food, etc; yet they became extremely independent and unconventional when they felt basic principles were involved.

12. For these individuals self-discipline was relatively easy because what they desired to do agreed with what they believed was right. Their values were based on what was real for them, rather than what others told them.

13. Healthy persons were "primarily motivated by their need to develop and actualize their fullest potentialities and capacities." Whereas average individuals were motivated by deficiencies as they were seeking to fulfill their basic needs for safety, belongingness, love, respect, and self-esteem.

14. These healthy individuals were very tolerant of others' shortcomings, and yet they were very intolerant about dishonesty, lying, cheating, cruelty, and hypocrisy.

15. The relationships that fully mature people developed were better for themselves and for others. Relationships were never exploitive.

16. The superior persons sometimes found it desirable to be constructively critical.

17. The healthy individual showed far less fear than the average adult who was less influenced by truth, logic, justice, reality and beauty. "Self-actualizing people enjoyed life in general and in practically all its aspects, while most other people enjoyed only stray moments of triumph, of achievement or of climax or peak experience."

18. The outstanding people that were studied had a number of other common characteristics. They had the ability to be objective and problem centered. There was detachment in social relationships occasionally causing trouble because it was interpreted as coldness, aloofness, snobbishness, even hostility. They had an unusual ability to concentrate, and this sometimes produced absent mindedness. Because they had fewer problems of their own, they tended to work to solve

problems of society; they had some mission in life. They were more concerned with ends rather than means. They were sufficiently philosophical to be patient and seek or accept slow orderly change rather than sudden change.

In pulling out this digest of characteristics of self-actualizing, fully human individuals, many aspects of the lengthy discussion have been omitted. Even then the list seems unreal and idealistic. For most of us the hopes of living up to such qualities would seem to be an impossibility. Yet, how well we do in reaching what would seem to be unattainable goals is largely up to our own degree of motivation. Can we muster the will power and determination to achieve enough of them to find the joy of being creative, self-fulfilled persons?

7-5 MOTIVATION

The concept of motivation is used to explain why human behavior occurs (not as a direct cause of all behavior). Wlodkowski (1977, 6) indicated that the general definition used by most psychologists and educators is that:

Motivation is the word used to describe those processes that can; (a) arouse and instigate behavior; (b) give direction or purpose to behavior; (c) continue to allow behavior to persist; and (d) lead to choosing or preferring a particular behavior. A motive is any condition within persons that affects their readiness to initiate or continue any activity or sequence of activities.

Self-preservation is probably the primary factor in driving people to fulfill their basic physiological, safety and association needs. It seems logical that self-fulfillment and self-actualization, judging from the list of characteristics discussed above, are motivated by other factors as well. Tournier (1965a, 5) believed adventure to be one of the great motivating forces of people. He said:

I even think that the urge to adventure must be considered an instinct, since it has the universality and the indominatable power characteristic of instinct, and because its satisfaction affords the specific joy which always accompanies the satisfaction of instinct.

Fromm (1947, 1990, 4) in *Man for Himself* said:

While becoming the master of nature he (man) has become the slave of the machine which his own hands built. With all his knowledge about matter, he is ignorant with regard to the most fundamental questions of human existence: what man is, how he ought to live and how the energies within man can be released and used productively.

A *Success* (Oct. 1981, p. A-4) article interpreting Fromm indicated:

An individual's productive character constitutes the source and basis of virtue. Self-love, self-esteem, are the supreme values of ethics. We (*Success*) extend this to conclude that belief - belief in one's self, in one's job, in one's purpose - is the essence of motivation. Motivation is grown in the heart and mind of the individual through the power of belief.

They suggest that belief is made up of such elements as knowledge, conviction, faith, confidence, and truth. Without knowledge, uncertainty, hesitation, and vacillation, are created. Conviction indicates the level of belief which starts at one end with obsession and goes to the other of casual interest. If faith is at the center of belief, confidence is its major support, for it springs from assurance and trust. From these we develop courage. For true happiness we must know truth, honesty, and integrity. From all of these and from knowing ourselves, we gain the strength that motivates us to move on. Most difficult of all is responding to criticism. We must know the basis of our beliefs and be able to substantiate them. We must also be able to overcome the inertia that exists in all of us to make motivation effective.

7-5.1 Adventure and Work as Motivational Forces

Curiosity and the desire for and the thrill of adventure tend to motivate people. Tournier (1965a, 85) said:

Adventure is first a form of self-manifestation.

He pointed out that expressing oneself to the outside world is a vital need for every person. People are driven to put their talents to use and do creative work or they ultimately feel a sense of guilt. He went on to say of adventure that:

It innovates and invents; it is ingenious. It is coherent, evolving in the pursuit of a single final goal. This goal is love;

it is love which suggests the goal, and love which directs and sustains the adventure. Lastly, it involves necessarily the running of a risk.

He believed that the instinct for adventure may also be the instinct for love which causes people to give of themselves, to dedicate themselves to pursuing worthwhile goals, and doing it for mankind. This would seem to be the ultimate in motivation. However, we are sometimes motivated by hate and a desire to seek revenge.

Doing for ourselves or for others usually involves work. "Why people work?", an interesting article in the *JD (John Deere) Journal* 3:No.1, 1974) suggested several reasons, some of which are similar to those relating to adventure: Work (like adventure) gives us an identity. It provides a good place to test and evaluate ourselves, to measure our achievements, to build self-esteem. Through work we gain a sense of competence and value. It indicates to us that we are needed, have something to offer. Work plays a major role in determining our status and that of our families. Work brings order to our lives. Tournier (1965a, 58) said that:

The meaning of man's work is the satisfaction of the instinct for adventure.

7-5.2 Individual Motivating Forces

Much has been written suggesting ways of motivating people. One study by David S. Brown, Professor of Public Administration at George Washington University, involved 1,522 responses by both government and private business employees. They each picked five items (from a list of 27) which they considered most important in motivating them to do their best work. The first five picked by the greatest number were:

1. feeling my job is important;
2. opportunity to do interesting work;
3. opportunity for self development and improvement;
4. respect for me as a person; and
5. a chance for promotion.

Their next five choices were:

6. good pay;
7. chance to turn out good work;
8. knowing what is going on in the organization;
9. large amount of freedom on the job; and
10. steady employment.

I presented this same list of 27 choices to several groups of graduate students and faculty from several different disciplines at Cornell University over a period of years. Tallies of their responses showed that chance for promotion, good pay, steady employment, and knowing what is going on in the organization, dropped out of the top ten and were replaced by getting along well with others on the job, chance to do work not under direct or close supervision, being told by my boss when I do a good job and having an efficient supervisor.

Lippitt (1982, 69) listed six motivational items which he considered most important if people are to give their best to the organization. His list included:

1. meaningful rewards;
2. relationship;
3. importance;
4. initial success (assignments within their skills and experience);
5. opportunity to grow; and
6. appropriate involvement in key decision-making.

One can readily see where this more general listing covers and over-laps most of those listed in the Brown survey.

7-6 MOTIVATIONAL THEORIES OF CREATIVITY

MacKinnon (1978, 196-197) indicated that the theories of creativity are many and varied with multiple driving forces usually working together. Among the things discussed, he indicated the following as important elements:

- Creativity serves as a defense.
- Creativity results from a compulsive need to order and control.
- It is often the expression for the wish fulfilling fantasies for someone who is dissatisfied.
- It may be the result of an attempt to avoid or overcome feelings of alienation.
- It may result in enjoyment and pleasure in exercising one's skills or competence.
- There is the aspect of self-rewarding activities for activities sake.
- It may be the result of the need for novelty or maybe the result of the need for play.

7-7 SELF-CONTROLLED BARRIERS

Creativity is largely self-controlled and implementing it is up to each of us. Leaders, managers or companies cannot initiate creativity, but they can help creativity thrive or unwittingly become idea-killers. We can be alert to and help ourselves to overcome some of the self-controlled barriers (see Table 7-2). A number of these were discussed in earlier chapters relating to intelligence, emotions and problem-solving.

Table 7-2
Inner (Self) Barriers to Creativity
(Chapter where the item is discussed is in parentheses.)

• Restricted thinking	(2-8)	• Mental distortions	(2-10)
• Lack of imagination	(3-4)	• Viewing too narrowly	(3-5)
• Over specialization	(3-5)	• Tradition bound	(4-4)
• Transferring habits	(4-4)	• Lack of flexibility	(4-4)
• Intolerant of ambiguity	(4-4)	• Fear of failure	(4-4)
• Unwilling to risk	(4-5)	• Lack of discipline	(5-3)
• Lack of challenge	(7-7)	• Over motivated	(7-7)
• Over saturated	(12-3)	• Inability to relax	(12-9)

- Trouble distinguishing reality from fantasy   (3-4)
- Inability to suspend critical judgement   (5-7; 6-14)
- Difficulty in seeing the problem   (3-5; 6-4; 6-6)
- Failing to view the problem from various ways   (6-4)

7-7.1 Lack of Challenge or Too Little Motivation

All too often we are in a position where there is a lack of challenge. This may sometimes be due to being in a role that is not in keeping with our own interests, or being over qualified for the assigned task. To counteract conditions where there is a lack of challenge and help ourselves, we must become self-starters and self-motivators. Morgan (1968, 100-111) made several suggestions for doing this. His ideas included such things as allowing ourselves to be dissatisfied and by breaking the monotony by finding new and different ways of doing things. We should not expect that every act is going to be a major one, and we need to accept modest accomplishments. We may often find satisfaction in a series of small successes. Actually for most creative persons, satisfaction and major accomplishments are apt to materialize out of persistent efforts with a long series of minor triumphs. We should not discount the idea of seeking a new approach or even seeking a new job.

7-7.2 Over-Motivation

Being unrealistic and succumbing to an urge to accomplish too much in too short a time can frequently cause us difficulties and maybe even failure. This may be caused by excessive pressure from our employer, a compulsive interest and narrowing our field of observation too much, from lack of experience, poor planning, or simply our inability to say no. These can diminish our creative abilities and may even lead us to "burnout." Among Morgan's (1968) suggestions to counteract over-motivation were such things as:

- Cooling an over-intense or compulsive interest.
- Reducing our competitive drive and ambition.
- Not seeking so many rapid successes.
- Seeking to cut down on excessive pressures from our employer.
- Broadening our views.
- Guarding against compulsion.
- Realizing that we are not going to win them all.
- Finding ways of relaxing.

7-7.3 Other Self-Imposed Barriers

We must be careful not to follow or transfer old habits to new problems or opportunities (see Chapter 4-4). Our old habits are difficult to break and may lead us into a blind alley. We must also take care to recognize the danger of not being able to tolerate ambiguity, as well as the importance of being flexible (refer to Chapter 4-4). We also need to guard against fixed approaches; all problems do not lend themselves to attack by the same procedure. Likewise, we must take care at times, to suspend critical judgement (see Chapter 6-6, 6-9). We should keep all of these in mind, as well as the others mentioned in Table 7-2, to avoid having our own makeup diminish our creative capabilities.

7-8 SELF-DEVELOPMENT

Although the development of creative potential is greatly influenced in early life (see Chapter 10-3), continuing development of the self is a constant, life-long challenge. Moustakas (1956, 9-11) has indicated a number of principles summarizing the basic approach and recognition of the self. These are important points to recognize in understanding our own role in enhancing our creative potential.

His points have been condensed and summarized below:

1. We know ourselves better than anyone else and therefore have a better perception of our own feelings, attitudes, and ideas than would result from any outside diagnosis.
2. We must respond in ways which are consistent with our own inner feelings, thus perception of ourselves determines how we will behave and this behavior can best be understood from our own point of view.
3. We are logical in the context of our own personal experience. These meanings reflect our own background. Our point of view may seem illogical to others if we are not understood.
4. We each want to grow toward self-fulfillment, and this will happen as long as we accept ourselves, otherwise much of our energies will be used in defense rather than exploring and actualizing ourselves.
5. Only we ourselves can develop our potentialities. Only those things which are involved in the maintenance and enhancement of ourselves will be learned. Any other learning is temporary for us and will disappear as soon as the threat is removed.
6. Under threat the self is less open to spontaneous expression and is therefore more passive and controlled and less free to be and to strive for self-actualization. We cannot teach another person directly. We can only facilitate real learning by providing information, the setting, atmosphere, materials, resources, and by being there. If learning threatens the maintenance or enhancement of the self, the learning experience will be of little relevance or consequence. The learning may be difficult for the individual person even if it has significance for the enhancement of self.

The self plays a central and controlling role in creativity, and we must be able to respond and react to the impact of others, society, and the environment in order to be productive and creative, to experience fulfillment and happiness, and to become fully human. The challenges to the individual are: Can one be a self-starter? A self-challenger? A self-motivator? A self-finisher?

7-9 HIGHLIGHTS OF CHAPTER SEVEN

1. Our productivity and self-fulfillment are highly dependent upon our opportunity to fulfill our basic and self-actualizing or growth needs.

2. Self-esteem; the need to be right, the need to understand, the need to feel good, the need for self worth, and the need to be ethical in each of us is critical if we are to be creative.

3. Belief in ourselves, in our purpose, and in our task or job is essential if we are to be motivated.

4. Belief seems to be made up of knowledge, conviction, faith, confidence and truth.

5. Although our creativity is greatly influenced by our early life, continuing development is largely up to each of us.

6. The individual is the center of the potential productivity and self-fulfillment mix but is highly influenced by other surrounding individuals and by the environment.

7. Even though we have an inherent drive for work and adventure, self-motivation and encouragement by others can greatly enhance our creativity.

8. We must constantly strive to control and overcome our internal barriers such as too much or too little motivation, perceptual blocks, habit transfer, intolerance of ambiguity, lack of flexibility, and a host of other creativity impeding factors.

7-10 AFTERGROWTH STIMULATORS

1. Have you taken time lately to assess how you, yourself, are contributing to your creativity?

2. Would you say your image of yourself is helpful or harmful to your creative abilities? Would you rate your self-esteem high or low?

3. Do you spend most of your time striving to fulfill your basic individual needs, or do you have time left to pursue your growth and self-fulfillment needs?

4. What motivates you to do your best in being creative?

5. What have been some of your own self-generated barriers to creativity? How are you doing in avoiding the inner barriers to creativity listed in Table 7-2?

6. In what ways are you a good self-motivator? Self-challenger? Self-starter? Self-finisher?

CHAPTER 8

THE IMPACT OF OTHERS: RELATIONAL POWER

8- 1   Introduction
8- 2   The Need for Interpersonal
        Relationships
8- 3   Separateness
8- 4   Aloneness and Loneliness
8- 5   Unilateral Power
8- 6   Relational Power
8- 7   Building a Lasting Relationship
8- 8   Love and Caring
8- 9   Building Trust
8-10   Communications
8-11   Relationships and Health
8-12   Relationships and Creativity
8-13   Barriers to Interpersonal Relationships
8-14   Highlights of Chapter Eight
8-15   Aftergrowth Stimulators

8-1 INTRODUCTION

In previous chapters (especially 7-3) we have emphasized how critical it is for us to feel that our presence on this earth counts for something. We must believe that what we have done and are doing is worthwhile. But if we are alone we have no reference point with which to judge our effectiveness. We must have others against whom we can measure and evaluate our actions and accomplishments. It means, like it or not, that we can not escape living in association with others to some degree.

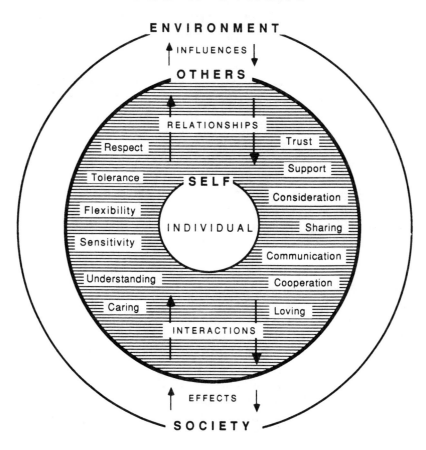

CREATIVITY and the ROLE of OTHERS

Fig. 8-1 The Impact of Others on Individual Creativity

We have a strong basic human need to be in association with others. This need may be so strong that much of our attention gets devoted to it, and if we are busy searching for relationships with others, we cannot be exerting much effort to production and creativity. The presence and behavior of others and the interrelationships we develop with them thus become extremely important factors in our own performance and creativity (refer to Table 1-2) and see Figure 8-1). Understanding our reaction to interpersonal relationships can determine whether the impact on our creative abilities will be positive or negative.

8-2 THE NEED FOR INTERPERSONAL RELATIONSHIPS

From the day of our conception until our birth we are an integral part of our mother. From birth until we are able to fend for ourselves, we continue in the presence of a mother and/or another caring person. In the early part of this century it was learned that just food and clothing (warmth) were not enough to keep an orphan alive. Being touched (fondled), talked to, loved, and made aware that they were a worthwhile being was necessary for the survival and well-being of an infant. Even after we are able to maintain ourselves, Block (1980, 3) has indicated that growth ceases if we cannot become involved outside ourselves.

As the population increases and our mobility becomes more rapid and global, we will be practically forced and guaranteed to have greater interpersonal contacts. Concurrent with population growth has also come a greater interdependency for the necessities of life, again continually forcing us to more and more interaction. The possibilities of our living a completely isolated life are becoming less and less.

The complexity of modern civilization is presenting humanity with an increasing number of problems that are too broad in scope, and/or too technical to expect a solution from any single individual. Large problems often require a team approach. Opportunities for us to make discoveries and contributions while working alone are still great, but even then we need interaction with many others, if survival and maximum progress are to be made. In essence this means that if we are starting a career today we can anticipate the need for greater skills in dealing with interpersonal relationships in our lives than has been the case even in the immediate previous generation. This then means that we will need a greater understanding of interpersonal relationships in the future.

8-3 SEPARATENESS

Perhaps initially we need to become more aware of why we have great fears of being isolated, alienated, not measuring up, and out of control of our own lives. Thus our great need to relate to others. Fromm (1956, 6-8) has indicated that at birth we are brought into a situation that is indefinite, uncertain and open. With the ability to reason we become aware of ourselves, of others, and the possibilities of the future. Fromm said:

> The awareness of himself (mankind) as a separate entity, the awareness of his own short life span, of the fact that without his will he is born and against his will he dies, that he will die before those whom he loves, or they before him, the awareness of his aloneness and separateness, of his helplessness before the forces of nature and of society, all this makes his separate, disunited existence an unbearable prison.

Thus separation, our greatest fear, is manifested in such things as:

- fear of loss of life (self and others);
- loss of friends;
- loss of job, home, possessions, etc.;
- being unlovable - rejected, inferior, not measuring up;
- being vulnerable - not able to compete, not able to cope; and
- being out of control - especially control of our lives, decisions, health, etc.

Fromm said people of all ages and cultures have been faced with "...how to avoid separateness, achieve union, transcend one's own individual life and find at-onement." This fear of separateness causes intense anxiety "...the source of all anxiety," as Fromm said.

8-4 ALONENESS AND LONELINESS

Because of fear of separation we often choose aloneness, especially if we have experienced the pain of separation before. Separation, if not wanted, results in loneliness and pain of the worst kind. Morris (1971, 106-107) commented:

> Short of physical torture or death, solitary confinement is the worst agony that can be inflicted on a prisoner (person). He is driven eventually into near-madness. Intimacy needs understanding, and most of us do want to be understood, at

least by a few people.

Fear of failure, fear of rejection, fear of not measuring up, all tend to make us feel unworthy and then to seek isolation. In turn, these feelings of inferiority result in anxiety which can only be removed by seeking and removing the source. Anxiousness is a component of fear and will get progressively worse if we do not acknowledge and deal with it, according to Gaylin (1979, 19). Levels of fear, as I cited in Chapter 4-4.1, can vary and may range from mild to severe and are destructive because of our anticipation of pain (painful in the broadest sense).

Being alone does not necessarily lead us to loneliness. There are times when we may need to be away from others and have time to deal with our own thoughts. Advantages of being alone suggested by Burns (1980, 285) included that it:

1. Gives us the opportunity to explore what we really think, feel, and know.
2. Gives us a chance to try all sorts of new things that might be harder to try if we were tied too close to another.
3. Forces us to develop our own personal strengths.
4. Enables us to put aside excuses for taking responsibility for ourselves.
5. Is better than being with an unsuitable other person.
6. Gives us an opportunity to develop into our own fully human person.
7. Can help us understand and be supportive of others who may have been forced to be alone.
8. Can help us to gain confidence that we can make it on our own and not be overly dependent on some other person.

Being alone may often be advantageous, particularly if we feel free and do not develop anxieties over the situation. A major contributing factor to much of our anxiety from being with others stems from interpersonal relationships which are based on unilateral power.

8-5 UNILATERAL POWER

The concept of power that predominates in much of the world is the kind that is essentially one directional. It is a kind of political power. More specifically, this kind of linear power focuses on our influencing, guiding, adjusting, manipulating, shaping, controlling or transforming the human or natural environment with little or no attention to feedback (Loomer, 1976, 5-32). This results in our exercising our influence over another with no attention to the points of view, feelings or wishes of others. We do not seek feedback nor do we acknowledge feedback even if the other persons attempt to express opposing or competing points of view. When we practice this kind of power it leads us to insensitivity to the presence of others whether it be another person, nature or a god. It is the antithesis of love. Unfortunately it is the kind of power that predominates in much of the world between nations, governments, groups and all too frequently between and among individuals. It is destructive of trust and respect and therefore tends to destroy good interpersonal relationships and thus can be extremely detrimental to our creative and innovative capabilities.

8-6 RELATIONAL POWER

Relational power focuses on our mutually influencing and being influenced, on mutually giving and receiving, and on mutually making claims and permitting and enabling others to make their claims on us. It carries with it the concept that there is the capacity to absorb an influence as well as attempting to exert an influence. In it we acknowledge and affirm others, and recognize that the energy generated in the relationship will likely far exceed unilateral power. It is the kind of power relationship that is essential if we are to enjoy successful interpersonal relationships. The key in this kind of a relationship may well be that we neither fear nor destroy any aspect of the other, whether it be persons or nature. Loomer indicated that the ultimate aim of relational power is the creation and enhancement of those relationships in which all participating members are transformed into individuals and groups of greater stature. In practice this is essentially following and living by the "Golden Rule" of "Do unto others as you would have them do unto you."

8-7 BUILDING A LASTING RELATIONSHIP

We cannot build strong relationships with other individuals quickly nor without conscious efforts and reliable behavior by all those involved. In the early stages of building a relationship there is often a tendency to attempt to be what we think the other(s) expect(s) us to be. That means we are apt to do a great deal of faking, avoiding disagreement and being overly pleasant with one another. Just as usually occurs in group formation (see Chapter 9-2), this means there likely will be little progress in solving a problem or building the relationship until some changes take place.

Gradually we each will begin to reveal our real, and maybe selfish, views and who we are. We each begin to feel that, "If we are going to have a relationship that I can tolerate, I'm going to have to change this other person to my way of thinking." This obviously leads to confusion, conflict and maybe even chaos. Only as we each reach a state where we are willing to be honest with one another, give up the notion that we must change the other, be willing to let go of our pet ideas, and finally see that we must resolve differences by compromise and agreement will the bonds of a true relationship begin to form.

True and lasting relationships require a number of things from each of us involved. Some are:

- developing a relationship that goes deeper than our outward masks of composure;
- having a deep respect and trust for one another;
- being our own true self in all circumstances;
- honoring each other's individual differences;
- giving and encouraging each other to exercise the freedom to be our own independent selves;
- being absolutely honest, even if it hurts at the time;
- affirming one another frequently;
- showing genuine "brotherly" love; and
- learning how to communicate openly and honestly with each other.

8-8 LOVE AND CARING

Love was defined by Fromm (1956, 22) as:

... the active concern for the life and the growth of that which we love.

The above listed requirements for a lasting relationship incorporate those elements indicative of love and caring. The Biblical description of love is:

Love is very patient and kind, never jealous or envious, never boastful or proud, never haughty or selfish or rude. Love does not demand its own way. It is not irritable or touchy. It does not hold grudges and will hardly even notice when others do it wrong. It is never glad about injustice, but rejoices whenever truth wins out. If you love someone you will be loyal to him no matter what the cost. You will always believe in him, always expect the best of him, and always stand your ground in defending him. (1 Corinthians 13:4-7, Living Bible)."

Fromm suggested four basic elements common to all love - care, responsibility, respect and knowledge. In love we must care for one another, be responsibile and ready to respond, and respect one another. Fromm described this as:

The ability to see a person as he is, to be aware of his unique individuality. Respect means the concern that the other person should grow and unfold as he is. Respect, thus, implies the absence of exploitation.

To respect another, we must know the other. Care and responsibility are not possible without knowledge of one another.

Buscaglia (1984, 36) reported a study of the qualities viewed by a large number of people to be enhancing or destructive of loving, growing relationships. His findings are listed in Table 8-1.

Table 8-1
Factors Affecting Loving, Growing Relationships

Enhancing Factors	Destructive Factors
Communication	Lack of communication
Affection	Selfishness/Unforgiving
Compassion/Forgiveness	Dishonesty
Honesty	Jealousy
Acceptance	Lack of trust
Dependability	Perfectionism
Sense of humor	Lack of flexibility
Romance (including sex)	Lack of understanding
Patience	Lack of respect
Freedom	Apathy

Constructed from text of Buscaglia, 1984, 36-37.

8-9 BUILDING TRUST

To become mature, productive and healthy persons, we must trust and be trusted. Deshler (no pub. date, 32) said;

We enter into one another's lives only insofar as we trust each other. Again, it is apparent that the love which develops in an intimate group is the main source of the release and healing that take place in the lives of the members. There is no fear of love. As the group members learn to love one another, they learn to trust one another; for they no longer fear rejection or disapproval.

Buscaglia (1984, 80) indicated that:

We have a very human need to believe, to trust each other. I think we'd go mad if we felt there was no one we could trust. It is through trust that our value systems grow and change. With the security and reassurance arising from trust we become more open to risk.

8-9.1 The Importance of Honesty

Honesty is essential for, whereas dishonesty is extremely destructive of, trusting interpersonal relationships. Two books are of help in considering honesty or dishonesty in relationships (see both Buscaglia, and White, 1979).

Buscaglia's (1984) report showed honesty high on the list of essentials for good interpersonal relationships (see Table 8-1). All too often we avoid the truth because we think we might cause a minor crisis. So we resort to telling a "little white lie." We teach that honesty is the best policy, but convey to others by our actions that lying is a condoned and necessary social skill. When we punish our children or cause them to lose face for telling the truth, they soon learn to protect themselves by lying.

If we try to build a relationship on lies, we run the risk of the deception destroying future interactions by forcing a continuing series of lies. This risk of discovery means that we, as the perpetrators, must overload our memory system to avoid being caught. And, if caught, our credibility can be forever in question. Buscaglia emphasized this by saying:

... seemingly insignificant experiences mushroom, escalate, and finally create complicated and tangled webs of distrust that capture and destroy.

Thus even the "little white lie" can cause unlimited detrimental effects on our human behavior.

Buscaglia also said:

Only the truth can help us feel secure. Only truth can bring us the necessary trust needed for long-lasting relationships.

Only truth, painful though it may sometimes be, can create a safe environment of unity and growth. Trust is impossible without truth. Where there is no trust there can be no love.

Not only is our potential for interpersonal relationships impaired by dishonesty, but also the real self is, to some degree, violated. Thus the impact of dishonesty on individual creative abilities can be enormous. Buscaglia (1984, 84) cited R. Gould as having said:

Every self-deception causes erroneous judgments, and bad decisions follow, with unforeseen consequences to our lives. Every protective self-deception is a crevice in our psyche with a little demon lurking in it ready to become an episode of unexplained anxiety when life threatens. The larger the area of our mind we find it necessary to defend, the more our thinking processes will suffer, we will not allow our mind to roam freely because new information might contradict our self-deceptions. The larger the self-deceptions, the larger the section of the world we are excluded from.

Thus dishonesty not only lessens the possibilities for good interrelationships, which can contribute greatly to our creative storehouse, but is likely to clutter our minds with extraneous anxieties that will further diminish creative capabilities, possibly for a lifetime.

8-9.2 Other Factors Important to a Trusting Relationship

The importance of being affirmed by those close to us, such as family, close friends, peers or others is often over-looked. Criticism by these same persons is more devastating to us than it is if it comes from someone more distant. However, when given in love and in a relationship where closeness has been generated, openness and forthrightness can be quite helpful for our personal growth. We should make sure that such a relationship has plentiful affirmation and praise as well as open and constructive criticism.

Making ourselves available is an aspect that needs our careful consideration in close relationships and especially in subordinate and superior relationships. We must avoid being or projecting a superiority and dominant role, as well as projecting a view that "I don't have time for you." Both are detrimental to any close relationship. When, as parents, we fail to find time for our children, or when our bosses can't find time to interact with us, interpersonal relationships deteriorate. The same is true if we cause or show dominance, embarrassment of others, mistreatment or commit other disrespectful actions.

Reliability, openness, sensitivity, confidentiality, and accountability to others are additional all-important components for us in building trusting and lasting interpersonal relationships.

8-10 COMMUNICATION

Communications are essential in every walk of life. We get some idea of the rewards on a broad scale when broken or missing communications among and between groups are changed and healed by disasters such as earthquakes, tornadoes, hurricanes, wars, etc. On a smaller scale a communication breakdown between two of us can be just as devastating and in need of healing.

Too often we only think of communication as a process of telling someone something. Effective communication is not a monologue, rather it is a dialogue (two-way) which involves both persons as senders and receivers. At best, it is a sharing of our thoughts and ideas, and an expression of our feelings in an attempt to mutually understand one another.

We use communications to show who we are, and through communications we learn who others are. The authenticity of the revelations in both depends on how honestly we reveal ourselves. Open and honest communication between and among us is crucial for the development of strong and lasting interpersonal relationships (see discussion on honesty 8-9.1). Moustakas (1972, 130) has depicted very clearly his frustrations with communications:

Increasingly, I have become painfully aware of the terribleness of most communication: of people talking but not saying what they mean; of the contradiction between the outward words and expressions and the inner meanings and messages; of people looking as if they were listening without any real connection or contact with one another. When I am with such persons I experience deep feelings of loneliness, and I want to break through the empty words and come into touch with the feelings; I want to go beyond the icebergs on top, and into what is actually happening deep down? I have become keenly aware that individuals rarely express what really matters: the tender, shy, reluctant feelings, the sensitive, fragile, intense feelings. Too often we receive the words but not the concrete, actual messages and meanings. What has happened to us as human beings that we can be so near and yet so far, that we can be so distant from each other and not even know? Where are we anyway in those hours when the human spirit cries out in despair, when the hunger for sharing and for loving comes through in disguised and devious forms? What has happened when we have become so radically cut off from our own humanity that we kill the human need for compassion and understanding, when the longing for response is not even recognized or noticed?

Deshler (no pub. date given, 35) has suggested that communication is basic. It is our power of self-expression to other people. He has indicated that without it we cannot develop a mature personality. He went on to say that we must develop the ability to convey our feelings and thoughts to others. Most of us can contribute far more than we think we can. If we are to develop good interpersonal relationships, we must be open and share our doubts, resentments, anger, and guilt. This we are not likely to do if there is not love, trust, honesty, and a certainty of confidentiality.

Some years ago it was estimated that approximately 45% of our communication time was spent in hearing, 30% in talking, 16% in reading, and 9% in writing. Although much of our communication involves the spoken word and listening, it is somewhat surprising how much we convey through vision, body language, and touching. We need (probably it has been done) a study now on how much of our total communication is received through vision. However, even with the visual part of television, much also comes through hearing.

8-10.1 Speaking (Conversing)

Language is the major basis of our ability to communicate. It is through words that we learn a lot of what we come to know, and through words we let others know and understand what we are and what we know. Howe (1963, 3) suggested that it is only through dialogue that we escape from the feeling that every other person is a potential adversary. He suggested that:

When dialogue stops, love dies and resentment and hate are born.

In dialogue there is a flow of meaning between us even in the presence of interactions which may block a relationship. In a monologue we, as speakers, become so preoccupied with ourselves that the spoken words flow in only one direction and there is no feedback heard or accepted. Thus, communication breaks down.

Powell's (1969, 54-62) discussion on level of communications makes it obvious that many of our exchanges are of little value in revealing who we are, where we stand, what we believe, etc., because our conversations are directed away from true meaning. He suggested the five levels of communication shown in Table 8-2.

Table 8-2
Levels of Communication

- Level 5 - Cliche conversation - Chit chat. How are you? How is your family? The non-communication of the cocktail party.
- Level 4 - Reporting the facts about others - I remain largely in the prison of my loneliness, exposing nothing of myself.
- Level 3 - Some communication of my person - I risk telling some of my ideas, decisions and judgments.
- Level 2 - Exposing my feelings and emotions - Showing things that are my unique person, my gut-level reactions and emotions.
- Level 1 - Peak communication - Absolute openness and honesty, basis for deep and authentic relationships.

Constructed from text of Powell, 1969, 54-62.

Little of what we are, what we know, or what we feel is conveyed in the lowest level (level five) of conversations. The highest level (level one), or peak communication, is not a level that we are likely to maintain over a long period of time. But, it will likely result in generating deep feelings of relationship which give us an ecstatic feeling of union and will be remembered and sought after over and over again. It is the kind of feeling which we may achieve with one other person, but would rarely experience in a group. Relatively few speakers have the capabilities of stirring the release to peak communication with a large audience.

Our tone of voice and our accompanying body language can greatly influence how well our message is received when we speak. Even a clearly worded conversation can be misunderstood if our body language (facial expression, etc.) conveys a different message than the spoken words. Words can be lies, and may often deceive, but body language usually reveals our true feelings. The Bible has said it clearly:

A soft answer turns away wrath, but harsh words cause quarrels (Proverbs 15:1. The Living Bible).

8-10.2 Lecturing (Speaking to Groups)

When we speak to a group, or lecture, we are essentially doing a monologue. Thus there is usually no chance for feedback, and we know that the most effective communication is a dialogue. However, we can be effective in lecturing if we manage to get and hold the alert attention of the listeners. Harding (1948) wrote a satirical article on speaking in which he pointed out that we could accomplish poor speaking to groups by:

1. making no preparations;
2. giving the speech no order, let it ramble;
3. avoiding conclusions or summaries;
4. mumbling and not looking directly at the audience; and
5. never analyzing an audience or evaluating our performance.

Other ways he mentioned for us to be poor speakers is by:

- keeping our audience guessing what point we are trying to make;
- trying to cover more than the time allows;
- reading our speech;
- not omitting detail;
- not rehearsing or listening to ourselves ahead of time;
- arriving late;
- not using the public address system;
- using an extremely fast or slow tempo to attract attention;
- using a flat monotone;
- dropping our voice or being loud;
- avoiding humor;
- drawing our speech out;
- repeating things several times;
- not leaving time for questions or discussion; and
- not worrying about insulting a few of the listeners.

DuBois (1942) discussed six audience enemies as including:

1. the mumbler or voice dropper;
2. the slide crowder who tries to cram all of his data in or uses too many slides;
3. the time ignorer;
4. the sloppy arranger who jumbles his material;
5. the lean producer who has poor and irrelevant material;
6. the grasping discussant who just happens to have a few slides and doesn't know when to stop talking.

If we pay attention to the warnings listed above and carefully prepare ahead of time, including being prepared for interruptions such as - slides being projected upside down, disturbances in the audience, improper room lighting, etc., we can become much better lecturers or paper presenters. We should strive to make a good appearance, avoid distracting actions and comments, get the audience involved by presenting pertinent materials and allow time for interaction; all of which can contribute to our giving a successful lecture or speech. We dare not leave the subject of speaking without a word about silence. All too often as speakers, facilitators, or discussion leaders we become embarrassed by silence. We may ask a question, set up a situation which is intended to stimulate the audience to think or ask questions, and then fail to allow enough time for reasonable thought to develop. We feel that the silence is a reflection on us, and it is our responsibility to fill in with something. We may even answer our own question, which really turns discussion off. Silence can often be more effective than the spoken word. Usually the participants (hopefully they have been stimulated to become participants) have as much responsibility in keeping the exchange going as we do as leaders, if listener involvement is hoped for and/or expected. Silence is a must for thinking. Remember as the old saying goes, "We can't think or hear with our mouths open."

8-10.3 Hearing - Listening

Whereas talking or speaking is one half of verbal communication, listening is the other half. Careful listening can help us in many ways. It can reduce the tension which is often generated if we have not heard correctly. We can learn and often win friends by listening. We may often be able to solve mutual problems and resolve differences if we hear what others are saying. Listening shows respect for others and can help increase cooperation. Attentiveness and listening encourage others to speak more openly. Knowing helps us make better decisions. All in all, this means we are likely to do a better job, gain more confidence, and enjoy life more fully if we listen.

We will make few changes in our interactions if we are not aware that good listening is important and make a practice of listening. Nichols and Stevens published an article on "Listening to People" in the *Harvard Business Review* (Sept.-Oct., 1957) which was reproduced in a booklet on *"Effective Listening: Listener's Response Book"*, put out by Xerox Corporation in 1963 and 1964. The following points are made in the booklet. The effective listener:

1. Constantly analyzes what is being said.
2. Organizes the statement into main points and supporting reasons.
3. Outlines by use of key words.
4. Organizes advantages from disadvantages.
5. Discriminates between relevancies and irrelevancies.
6. Cuts through distractions, such as:
   a. background noise;
   b. unusual accents and dialects;
   c. speaker disorganization and emotion; and
   d. superfluous material.

In general, people do not know how to listen today. The importance of listening is indicated by top executives who suggest that 80% of all that they do is dependent upon listening to someone or having someone listen to them. In studies by Nichols and Stevens at Florida State University and Michigan State University, it was found that as average listeners we will remember only about 25% (or maybe even less) of what we heard two months after we have listened to a talk or attended a meeting. They suggest that, in general, one-half to one-third of all that is heard is forgotten within eight hours (see Chapter 2-4.2).

False assumptions that we make regarding listening are:

1. It has been assumed that our listening ability depends on intelligence. Although intelligence is important to listening, there is no indication that high intelligence assures good listening.
2. The assumption that learning to read will help us learn to listen is false. Listening is not helped if only reading is taught. The improvement in listening ability has ranged from 25 to 40% in controlled experiments where listening training has been involved.

Two important factors in improving our listening include:

1. being aware that certain factors affect listening ability; and
2. practicing good listening habits.

One of the reasons good listening is hard for us to learn is that the average rate of speed of speech for most Americans is about 125 words per minute. Our brains work at a much faster rate, thus when we listen we ask the brain to slow down greatly, compared to its capabilities. The thing that happens then is that our brain gets side-tracked and goes off in tangential thoughts. A good way to counteract this and bring about effective listening is for us to:

1. use the capacity of our brain in trying to anticipate what the oral presentation is leading to;
2. weigh the spoken words to determine whether the facts or the evidence being presented are valid and complete;
3. review and summarize the points of the talk or conversation up to the particular point reached; and
4. attempt to "listen between the lines" so that the meaning of what is not being put into words can be determined.

Do we often skip some of these things? Two much attention to facts can lead us to confusion. It is far better for us to listen for principles, concepts, ideas, or general situations. Understanding the ideas can help us to recall the facts. We must be careful that our own emotional reactions do not turn us off mentally. We have a great tendency to listen to what we want to hear and to turn off what we do not want to hear. We must be careful to:

1. withhold evaluation until all of the conversation has been produced; and
2. look for negative evidence.

Seeking out evidence that shows we are wrong as well as hearing what we think is right can help us avoid the danger of missing what people are saying.

Good communication can lessen paperwork and improve upward and downward communication. This helps improve human relations and helps us sell ourselves and our ideas, thus getting in tune with those who are involved in the conversation.

8-10.4 Writing - Reading

Although early man relied on the spoken word to pass information on from generation to generation, the written word (and picture word) has for centuries been the means of communicating more precisely to each succeeding new generation. Of course movies, television and videos have now combined voice, writing and pictures to record things for posterity. However, writing and reading will likely be of major significance for years to come, and will remain our major historical record of the past. As individuals we still place a heavy reliance on writing and reading for communicating with those at a distance from us even though satellites and airwaves are available for properly equipped remote areas.

Personally, we write not only to preserve for posterity, but to assist us with our own memory. Written notes help us with names, places, ideas, spelling, thoughts, and even in developing concepts. Writing helps us to fix things in our memory. We often think we have things well in mind, until we are called upon to put them in writing. In the effort to put them in writing, we are forced to clarify and crystallize what we want to think, say, or remember. In fact when we write we may even find that we know more than we thought we knew.

Volumes have been written, and much advice has been given on how to communicate by writing. One set of recommendations has been given by Dale (Nov. 1969). He emphasized that writing can be difficult, and it is nearly impossible to write for everyone. His suggestions in abbreviated form include:

1. define your audience and purpose;
2. avoid a lengthy introduction;
3. tell a logical story;
4. make your key points visible;
5. be concise but clear;
6. make it personal;
7. invite reader participation and involvement;
8. use pointed examples;
9. simplify the vocabulary;
10. watch your sentence structure;
11. use visual material of various kinds; and
12. repeat and summarize thoughtfully.

Clear and concise scientific writing, just as most writing, does not come easily for many persons. Woodford (1967) wrote an article in *Science* on "Sounder Thinking through Clearer Writing." In it he declared:

Bad scientific writing involves more than stylistic inelegance; it is often the outward and visible form of an inward confusion of thought.

He emphasized that:

In the work to be described, what was the question asked and what are the answers obtained?

In a later book which he edited (Woodford, 1981), he has also pointed out that in scientific reports:

Writing is not extrinsic to research: it is inevitably a part of it, since research is not complete until it is published.

Poor writing and slow reading can both be great deterrents to many kinds of creativity. This is especially true since much of our thinking is based on transforming images into words and vice versa. Thus, increasing our capabilities in reading and writing can bolster our fluency with words, our potential avenues of flexibility, our thinking, and our creativity.

8-10.5 Vision - Seeing and Body Language

Reading is, of course, a visual means of receiving messages. We also communicate or perceive through images, pictures, illustrations (pictorially, demonstrationally, graphically, photographically, etc.). Certainly the old saying that "a picture is worth a thousand words" usually holds true. Visual perception has been defined as "the mind's interpretation of what the eyes see." How we interpret things often depends on factors such as their surroundings, the viewing conditions, whether or not they are in motion and even our needs, expectations and desires at the time.

We all communicate with others by our body language through our eye, facial and body messages. We often forget that the nonverbal communication signals we receive or send may be more honest than the words that are being spoken. As Fast (1977) has pointed out, it may be fairly easy at times to deceive with words, but our true feelings are frequently revealed by our body actions or responses. It boils down to something like the old saying: "Because of the way you are acting, I can't begin to believe what you are saying." Actions speak louder than words.

Eye, facial and other body movements and expressions can convey various messages indicative of another person's inner feelings. They can also be used to better communicate our own messages, whether we are involved in a one to one encounter or in a presentation or exchange with a group of participants. We are, in fact, constantly communicating to others via our body language no matter whether we intend to or not, whatever the situation. Our facial expressions, seeking space away from another, opening our arms, folding our arms, clenching our fists, shifting our eyes, and many other movements send messages of our inward thoughts and feelings (see Nierenberg and Calero, 1971).

If we pay closer attention and can become more sensitive, we may be able to improve our ability to read body language. Then through practice we may be able to better recognize and interpret nonverbal cues and feedback. Doing so can increase our ability to communicate more effectively.

Eye contact, or eye language as Fast (1978) referred to it, can be an extremely important part of communicating. He made the following suggestions for improving effectiveness with eye language:

1. Making and prolonging eye contact helps us to establish a warmer, closer business or social relationship with those we meet and pass providing the gaze is not so long as to be rude, aggressive, or intimate.
2. Looking into the other person's eyes as we are talking and listening helps to convince others of our interest and helps to show that we are telling the truth.
3. If we stop looking at the other person, we will soon bring the conversation to a close. This is particularly true if we are the dominant one in the conversation. If our superior does this to us, it is a likely time to exit.
4. If we want to create doubt about what another person is saying, look them in the eye, raise our eyebrows, then look away.
5. If we avert another person's gaze, we do a great deal to prevent the establishment of any kind of close or trusting communication or relationship.
6. If we use a fixed and extended gaze into the eyes of a person of the opposite sex, we may be interpreted as showing more than just a common, important or business interest.
7. We can tell a great deal about the honesty and sincerity of another person by watching their eyes and body language. If the other person cannot look us in the eye and tends to exhibit nervousness, they may be feeding us a line.
8. We can show and maintain attention by looking away or above or below the eyes from time to time when we want to show our interest without conveying the wrong message.

8-10.6 Touching

Touching is the only means of communication that involves body contact. Touching is a basic need of the newborn (Montague, 1971, 23-32). Unloved, rarely touched children in an institution (as late as the second decade of the 20th century) suffered nearly 100%

mortality. Mothered (handled, touched) children in similar institutions usually lived and even thrived. According to Montague and Matson (1979, 115):

> The absence or presence of mothering showed up in many ways but most comprehensively in the developmental quotient - mastery of perception, of bodily functions, of social relations, of memory and imitation, of manipulative ability, and of intelligence.

Obviously all of these are critical to the later development of creative capabilities.

Later in life many of our adult body contacts convey acceptance or rejection. The pat on the back, full embrace, shoulder embrace, hand-on-shoulder, arm-link, hand-in-hand (mutual consent), head contacts, kissing, the handshake (Morris, 1971), all signal openness and acceptance of varying degrees. All indicate that the paths for communication are open and welcome. Pulling away, grabbing, pushing, shoving, hitting, kicking, and biting, all clearly send the message of rejection. All convey our unwillingness to communicate.

8-10.7 Blocks to Communication

A number of blocks to our communications have been indicated in the foregoing discussions in this chapter. In Table 8-3 a number of these (primarily verbal) are summarized.

Our failure to communicate, according to Dale (Dec. 1970), may be the result of:

- lack of a democratic atmosphere;
- an unwillingness to share;
- an inability to share;
- differences in experiences;
- differences in age;
- stratification of classes and economic levels; and
- living in different geographical areas.

If we live differently we tend to think differently, possess differing native abilities, and we may have problems of attitude and emotions. To overcome these we each must be willing to:

- tolerate varying opinions;
- accept and respect the rights of others to have different views; and
- attempt to understand where the others are coming from.

Table 8-3
Blocks to Effective Communication

---

1. Ordering, directing, commanding
   ("You must... You have to...")
2. Warning, admonishing, threatening
   ("You had better... If you don't, then ...")
3. Moralizing, preaching, obliging
   ("You should... You ought to...")
4. Advising, giving suggestions or solutions
   ("What I would do is... Why don't you ..?"
   "It would be best ... Let me suggest ...")
5. Arguing, instructing, lecturing, persuading with logic
   ("Do you realize...? The facts are... Here
   is why you are wrong... Yes, but...")
6. Judging, criticizing, disagreeing, blaming
   ("You are acting foolishly... You are not thinking straight...")
7. Name-calling, ridiculing, shaming
   ("You're a sloppy worker... Who hired you..?
   You have loused up this whole program...")
8. Interpreting, analyzing, diagnosing
   ("What you need is... Your problem is ...,
   You really don't mean that...")
9. Probing, questioning, interrogating
   ("Who...? What...? Where...? When...? Why...?")
10. Withdrawing, distracting, humoring, diverting
    ("We can discuss it later... That reminds
    me... When did you read a newspaper last?")
11. Reassuring, sympathizing, consoling, supporting
    ("Don't worry... You'll feel better... It's not so bad...")
12. Praising, agreeing, evaluating positively, approving
    ("You've done a good job... I approve of...")

(Source unknown)
*Author's note: While most of the listings above are absolute blocks to
communication, several can be qualified. For example; there is nothing
wrong with praising people honestly. However, being patronizing or
giving praise when you have no strong positive opinion in the matter
leads to dealing thoughtlessly with people. If we do this habitually, we
become less effective communicators.*

8-11 RELATIONSHIPS AND HEALTH

Interpersonal relationships can result in many conditions that are
either beneficial or detrimental to physical as well as mental well-
being. Many social readjustments (good and bad and usually closely

tied to interpersonal relationships) and environmental conditions are stressful and detrimental to our health and well-being. Holmes and Rahe (see Mason, 1980, 7-8) showed that too many such stresses imposed in a short time may make us much more susceptible to illness. They developed a stress-rating scale ranging from 100 for death of a spouse, (divorce-73, fired-47, pregnancy-40, trouble with in-laws-29, change in sleeping habits-16, vacation-13), down to 11 for a minor violation of the law. If we accumulate under 150 points in one year, there is less than a 1 to 10 chance of illness within the next 12 months. But they found there was about a 50:50 chance of a hospitalizing illness within the next 12 months following the accumulation of over 250-300 points.

Love, acceptance and a close circle of persons to whom we can relate openly and with confidence seem to be not only comforting and rewarding but also seem to help one ward off and even recover from some illnesses (Cousins, 1979; Siegel, 1986). Humor is also believed to be a helpful factor. Humor usually comes from our interactions with others and/or seeing or visualizing ourselves in circumstances involving relationships to other persons or things.

Lynch (1977, 3-4, 181-182) presented evidence that companionship and a healthy relationship often seem to prolong life. Loneliness is detrimental. He showed that a lack of companionship and/or relationships, as well as losses through death or separation often bring us to what appear to be earlier than expected heart attacks and death.

8-12 RELATIONSHIPS AND CREATIVITY

Although the individual self is at the core of creativity for each of us (see Fig. 7-1), other people and interpersonal relationships can have an especially beneficial or detrimental influence on us (see Fig. 8-1). Thus there may be a real advantage for us, if we desire to be creative, to put forth extra efforts to build friendships. Block (1980) suggested three major points of emphasis needed in developing friendships:

1. We need the "courage to be, to be authentic." We fear we will be found to be undesirable and this fear of rejection causes us to put forth a false front, to put on a mask, to avoid being known.
2. We must accept that "What is, is." A healthy relationship precludes the demand that "you must think, feel, act like me." Respect and value for another as a separate unique

person is essential.
3. "Please, tell me what you want." Our direct expression of words (communication) can be used to hurt, calm, nurture, confuse, anger, provoke, deceive, dominate, manipulate - even silence conveys a message as does body language. Camouflaged, hidden and indirect messages confuse.

We reap many real rewards when we are willing to be ourselves and simultaneously be in relationship with others. Some of the rewards have been expressed by Thomas (1971, 102-104). These are summarized in Table 8-4.

Table 8-4
Fruits of Courage to Be Self and in Relationship to Others

Independent	In-relationship
Self-awareness	Awareness of others
Self-confidence	Confidence in others
Self-respect	Respect for others
Respect from others	Support and approval
Self-importance	of others
Ego	Strength and power
Freedom	received from others
Personal power	Group strength

Constructed from text of Thomas, 1971, 102-104.

Rogers (1961, 37-38) has suggested that we can be of help in creating a relationship if we are willing to:

1. Show a genuineness and transparency in which we are our own real feelings.
2. Show a warm acceptance of and prizing of other persons as separate individuals.
3. Develop a sensitive ability to see their world and them as they see themselves.

Hopefully, in response, the other persons in the relationship will:

1. Experience and understand aspects of themselves which previously they have repressed.
2. Find themselves becoming better integrated, more able to function effectively.

3. Become more similar to the persons we would like to be.
4. Be more self-directing and self-confident.
5. Become more of a person, more unique and more self-expressive.
6. Be more understanding, more acceptant of others.
7. Be able to cope with the problems of life more adequately and more comfortably.

All of this is in contrast to the negative and lone-individual approach which is so often seen. Individuals who isolate themselves often distrust others and if involved like to blame others when things don't go well. I saw this kind of individual suffer in his aloneness for several years. He was so secretive that he refused to share anything about what he was doing. He seemed not to trust anyone. He contributed little, and even his superiors had difficulty learning just what he was spending his time doing. He stood out in the group only because he constantly thought others were getting all the recognition and rewards while he was being short changed. He had a heart attack and died at an early age.

Blame and overdemanding dependency wear us down and inhibit real intimacy. Energy used in blaming, as well as that of trying to please an over-dependent person, is energy lost for our constructive efforts and thus diminishes our energy for creativity.

Our attitudes (of being a "whole person") toward others are extremely important. Respect, tolerance, trust, and communications head the list of attitudes towards others that are most important for us in interpersonal relationships. Trust has been indicated by some as the most critical factor.

8-13 BARRIERS TO INTERPERSONAL RELATIONSHIPS

Relationship blocks to creativity are generated both by us and those with whom a satisfying interpersonal relationship is sought. Some of the types of barriers may be:

1. Disrespect, distrust and disregard for others with whom intentional or unintentional close contact is made (see Table 4-1 and Chapter 4-5).
2. Intentional efforts to manipulate, guide, control, convert or force others (see 8-5).
3. A lack of tolerance, flexibility, cooperation and trust among colleagues (see 8-9).

4. Autocratic leaders, superiors or peers who are stubborn and value only their own ideas (see 12-2.4).
5. A boss who is unfair and does not reward others (see 12-2).
6. The presence of persistent distractions - difficult persons, telephone, easy intrusions, etc. (see 10-7).
7. A lack of support and enthusiasm for bringing new ideas into consideration and action (see 6-11).
8. Feeling that we must conform to the beliefs and practices of others, or that they must conform to ours (see 9-7).
9. Fear of risk, criticism, not being right, becoming trapped or dominated (see 4-5).
10. Blocks to communication (see Table 8-3).

Many additional barriers to good interpersonal relationships can likely be identified with a little effort. We can often avoid most, or at least minimize their impact by conscious effort and practice. Increasing our flexibility and tolerance, suspending and modifying our critical judgement, avoiding efforts in which we appear to force, manipulate and control others, and making sure clear communications are being achieved, can help in building good relationships with others.

Building satisfying and productive interpersonal relationships usually requires us to exert almost constant, purposeful effort. It is easy for us to become a "mission impossible" without realizing it. Yet close relationships with others who are desirous of and striving for them can result in some of our lives' greatest rewards. This was well said by Deshler (no publication date given, 25) in the following:

It is one of life's greatest discoveries to find a fellowship where there are no barriers and no pretensions, where one need not live in fear that someone might get a glimpse into his heart. As the members open their lives to one another, they find themselves responding with sympathetic interest and then with love. Nothing more wonderful can happen to a person than for him to realize that people love him, not for what he pretends to be, but for himself - not because he is good or bad, but because he is a person whom God loves.

8-14 HIGHLIGHTS OF CHAPTER EIGHT

1. Population growth and our interdependency on each other for the necessities of life force us to greater and greater interpersonal contacts.

2. Growth ceases if we cannot become involved outside ourselves.
3. Our greatest fear is separation. Thus we seek community and go to great extremes to avoid rejection, loss of control, becoming vulnerable, feeling inferior and being accused of not conforming.
4. Building relationships is greatly impaired for those of us who resort to a unilateral type of power in which we attempt to manipulate and control others, for it usually leads to distrust.
5. Relationships come more easily for those of us who rely on a pattern of relational power - in which mutually influencing and being influenced, giving and receiving, making claims and permitting others to make their claims by way of feedback is practiced, for it serves to build trust.
6. Honesty, openness and consideration for others are essential if we are to realize lasting interpersonal relationships.
7. We are highly dependent on establishing good communications when we wish to build relationships and community between and among group members.
8. Good relationships can improve our health and creativity.
9. We must resist pressures to conform in many situations if we want our own creativity to flourish.

8-15 AFTERGROWTH STIMULATORS

1. Describe how you felt when you had fears of being rejected by, unloved by, losing control to, or not fitting in with those close around you?
2. What is the most memorable situation in which you felt that unilateral power was being inflicted on you? How were you treated? How did it make you feel? What did you do about it?
3. Describe someone with whom you found it difficult (or impossible) to build a reasonable level of trust and respect? What tactics did you try to change the situation?
4. In what ways have interpersonal relationships affected your opportunities to be creative?
5. Do you feel that interpersonal relationships have ever affected your health and well being, either positively or negatively?
6. Describe what you believe is (was) the best working relationship you have ever experienced? What made it so great?

CHAPTER 9

TEAM EFFORTS:
GROUP INFLUENCES

9- 1   Introduction
9- 2   Stages In Building
        Community or Teams
9- 3   The True Meaning of Community
9- 4   When Teams Are Needed
9- 5   Advantages of Having Teams
9- 6   Disadvantages of Team Efforts
9- 7   Common Problems in Group Efforts
9- 8   Why People Do Not Like to
        Work in Groups
9- 9   Required Characteristics for an
        Effective Team
9-10   How to Have a Successful
        Group Meeting
9-11   Group Impact on Creativity
9-12   Highlights of Chapter Nine
9-13   Aftergrowth Stimulators

9-1 INTRODUCTION

The complexity of problems and opportunities today practically insures that we must rely on the skills of more than single individuals if timely solutions are to be found. Therefore, effective team building becomes a major task for us when we need to assemble a working group.

In developing an effective team one of the most challenging situations we face is that of getting a group that will work together. Another challenging problem is that of convincing individuals to set aside their separate goals and to commit themselves to the group effort. Several writers, in discussing management challenges, have indicated that the more outstanding the participants in a working group, the greater the need for outstanding leadership and creativity in managing the unit.

We need to select individuals with self-actualizing characteristics and the ability to create as members of the team. Special efforts then need to be made to avoid conditions which block their potential creativity. An awareness by us, as leaders, of these needs and deterrents can help in enabling members to reach their greatest potential.

It is not always easy for us to bring together individuals with the appropriate knowledge and skills to most effectively take advantage of an opportunity or to solve a problem. Developing understanding, trust, and a spirit of cooperation demands real effort and commitment on our part and from each of the individuals involved in the group.

If a unit leader is successful in developing an effective team, it is often possible to capitalize on opportunities and reach solutions to problems much more rapidly than if the unit is depending upon individual contributions alone.

9-2 STAGES IN BUILDING COMMUNITY OR TEAMS

Much of the discussion in previous chapters has focused on rugged individualism, individual creative potential and factors affecting these items. However, throughout we have been indicating that there is great impact on the individual from other persons. As Peck (1987, 56) has said regarding rugged individualism:

It denies entirely the other part of the human story: that we can never fully get there (alone) and that we are, of necessity in our uniqueness, weak and imperfect creatures who need each other.

To survive we must form partnerships, teams and communities. Team building (community building) is characterized, as Johnson and Johnson (1987), Peck (1987) and many others have shown, by various kinds of human behavior. Peck (1987, 86-106) called these stages of community-making. His points are summarized in Table 9-1.

Table 9-1
Stages of Community Making

1. **Pseudocommunity** - Forming
   Pretend; fake it; avoid disagreement and conflict; tell white lies; withhold some of the truth; be pleasant with one another no matter what.
2. **Chaos** - Storming
   Hold to individual legalistic, parochial and dogmatic views; attack opposing views; win all to your way of thinking.
3. **Emptiness** - Norming
   All (including the leader) must empty themselves of barriers to communications; give up anything that stands in the way (expectations, preconceptions, prejudices, need to heal, convert, fix, solve, control, etc.); examine our deepest motives openly.
4. **Community** - Performing
   Resolve conflict; incorporate individual differences; be real and open-minded; create an atmosphere of respect and safety.

Modified and constructed from text of Peck, 1987, 86-106.

Initially, as group members, many of us come together expecting that everything is going to be "rosy." We think that we must be on our good behavior and that no one should "rock the boat" or upset the equilibrium of the group in any way. This results in pseudocommunity; it is not real. Soon, as individual members, we decide that we must try to get things moving. We begin to express our own self-determined legalistic, parochial or dogmatic views and try to control and win all to our way of thinking. This results in many fixed and different views, resulting in the group being pulled and pushed in all directions. Chaos results.

During these early stages of community building, we, as members of the group, are apt to find ourselves in various forms of what Peck (1987, 107-118) called "task avoidance" behavior patterns. We come together thinking that we should avoid troublesome issues, problems and individual differences. As a result we usually ignore and avoid anything that causes or triggers emotional pain. To avoid pain when it occurs we often resort to noisiness, changing the subject or simply ignoring the hurting person. These moves are referred to as "flight" patterns. Another pattern is one of "fight." This comes when we try to make everyone normal (fit our view), or when they avoid listening and integrating their individual differences and try to heal or convert one another instead. Usually these tactics lead to attacking one another and the leader when there is lack of direction.

Forming alliances (conscious or not) between two or a few in the group will also be highly likely to hinder mature group development. Still another counterforce, which may be the most destructive of all to true community development, comes from the group becoming overly dependent on the leader. In essence each of us is equally responsible for the success or failure of the group. As true leaders we must discourage dependency, and encourage all to carry their share of the load. As true leaders, we must be willing to accept - even welcome - the accusation of failing to lead. Peck has said, "It is far easier as leaders to teach and preach than to not speak." Obviously we, as leaders must shed our desire, and need, to control.

Gradually we must come to realize the chaotic nature of the situation, and that we are getting nowhere. It becomes obvious that we must compromise, if we are to get anywhere. Peck has indicated that all members, including the leader, must give up anything that stands in the way of, or serves as a barrier to, communications. This includes pet ideas, prejudices, preconceptions, needs to control, guide, fix, solve, etc. (see Table 9-1). He called this stage "emptiness." Once that has been accomplished, the group can begin to compromise, resolve conflicts and incorporate individual differences. They can then begin to come into community.

9-3 THE TRUE MEANING OF COMMUNITY

To reach a state of genuine community, we must learn to treat each other with respect even though we have differences in our views. Evans (1982) has suggested some principles for relating which every individual should learn and exhibit. He considered these essential if groups are to become genuine and really productive in their endeavors. These are paraphrased and presented in Table 9-2.

If as members of the team we do exhibit and practice these principles, we are much more apt to become satisfied with our membership in the group, and will become committed to implementing group decisions. If all become involved in helping the group to reach decisions, there is an equalization of power among us, and even productive controversy is encouraged.

Peck indicated that he believed the members of the true community must strive to help it maintain the qualities shown in Table 9-3.

Table 9-2
Essential Principles for Effective Groups

- Affirmation - Unconditionally agree to support each other, even though we disagree.
- Availability - Agree to give time, energy, insight, and maybe even possessions to support the group.
- Openness - Realize they must discard their masks and become more open in expressing their feelings.
- Honesty - Promise to be completely truthful even though it may be painful at times.
- Sensitivity - Be ever aware of others' feelings and needs.
- Confidentiality - Keep things that are shared within the confines of the group in confidence.
- Accountability - Strive to be accountable to ourselves, our partners, and to the group.

Compiled and paraphrased from Evans, 1982.

Table 9-3
What the True Community Must Be

Inclusive - Always reaching to extend themselves. Shows a willingness to coexist (crucial). Does not exclude self or others. Celebrates human differences as gifts.

Realistic - Shows humility. Fully aware of human differences. Recognizes the interdependence of humanity.

Contemplative - Shows increased awareness of: The world outside oneself. The world inside oneself. The relationship between the two.

A safe place - Where healing and converting can occur without fear and/or pressure. Customary defenses and threatened postures, barriers of distrust, fear, resentment, and prejudice are dropped. There is total decentralization of authority. The group can fight gracefully.

A place where there is a dramatic change of spirit.

Constructed from text of Peck, 1987, 61-76.

If a group can attain and hold to these several characteristics, it can become what Peck (1987, 59) called the true community. It then becomes a group of individuals who have:

1. learned how to communicate honestly with each other;

2. whose relationships go deeper than their masks of composure; and

3. who have developed some significant commitment to rejoice together, mourn together, delight in each other, make others' conditions their own.

Under these conditions, individuality and creativeness can thrive; there can be conflicts of ideas and opinions, yet growth and change can occur and psychological safety can prevail.

The true and lasting community honors all its members, not just a few. As Dale (May, 1969) indicated regarding the good society:

It builds self-respect by respecting itself. It takes pride in what it has done, is doing, and plans to do in the future. It does not manipulate people, using them as means for the ends of others. It does not deal with people as if they were things; to pick them up and set them down without respect for their uniqueness.

He went on to quote Judge Learned Hand as having said:

That community is already in the process of dissolution where each man begins to eye his neighbor as a possible enemy.

9-4 WHEN TEAMS ARE NEEDED

Often in the unmonitored and uncontrolled group situation, there are those who are uncertain about what their individual responsibilities are. These individuals are apt to be afraid to ask questions which they should be asking because they think it will make them look stupid. There may be others who always want to stick to the old way of doing things, while others believe there are new and better ways. Factions and cliques may be quarreling frequently. There may be a lot of jealousy between individuals and among factions within the group. The group does not seem to have clearly established goals which are understood by the members. Many may be aware that things are not going well, but no one is quite sure what the problem is. These conditions and the symptoms, which Lippitt (1982, 209-210) suggested, indicate situations where formation of a team may be needed. These include such things as:

1. loss or decrease in quantity and/or quality of output or service;

2. increase in discontent, grievances, complaints, and turnover of personnel;

3. hostility, conflict and resistance among group members;
4. lack of interest in properly implementing management decisions;
5. apathy and lack of interest and creativity within the group; and
6. communication failures and ineffective meetings.

If the atmosphere among the members of a team is relaxed, informal, and appears to be comfortable for those involved, and the task and objectives of the group appear to be clear to everyone, then productivity will likely be good. The group would appear to have already developed a pattern of working together with a team approach and a team atmosphere. Then the formation of a team may be contra-indicated and might even slow progress. Lippitt (1982, 210) listed a number of conditions under which a team should not be formed. These include such things as:

1. when no felt need for improvement exists;
2. when it is a management problem that team building cannot solve;
3. when the manager is using team building to achieve an ulterior motive;
4. when the manager is not well prepared to change or heed feedback;
5. when the manager is not willing to share leadership and decision-making;
6. if work is done primarily on an individual basis and members interact only on a limited basis;
7. if the manager and/or group does not fully understand the commitment of time and energy or the long-term nature of team development;
8. lack of time and availability of personnel to work in the program;
9. lack of willingness to look at one's own behavior, to analyze group process, to give and get feedback; and
10. people in power will not back up team solutions and team development activities.

Dyer (1977, 35) has indicated:

(that a team building)...program should not begin unless there is clear evidence that a lack of effective teamwork is the fundamental problem. If the problem is an intergroup issue, a technical difficulty, or an administrative foul-up, team building would not be an appropriate change strategy.

He also presented an extensive checklist (pp. 36-40) for assessing the need for team formation.

9-5 ADVANTAGES OF HAVING TEAMS

We frequently find there are a number of advantages and benefits that can result from forming teams to solve problems and develop ideas for seizing opportunities. If ours is a task-oriented point of view, having more people working on a problem can often reduce the time required to pull together the data or information needed. If we need expertise in a number of areas for complex problems, bringing in persons from several disciplines may be necessary.

From the interpersonal point of view, thinking, imagination, initiative, and innovation tend to be stimulated by the presence of others who are concentrating on the same issue. Combine these with the potential for better communications and the stimulus of competitiveness, and our group efforts are likely to produce more ideas.

Capener and Young (1975, 354-356) discussed some of the advantages of team efforts. Their points along with others are incorporated in Table 9-4.

Table 9-4
Some Advantages Provided by Team Efforts

1. An opportunity for comprehensive and unique views being applied to attacking complex problems.
2. Problems will likely be looked at in greater breadth and possibly in even greater depth, depending on the make-up of the team. Thus a better understanding of the whole problem.
3. More persons get the challenge and opportunity to participate in all phases (from planning to completion) of the problem-solving task. Thus less chance of an important aspect being overlooked.
4. The product resulting is likely to be in response to the needs and potential interest of a wider group.
5. A broader set of products, policies, publications, etc. are likely to be produced.
6. An opportunity to gain experience, insight, understanding and ability in working with others with varying backgrounds.
7. Inexperienced persons get an opportunity for leadership training and experience.
8. Participants gain valuable group experiences that will be of future benefit.

Constructed from text of Capener and Young, 1975, 354-356.

Participants new to team efforts are likely to be surprised at what they learn from others. New approaches and ways of thinking and viewing certain situations come to light. Often, if we have experts in a field present, they will have certain fixed ideas about what is possible or impossible and their thinking may be blocked to new approaches. Persons from other fields may not have those blocks regarding a field foreign to them, and thus may open new avenues of approach that would otherwise be ruled out without testing.

9-6 DISADVANTAGES OF TEAM EFFORTS

We can expect some things to occur when teams are formed and should plan for in order that we not be surprised when they do happen. Several of these disadvantages, based in part on the Capener and Young (1975, 356) discussion, are brought together here. These disadvantages of team effort include:

1. It takes more time and effort to get started and things progress more slowly because of the usual initial community building and communication difficulties.
2. Finding a leader with experience and skill may be difficult.
3. An individual's professional reputation, status, feelings of support and competency may be challenged (especially when the problem and team covers a wide range of disciplines). Thus there may be participation resistance.
4. Participants may be reluctant to be taken away from their own self-directed programs.
5. Total time required is usually longer and results are slower in coming.
6. Definition, delineation and explication of the problem are usually more complex and difficult.
7. Understanding concepts, terminology, meanings, standards and differences in other disciplines (fields, etc.) may cause difficulties.
8. Feedback on progress, awareness, and growth of the group is more difficult.
9. Recognition and rewards for participants may seem to be inadequate.
10. Diffusion of responsibility may lead to no one being responsible.
11. The threat of a breakdown in the actions of the group can threaten the goal of meeting the charge of the group.

9-7 COMMON PROBLEMS IN GROUP EFFORTS

There are a number of kinds of problems we can expect in all kinds of teams, groups and in meetings in general. Some of those discussed in some detail by Doyle and Strauss (1976, 83-84) have been modified and added to and are presented in Table 9-5.

Table 9-5
Common Problems in Group Efforts

1. Everybody going off in different directions at the same time.
2. Confusion over objectives and expectations.
3. Confusion between process and content. Is it what to do? Or is it how to do it?
4. Unclear roles and responsibilities.
5. Manipulation by group leader. Rubber-stamp and abuse of power to achieve personal objectives.
6. Unresolved questions of power and authority. Do we have the power to make this decision? Will our action be acted upon?
7. Win/lose approaches to decision-making. Partial solutions, compromises, polarization, and low commitment.
8. Personal attacks on individuals rather than on ideas?
9. Personality conflicts. Lack of openness and trust. Underlying tension, racism, and sexism.
10. Communication problems. Not listening to or understanding what others are saying (use of field jargon, etc.). Making false assumptions.
11. Having to hold on to too many ideas at one time.
12. Difficulty in leaping into the conversational flow and getting a chance to participate.
13. Repetition and wheelspinning, going over the same old ideas again and again.
14. Problem avoidance; "everything is fine"; "There are no problems around here."
15. General negativity and lack of challenge.
16. Being mislead or put down by an over-dominant participant.
17. Poor meeting environments. Can't hear, can't see, too stuffy, etc.

Constructed from text of Doyle and Strauss, 1976, 83-84.

9-8 WHY PEOPLE DO NOT LIKE TO WORK IN GROUPS

Many of us do not like to work in groups. We may prefer to concentrate on our own agenda. Others may be concerned about losing their independence and identity if they must work with a group of other people. Fears also are major factors causing us to dislike working in groups. Fear of risking and speculating (see Chapter 4-5.4), fear of criticism (see Chapter 4-5.5), fear of failure due to someone else (see Chapter 4-5.6), fear of not measuring up (see Chapter 8-3), fear of rejection and ridicule (see Chapter 8-4), and fear of loss of individual recognition, all are issues that need to be considered. We may find difficulties when there is need to develop or build consensus: teams, like committees, may be less willing to take risks. Finally, the pressure to conform must also be taken into account.

If we are to become good team workers, we must commit ourselves to the group. The struggle then becomes one of how to hang on to our own independence and still be loyal to the group; and how can we merit individual recognition in the midst of a host of others, many of whom may be stars in their own fields. The solution would seem to be to maintain our own individuality and self-esteem and be willing to risk them by being ourselves without being over-bearing and obnoxious in the activities of the team. Leaders of teams need to see to it that all members of a team get properly recognized for their contribution to the team if we hope to have the cooperation of those team members another time. The part of the team effort that each member is responsible for should be clearly defined at the onset of the team effort, and all members should know at that stage what the rewards are likely to be, providing they fulfill their role in the total effort.

According to Morgan (1968, 71-73) the real problem for us of the compulsion to conform lies mainly in:

1. dependence on the opinions of others;
2. feeling our reputation is at stake;
3. our tendency to act and think like others:
4. pressure to conform to other's rules;
5. our hesitancy to question views and ideas of others; and
6. being passive rather than actively participating.

Morgan (pp.73-76) has described three types of conformers. In the first type we are *consensus conformers*, we look for a solution, need information, and accept the opinion of the group as the most likely answer. In the second type, we are *expedient conformers*, we believe we have the right answer, but go along with the group on what we think is the wrong approach because we "don't want to rock the boat." In the third type, we are *passive conformers*, we lack confidence and accept group opinion.

Dyer (1977, 74-75) suggested a number of factors that cause us to develop a dislike for working in groups. These factors are abbreviated and presented in Table 9-6. The factors listed as causing us to dislike working in groups are similar to and in some respects duplications of common problems that occur in groups. Problems in groups trigger the dislikes.

Table 9-6
Factors Causing People to Dislike Working in Groups

1. Poor leadership; weak or undemocratic; lets discussion get off track; plays favorites; dominates discussion; is disrespectful; fails to keep things moving.
2. Purpose and goals unclear; members not really sure what they should be doing today; what are the ultimate goals?
3. Some members do not take assignments seriously; lack of commitment on the part of some.
4. Lack of preparation and default by chairperson and/or some members in carrying out responsibilities.
5. Waste of time; undirected and nonproductive discussions; no conclusions drawn; no assignments made; No action taken; group's recommendations ignored by superiors.
6. Special interest cliques, negative and super-critical persons dominate.
7. Placing personal interests ahead of, and to the detriment of, the group's goals and objectives.

Constructed from text of Dyer, 1977, 74-75.

9-9 REQUIRED CHARACTERISTICS FOR AN EFFECTIVE TEAM

From the foregoing discussions it appears that we can come up with some generalizations required to have an effective team. It's important that we have the right people, no more than needed, and a clear assignment for each. Openness, trust, mutual respect, and an ability to deal with conflict are characteristics that we must develop for maximum productivity. We must have skilled, democratic leadership. Some more detailed requirements (compiled from several sources) are presented in Table 9-7.

Table 9-7
Required Characteristics for an Effective Team

1. It is essential that there be a clear understanding and a unity of purpose in the endeavor.
2. There should be a strong sense of belonging and commitment to the group.
3. There must be a high degree of trust and confidence in one another.
4. The team needs to be made up of individuals with appropriate capabilities and each utilized maximally in the effort.
5. There must be a high degree of cooperation with flexibility and sensitivity to the needs of others without letting conformity adversely affect individual creativity.
6. A clear assignment and assumption of responsibilities is required of each team member.
7. There needs to be full, free and open communication of ideas, and feelings as well, among all members.
8. A respect for and willingness to share in a participative leadership is needed.
9. There needs to be frequent, extensive discussion of plans, progress, responsibilities and results.
10. Frequent, frank, constructive criticism and a willingness to discuss disagreements is imperative.
11. Visibility and reward for individuals wherever possible as well as overall team accomplishments should be highlighted.
12. All members must remember that each is responsible for a special part of the effort, but each is also 100% responsible for the success of the team as a whole.

9-10 HOW TO HAVE A
SUCCESSFUL GROUP MEETING

When we have teams or groups working together they must, of necessity, come together to communicate. This likely means frequent meetings are necessary, at least at the start of the teamwork effort. We can make these frequent meetings fruitful or disastrous, depending on how we conduct them. A number of things can be done prior to each meeting to help us insure success and effectiveness.

First, and of utmost importance, we need to be sure to pick appropriate participants for the group. Every person should have been selected to fulfill a specific need on the team. In some cases that may be a communication, information, and maybe even a political need. However, caution should be used to not put people on the committee or team just because they should ultimately know the results of the team's actions. Extra persons not needed to carry out the primary function of the team simply complicate our communication and decision-making, thus slowing and maybe even stymying our team action.

Since there are specific purposes for all team members, all should know, prior to the first meeting, the general purpose of the team, what role they will be expected to play, and who else is on the team. In fact, prior to each meeting an agenda should be developed to include what items are to be discussed, what is hoped to be accomplished, and which members of the team can and should be prepared to contribute (including materials that everyone should be familiar with before the meeting). Meeting notices should be in the hands of every member far enough in advance so that all can make appropriate preparations and clear their calendars. It is important also to make the expected meeting duration known.

At meeting time be sure to:

- start promptly;
- introduce every one to the other team members;
- stick to the agenda, but be flexible;
- keep the discussion on track;
- give everyone a chance to participate;
- politely cut off repetitive discussions;
- use subcommittees to work out lengthy details, suggest alternatives, and report back at the next meeting;
- call on those who were asked at the last meeting to report at this meeting;
- repeat and clarify decisions;
- make assignments;
- clarify what actions are expected of all members, and on what time schedule;
- let all know the importance of their contribution to the over-all effort of the team (whether it is a large or small contribution);
- encourage everyone with the progress that has been made, and express expectations for future reports of progress;
- don't let the meeting drag on; and
- close on time.

As leaders we often have a great tendency to become lax with many of the above items. If that happens, we may cause team members to become disenchanted with the team effort because they feel there is such a waste of time and that there is little recognition of their input.

9-11   GROUP IMPACT ON CREATIVITY

Many of the references cited throughout this book point out that creativity can either be helped or hindered by the presence of others around the potentially creative person. Comparisons have been made of effective and ineffective groups (Lippitt, 1982, 196-232; Johnson & Johnson, 1987, 1-33), which show that conditions which enhance and encourage the individual to be open and free, with concurrent respect to allow others in the group do the same, usually results, not only in productive and creative individuals, but also creative groups. However, no group is perfect in its performance, so some negative effects on creativity can be expected. Morgan (1968) suggested a number of effects of groups on the creativity of the individual. His points focused mainly on the pressures to conform that accompany group or team effort. Groups tend to discourage different and divergent opinions and ideas and directly or indirectly put pressure on individuals to conform. His discussion has been abbreviated and summarized in Table 9-8.

Table 9-8
Group Impact on Creativity

1. Group pressures inhibit originality.
2. Even creative people conform to group pressures.
3. Deviant support reduces the amount of conformity.
4. Expert opinion tends to increase conformity.
5. People conform more when actions affect others than when they alone are affected.
6. Status differences increase conformity, discourage deviant opinions, and reduce creative effectiveness of group work.
7. People who feel rejected conform more than people who feel accepted.
8. There may be times when a group is attempting to build "consensus" on goals and directions and conforming is required for the best of reasons.

Constructed from text of Morgan, 1968, 73-76.

Over the years in hundreds of group meetings and team efforts, I have seen nearly everything mentioned in this chapter happen. Member cooperation and effective leadership are critical to the success of group efforts. Group leaders need to be sure that individuals:

1. do not get lost in the crowd or upstaged by more senior members;
2. do get their share of individual credit;
3. do feel free and willing to share ideas and opinions;
4. do know and carry out their individual responsibilities;
5. do have a sense of responsibility for the total effort as well as for their portion of the effort; and
6. are recognized for their cooperation as well as for their efforts.

If this happens, then group efforts will usually pay off.

9-12 HIGHLIGHTS OF CHAPTER NINE

1. Many of today's problems and opportunities are so complex that the efforts of individuals with many different backgrounds, training and experience are required to have any hope of finding a solution.
2. We need to exercise care to be sure the situation calls for forming a group or team and that independent action cannot complete the task more rapidly.
3. In some situations help or time restrictions may dictate that we use a team to complete a task most effectively.
4. We need to exercise care in selecting a good group leader and appropriate group members, if an effective, community-minded team is to be realized.
5. A true community must be inclusive, realistic, contemplative, and a safe place where trust can be developed.
6. Initiative, imagination, and productivity are often stimulated in the competitive atmosphere of an effective team.
7. We need to impress team members with the importance and necessity for clear communications, trust, cooperation, and the assumption of responsibilities in order for the team effort to be successful.
8. Care needs to be taken to insure, in so far as possible, that individual team members are recognized for their input.
9. Team members need to remember that even though they are responsible for a special part of the team effort, each is also 100 percent responsible for the success of the over-all effort.

9-13 AFTERGROWTH STIMULATORS

1. What would be your major concerns if you were selected as a member of a group assigned to work on a problem in your field?
2. What would be your major concerns if you were asked to organize such a team?
3. What could you do to encourage a reluctant team member to cooperate if you were another team member? The team leader?
4. As a team leader, how would you go about dealing with an excessively dominant group member?
5. As a team member you find your leader is repeatedly ignoring your ideas, most of which you believe to be especially promising. What would you do?
6. Brainstorm with a friend ways you might use to resolve among team members a severe disagreement that arose during the early planning stages.

CHAPTER 10

SOCIETAL AND ENVIRONMENTAL INFLUENCES

10 - 1   Introduction
10 - 2   Culture
10 - 3   Parental Influence
10 - 4   Education
10 - 5   Institutions and Organizations
10 - 6   Creating an Open and
          Supportive Environment
10 - 7   Dealing with Stress
10 - 8   Highlights of Chapter Ten
10 - 9   Aftergrowth Stimulators

10-1 INTRODUCTION

Many societal and environmental factors greatly influence our creativity as they impact on us and the people around us. Our upbringing, educational, and cultural backgrounds and our experi-

CREATIVITY
and
ENVIRONMENTAL INFLUENCES

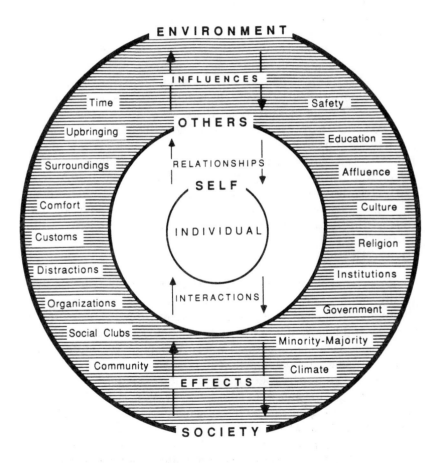

Fig. 10-1 Societal and Environmental Factors Influencing the Creativity of the Individual

ences, as well as, encouraging or discouraging atmospheres (environments) generated by governmental, community, and institutional influences, contribute immensely to making all of us what we are (see Table 1-2 and Figure 10-1). The negative impact of these factors can bring a stalemating of ambitions. Whereas, striving for improvement and continuing changes will often result in enhancing our creativity and promoting our growth.

We have a tendency to identify many of these influences of everyday life as negative or even perhaps almost complete blocks. However, many of these factors which block one of us may actually not affect or may even stimulate and encourage others. Both the positive and the negative forces may act directly on us or indirectly by affecting others who then influence our creativity.

Many societal and environmental factors are closely tied to our interpersonal relational interactions, or the lack thereof, with parents, teachers, co-workers, subordinates, superiors, families, and all sorts of other groups. We can easily find ourselves involved with persons, or caught in situations, where we are distracted or even blocked in our attempts to be creative. Other things may demand so much of our time that we cannot do what we would like to be doing that is more creative. An excellent example of getting ourselves spread too thin is cited in Chapter 11-8.4 (Dragstedt, 1962, 364-376). Over the years I have witnessed many cases where individuals were up against barriers generated by society and the environment. Thus it is important that we be on the lookout for such items.

10-2 CULTURE

Every society develops a wide array of cultural patterns that greatly influence those living in that society. In some countries, communities, or even family groups, there are extreme pressures to conform and live by the moral or amoral, ethical or unethical and general living standards of that society. Violating the cultural practices can cause possible rejection and ostracism.

The term culture has been defined as the distinguishing characteristics of a group, society or specific civilization. B. F. Skinner has been quoted as saying that a culture is not the behavior of us "living in it", but the "it" in which we live.

The "it" becomes the social and other forces which generate and sustain our behavior. These forces then affect our language, dress, patterns of behavior, feelings, attitudes, interactions, value systems, religion, education, group norms, and almost all aspects of our lives. Guidelines are generated and sustained relating to what we should feel and do if we are to be accepted in that culture. Being creative in that kind of a situation often means we must risk losing our cherished membership.

Growing up and living in the culture of a family and a country, as we all do, makes a deep impression on each of us, and it is next to impossible to shed some of the deeply ingrained beliefs and opinions. Short (1965, 305)in *The Gospel According to Peanuts*, quoted Bethell (*Essays on Literary Criticism and the English Tradition*, Hillary House Pub., Ltd., 1948, 25) as saying;

There is no impartial criticism...there is no critical neutrality... there are only critics who think themselves disinterested, but who are really swayed unconsciously by the belief they have necessarily acquired by being members of a particular society in a particular place and time.

Thus each of us must be especially insightful to be sure that we are not letting our cultural and environmental practices inhibit our freedom of thought and action. There have been many times over the years when the "work before play" practice, that was so deeply impressed upon me during my early years, kept me from relaxing when my performance would likely have been better if I had played more.

In some parts of the world culture, religion, tradition and education have caused people to fail to change their practices over long periods of time. For the most part, much of the western world and some parts of the eastern have largely broken out of that pattern.

10-2.1 Cultural Blocks

The widespread cultural blocks to creativity, which Adams (1986, 53-69) mentioned, include:

1. taboos;
2. fantasy and reflection are a waste of time, lazy, even crazy;
3. playfulness is for children only;
4. tradition is preferable to change;
5. reason, logic, numbers, utility, practicality are good;
6. feeling, intuition, qualitative judgments, pleasure are bad;
7. problem solving is a serious business and humor is out of place; and
8. any problem can be solved by scientific thinking and lots of money.

Undoubtedly, many of us have experienced some or many of these, perhaps without being aware of their impact on our own creative abilities.

10-2.2 The Impact of Religion

Religious teaching and training usually are started and encouraged by the parent(s) or care-person(s) in the home. It is difficult to say whether religious teaching will be helpful or harmful to the development of creative abilities. The roster of Nobel laureates has proportionately more Jews than expected, about the expected number of Protestant, and fewer Catholic representatives than expected (Amabile, 1983, 165). Some claim, and strongly believe, that they get messages from a higher power through intuition. Others seriously doubt that. It would seem that an important factor, as far as religion is concerned, is whether or not it teaches and insists on inerrancy, thus discouraging us from doubting and questioning. If that leads us to believe that everything in print is the truth and should never be questioned, then we may have real troubles being creative.

Some years ago I talked to a person who, after a few years in a responsible role following obtaining a Ph.D. degree, complained bitterly that his religious background greatly impaired his ability to be creative. He felt he had been admonished for years not to think, question or doubt. He also felt that his Ph.D. training had been too narrow.

In recent years in the U.S. there have been a number of religious oriented conservative groups who have tended to equate humanistic education with "secular humanism" (a philosophical religious movement). As Rogers (1983, 12) said:

The effort is made (by them) to discredit everything humanistic in education.

They blame the schools for practically all of the country's evils, and therefore attempt to censor and remove portions of the curricula, text books, library holdings, and even teachers who do not concur with their religious beliefs. They claim they know the truth about what is right and wrong, and insist that their view be the only one taught in the schools. They want to give no opportunity for examination or discussion of opposing views. Sometimes they go so far as to label as "anti-God, anti-family," and even "anti-American," those who stand up for free choice, free discussion and looking into the broad aspects of social, economic and moral issues. Rogers (pp. 13-14) summed up this issue well when he said:

Learning to solve complex problems, social and scientific, is a primary objective for education. And it cannot be achieved in a situation where conformity to one dogmatic view is demanded. It cannot be achieved when free and open discussion is in any way inhibited. This is the very real danger posed by the aims of the conservative movement. Whenever one group in society (a) has proclaimed itself as having the moral truth, and (b) has insisted on imposing its view of the truth upon all, the result has been a tyranny over the human mind and often over the human body as well.

The individual and the group must be free, but also responsible in evaluating differing views.

10-3 PARENTAL INFLUENCE

Parents and family are strong influences on us during our early life. Parents or those rearing us generally served as role models, set standards and patterns for us as growing infants, and generally promoted interest or disinterest in life patterns for us as developing youngsters.

I owe much to my parents, especially to my father, for his wise consul in my early years. He rarely gave me advice. But he seemed always to cleverly lead me into making decisions for myself by getting me to consider what alternatives were available to me. He then would encourage me to weigh and see the consequences of each of the choices. He encouraged me to not be afraid to try something new. He would often say, "You won't learn any younger." I was fortunate to have gotten such a start.

In our early years there are usually many dangers from which we had to be protected. As a result we heard "no, no, no" over and over again. Bettelheim (1950, 16-17) in his book on *Love Is Not Enough*, said:

The result is that frequent and often angry "no's" convince the child that finding things out for himself is dangerous and disapproved of by parents; that this is a world full of incomprehensible dangers where the safe thing to do is to do nothing, or only what parents explicitly permit. Often too, the child is convinced in the end that to try to find out for oneself is something bad.

How then can we expect children to be adventuresome, become creative and make discoveries on their own?

What occurs in the early life of children that helps them develop the domain-relevant and creativity-relevant skills and task motivation (see Chapter 1-7) that lead to creative productivity? Amabile (1983, 167-169) has reviewed several pieces of research in this area and points out that a disproportionately large number of eminent scientists are either firstborn or an only child. She pointed out other studies that suggested it is more a matter of special position within the family, like only son, first son, last child, last son, or a child who loses a parent early in life. Studies of Nobel laureates and eminent scientists showed that about three fourths of them occupied special family positions, and three times as many experienced early parental death as the average of eight percent for the general population.

10-3.1 Parental Characteristics and Behavior

Of considerable concern is what parental characteristics and behavior do to affect our early creativity. MacKinnon's (1978, 199-200) studies showed some generalities regarding kinds of home and educational environments that tend to nurture and develop creative potential. He stated:

If we look only at the generality, ignoring for the moment wide diversity and individual exceptions, we may note that the biographies of our creative subjects reveal several recurrent themes:

1. An early development of interest in and sensitive awareness of their inner experience, and of their ideational, imaginal, and symbolic processes, such introversion of interest often stemming from an unhappiness or loneliness in childhood due to sickness, a lack of siblings or companions, a natural shyness, etc.
2. The position of special skills and abilities which the child enjoyed exercising and the expression of which was encouraged and rewarded by one parent or the other or some other adult.
3. Aesthetic and intellectual interests of one or both parents similar to those of the child.
4. An unusual freedom for the child in making his own decisions and exploring his universe, whether granted by the parents or asserted by the child, in other words an early and unusual amount of independence both in thought and action.

5. A lack of intense closeness between parent and child so that neither overdependence was fostered nor a feeling of rejection experienced. In short, a kind of parent-child relationship that had a liberating effect on the child.
6. A lack of anxious concern on the part of the parents.
7. The presence of effective adults of both sexes, not necessarily the father or the mother, with whom identification could be made and who offered effective models for the development of positive ego-ideals.
8. Frequent moving during the early years, often from abroad to this country, providing both personal and cultural enrichment for the child.
9. Freedom from pressure to establish prematurely one's professional identity.

The impact on child development that the role model set by parents by their own adult behavior, is grossly underestimated and ignored by many parents. As children, most of us at some stage of our lives desired to be like our parents. As the words of the Nolte poem go:

Children learn what they live, children live what they learn.

If they live with reading, they will read as they live. If they are treated with respect, they learn to treat others with respect. It is unfortunate that more parents do not realize that a most effective way of helping their children to be what they would like them to be, is to demonstrate it by their own everyday living.

10-3.2 Mistreatment of Children

Missildine (1963) in his book, *The Inner Child of the Past,* has pointed out clearly how the way our parents or caretakers treated us in early childhood can be picked up by us. Negative experiences can lead to the developing of undesirabe traits that can be carried over into the remainder of our lives (see Table 10-1), unless we make a sincere effort to overcome them.

Missildine (1982, 289-290) suggested that if in childhood we experienced perfectionism or overcoersion, we can help ourselves today if we shed some of the pressure and demands we put on ourselves. If rejection, perfectionism and punitiveness occurred, we should put our emphasis on kindliness, respect and gentleness in the way we treat ourselves and limit our self-criticism. For overindulgence - make demands on ourselves to accomplish things; limit our dependence on others. For oversubmission - enforce firm limits on our impulsiveness, work to overcome our tendency not to respect feelings and rights of others. And, if neglect and rejection occurred - consciously do little kindnesses for ourselves; indulge ourselves when we can and reduce our self-criticism. He has indicated that in family life, limits must be set firmly; each family member, from father to baby, must be respected; there must be continuing firm limits against infringement on the rights of others, and these limits must be reinforced with a willingness and expectation of conflict when they are violated. Missildine (pp. 292-293) formulated six rules for a happy family life which can aid in avoiding the kind of treatments and responses which are so detrimental to child development. These rules are:

1. *Limits for children* whenever adults feel that their rights or dignity are intruded upon. Children may be isolated, sent to their room, until they are ready to come around without infringing on other people's rights. Respectful limits are not punitive. Children must make at least partial restitution for anything stolen, broken carelessly or lost. In the preschool years firm limits must be placed to protect children from common dangers, (i.e., streets, medicine cabinets, light sockets, stoves, knives, needles, scissors, open stairways, cleaning fluids, etc.)
2. *Chores*, beginning at school years, increasing as children get older, in order to develop work habits, self-respect and satisfaction in accomplishments. Children have a right to grumble about them, but parents have the right to insist.
3. *Study hours for children*, particularly older ones, with TV and radio turned off and an interested adult available as a consultant but not to do the work.
4. *Freedom for all* to pursue individual interests from mudpies to serious hobbies without anxious admonitions, pressure, lectures or criticism from others as long as these efforts do not infringe on the rights of others.
5. *When children quarrel* - and they do quarrel - isolation for both in separate rooms until they can agree to come together peaceably again.
6. *Adult recreation is necessary.* Adults can be more capable of maintaining a mutual respect balance if they can get away from the children for an evening with a fair degree of regularity. And children need to experience the

fact that parents have a vigorous life of their own to pursue - that adults weren't put on earth solely to administer to the needs of children.

Table 10-1
The Way Our Parents (Caretakers) Treated Us May Carry Over into Our Adult Lives

If our parents were...	As adults we may be...
Perfectionist	Overly preoccupied with accomplishments - physical, intellectual, social.
Oversubmissive	Inconsiderate, impulsive, and quick tempered with others.
Overindulgent	Easily bored and have trouble in initiating and carrying through with our individual efforts.
Overcoercive	Constantly tempted to resist, procrastinate, and unable to accomplish what we would like.
Punitive	Incorrectly thinking we are being punished, always seeking to get revenge for past actions and offenses.
Neglectful	Constantly feeling anxious, lonely, and as though we do not belong.
Rejective	An isolationist, lacking in self-esteem, often feeling unaccepted and accused of being self-centered.
Hypochondriacal	Easily fatigued, habitually worrying about our health.
Sexually	Overly obsessed with finding meaningful stimulating relationships and satisfying sex.

Constructed from text of Missildine, 1963, 85-301.

10-3.3 Effect of Poverty and Neglect

The severe detrimental effects of neglect (and the likely stress and mistreatment of living in poverty) during early childhood were clearly demonstrated by University of Wisconsin studies (Whimbey and Whimbey, 1975, 42-46). Children of low IQ mothers were given close attention and care from birth to five years of age. A teacher visited each infant for several hours each day during the first three months of the infant's life and instructed the mothers in homemaking and baby-care skills. After that the mothers took the children to a center where they both continued to receive stimulation and instruction until the children were two years of age. From age two to five they were placed in classes where language development and expression, reading, and mathematics/problem-solving were taught. The test group and a control group were evaluated at regular intervals throughout the investigation. At one year of age the two groups rated nearly the same on IQ test scores, both rating above 110. By the third year the test group had risen to an IQ above 120, the controls had dropped to about 95. These differences persisted throughout the trial. Considering that the mothers of both groups all were below an IQ of 75, the tremendous effect of attention and training on the intelligence of these children from a low income, poor housing environment is truly amazing.

This overwhelming evidence demonstrates that early home life dramatically affects the child's later academic abilities. These findings have led Whimbey and Whimbey (1975, Preface) to make several suggestions for all parents in being effective teachers and helping children develop effective thinking habits early in life. They suggested:

a. Talk to children, even when they are very small. Explain and describe things that you do with and to them.

b. Select and read books appropriate to children's ages, (maybe even start by leafing through magazines and naming the objects in the pictures - do this even before they can speak).

c. Don't prolong reading or talking to children who don't welcome it (don't make lessons out of the activity).

d. Don't curtail curiosity and the desire to climb and explore. Do take precautions to accident-proof the home and let children explore on their own.

Doing is an important part of learning. Thus the home environment during the early years is important in teaching children to think for themselves, learn motor skills, discover things, exercise their imagination, develop good work habits, learn to respect one another, and learn to discipline themselves.

10-4 EDUCATION

One of the great challenges of the future for all parts of the world will be education for oncoming generations. Few areas of the world will be able to escape the unbelievable changes that come with modernization and technological development. Bridging the gap among the primitive, the partially developed and the highly technical countries will pose seemingly unsurmountable difficulties. Only through creative efforts of all sorts will both ends of the educational and technological spectrums with these vast differences be brought to maximum fruition. We must change education for focus on changes, for openness of minds and acceptance of cultures and customs. Even in our highly developed countries where an attitude of "we've got it made," and a laxity of care for each other and the environment, of discipline and ethics, and general greed and selfishness are becoming more prevailing, we must return to greater emphasis on effective education and continuing to learn throughout our lives.

The importance of the role of education on creativity has been mentioned several times in other parts of this book. Comments were made in Chapter 2 suggesting that much of our educational effort is wasted because of the insistence on directed and conditioned thinking rather than on free and creative thinking. The failure of educational efforts to produce a well-balanced person was cited in Chapter 5.

One of the serious consequences of educational systems today, that is especially detrimental to our creativity, is the constant effort to standardize educational programs and trying to fit everyone into the same mold. Over the last few decades more and more persons have been questioning our educational systems in the U.S. and elsewhere. In 1969 Carl Rogers in the front piece of his first edition of *Freedom to Learn*, quoted Albert Einstein as having said:

It is in fact nothing short of a miracle that the modern methods of instruction have not yet entirely strangled the holy curiosity of inquiry; for this delicate little plant, aside from stimulation, stands mainly in need of freedom; without this it goes to wrack and ruin without fail.

In 1975 Evans (p. 37) recorded a Carl Rogers' response to questions about education in which he said:

I feel that conventional education from primary school through graduate school is probably the most outdated, incompetent, and bureaucratic institution of our culture.

In his book *Freedom to Learn*, Rogers (1983, 1), speaking about education, added, "(it was the)...most traditional, conservative, rigid..., and the institution most resistant to change."

H.J.M. Nouwen (1975), noted religious philosopher, has said:

If there is any area that needs a new spirit, a redemptive and liberating spirituality, it is the area of education in which so many people spend their lives, or at least crucial parts of their lives, as students or teachers or both. One of the greatest tragedies of our culture is that millions of young people spend many hours, days, weeks and years listening to lectures, reading books, and writing papers with a constantly increasing resistance. Practically every student perceives his education as a long, endless role of obligations to be fulfilled. If there is any culture that has succeeded in killing the natural spontaneous curiosity of people and dulling the human desire to know it is our technocratic society.

More recently Gowin (1981, 10) cited works which declared:

Our educational system tells a sorry story of our schools. The story it tells is one of education for non-citizenship, of education for apathy.and concludes that traditional high school education serves no very useful purpose for the majority of the people.

The folly of all the efforts to standardize us and our children is clearly illustrated by the following fable, supposedly written by a Cincinnati school superintendent.

The Animal School
Once upon a time the animals decided they must do something to meet the problems of the "New World." They adopted an activity curriculum consisting of running, climbing, swimming and flying. To make it easier to administer the curriculum, all the animals took all the subjects.

The duck was excellent in swimming, in fact better than his instructor, but he made only passing grades in flying and was poor in running. Since he was slow in running, he had to stay after school and drop swimming in order to practice running. This was kept up until his web feet were badly worn and he was only average in swimming. But average was acceptable in school, so nobody worried about that except the duck.

The rabbit started at the top of the class in running, but had a nervous breakdown because of so much makeup work in swimming.

The squirrel was excellent in climbing until he developed frustration in the flying class where his teacher made him start from the ground up instead of from the tree-top down.

He also developed "Charlie Horses" from over-exertion and then got a "C" in climbing and running.

The eagle was a problem child and was disciplined severely. In the climbing class he beat all the others to the top of the tree, but insisted on using his own way to get there. At the end of the year, an abnormal eel that could swim exceedingly well, run, climb and fly a little had the highest average and was valedictorian.

The prairie dog stayed out of school and fought the tax levy because the administration would not add digging and burrowing to the curriculum. They apprenticed their child to a badger and joined the ground hogs and gophers to start a successful private school.

Does this fable have a moral?????

The warnings and concerns about our educational systems have been sounded for decades, and in the last 30 years many experimental efforts have shown that these difficulties can be countered. Yet, the efforts to make changes in these conditions have generally been cosmetic, resulting in no overall improvement in the situation. In my own experience, several years ago, on a committee to suggest long range changes in a college curriculum for a point to be reached sometime early in the next century, committee members refused to accept my suggestion of setting aside all present courses and starting from scratch as worthy of discussing. All the members of the committee would have long since been retired by the target date (and some even expired). But the thoughts of removing everything and then putting back in those things that might be deemed essential for the next century must have been too frightening for most. True, all their own special interests might not have been considered important enough to have been included (and mine might not have been included). As a result practically no changes of any great consequence were proposed and adopted. We face great resistance to change in educational circles and on many other fronts.

10-4.1 Student Reactions

Many of our students have become highly resistant and critical of schooling today. Rogers (1983, 15) cited a report on the reactions of 3,157 students (male and female, black and white, public and private, rich and poor, from middle school through graduate school in the U.S. and Canada) who said school was "A BORE." Even 200 students from a "good" medical school expressed an outpouring of frustration, disappointment, and rage. They felt they were being overwhelmed with poor quality lectures spewing large quantities of facts (easily retrievable from printed materials), insufficient study time, absence of personal contact with the faculty, and a faculty and administration unresponsive to their needs or their pleas and complaints.

The over-all studies showed that many students at all levels were angry, frustrated and ready to give up hope or were already there. Many felt trapped, being stuffed with irrelevant materials, and showed no joy or enthusiasm for learning. Most alarming was the fact that a large number felt that nobody cared.

Dale (Oct., 1970) said if he were a student, he would ask faculty:

> Why can't we have superb teaching materials skillfully used by an able teacher who puts a maximum responsibility on me to educate myself? Why can't I learn more of this material independently? Why don't you help me become more independent day-by-day, instead of keeping me dependent?

10-4.2 Helping Students Learn

For years Rogers has said, "Why don't we listen to what the students are saying?" In his first edition of *Freedom to Learn* he indicated the need for focusing on how, why, and when students learn and how learning seems and feels from the inside. A summary of his views (1969, 157-163) on the essential elements needed for learning are given in Table 10-2.

In his 1983 revision of *Freedom to Learn*, Rogers said:

> I deeply believe that traditional teaching is an almost completely futile, wasteful, overrated function in today's changing world. It is successful mostly in giving children who can't grasp the material, a sense of failure. It also succeeds in persuading students to drop out when they realize that the material taught is almost completely irrelevant to their lives. No one should ever be trying to learn something for which one sees no relevance. No child should ever experience the sense of failure imposed by our grading system, by criticism and ridicule from teachers and others, by rejection when he or she is slow to comprehend. The sense of failure experienced when one tries something one wants to achieve that is actually too difficult is a healthy one that drives him or her

to further learning. It is a very different thing from a person-imposed failure, which must devalue him or her as a person.

Table 10-2
Rogers' Principles of Learning

1. Human beings have a natural potentiality for learning.
2. Significant learning takes place when the subject matter is perceived by the student as having relevance for his/her own purposes.
3. Learning which involves a change of self organization - in the perception of oneself - is threatening and tends to be resented.
4. Those learnings which are threatening to the self are more easily perceived and assimilated when external threats are at a minimum.
5. When threat to the self is low, experience can be perceived in differentiated fashion and learning can proceed.
6. Much significant learning is acquired through doing.
7. Learning is facilitated when the student participates responsibly in the learning process.
8. Self-initiated learning which involves the whole person of the learner - feelings as well as intellect - is the most lasting and pervasive.
9. Independence, creativity, and self-reliance are all facilitated when self-criticism and self-evaluation are basic and evaluation by others is of secondary importance.
10. The most socially useful learning in the modern world is the learning of the process of learning; a continuing openness to experience and incorporation into oneself of the process of change.

Constructed from text of Rogers, 1969, 157-163.

Putting the principles suggested in Table 10-2 into practice have proven to be quite effective (Rogers, 1983, 197-224) when incorporated with an overall effort to improve education, including joint efforts of teachers, students, administration and parents.

10-4.3 Effective Teaching - Facilitating

When we come to appreciate how students feel about their education, it is no wonder that discipline problems are enormous, that teachers feel over-worked and underpaid, and that they experience great frustration and little joy in teaching. The discipline problems have brought ever-increasing demands on the teachers' time for extra duty. In addition to problems with the students, administrators and teachers have had an inordinate amount of interference with extensive report writing and attempted regulation by special interest groups and by state and federal government agencies. Keeping up with these demands has placed an additional heavy burden on the teachers.

In his book "*The Art of Teaching*", Highet (1950, 12-57) did not have to include all these extras. He indicated that as teachers we must have a thorough knowledge of the subject matter, a mature mastery of teaching procedures, a love and understanding of our pupils (audience), and an ability to blend all with the highest quality of judgement.

Research has shown some aspects which are important for learning to occur. Those which are essential in the teacher-learner relationship to facilitate significant learning according to Rogers (1969, 106-112) are:

1. Realness in the Facilitator - When a facilitator is a real person, being what he is, entering into a relationship with a learner without presenting a front or a facade, he is much more likely to be effective... he can be enthusiastic,... bored,.. interested,... angry,... sensitive and sympathetic. Because he accepts these feelings as his own he has no need to impose them on his students... Thus, he is a person to his students, not a faceless embodiment of a curricular requirement nor a sterile tube through which knowledge is passed from one generation to the next.

2. Prizing, Acceptance, Trust - I think of it as prizing the learner, prizing his feelings, his opinions, his person. It is a caring for the learner, but a non-possessive caring. It is an acceptance of this other individual as a separate person, having worth in his own right. It is a basic trust - a belief that this other person is somehow fundamentally trustworthy...an imperfect being with many feelings, many potentialities.

3. Empathetic Understanding - When the teacher has the ability to understand the student's reactions from the inside, has a sensitive awareness of the way the process of education and learning seems to the student, then again the likelihood of significant learning is increased. This kind of understanding is sharply different from the usual evaluative understanding, which follows the pattern of, "I understand what is wrong with you."

"A wise teacher makes learning a joy; a rebellious teacher spouts foolishness (Proverbs 15:2, Living Bible)."

There are a number of things we can do to build a classroom atmosphere where freedom and providing opportunities for more self-reliant learning can occur. Rogers (1969, 130-145) suggested:

a. focus on a problem that has real meaning for the student (audience);
b. provide as many and all kinds of resources (as and if possible); This should include the instructor's time, too!!
c. let (and help) students set up their own goals (schedules, and contracts);
d. divide larger classes into groups (facilitator - learning groups, student discussion groups, etc.);
e. actually do experiments and research;
f. simulate situations;
g. use programmed instruction; and
h. employ self-evaluation.

Rogers also suggested a number of traditional things that are usually detrimental to building a facilitative atmosphere and should be avoided. Some of these are:

a. do not set lesson tasks;
b. do not assign readings (suggest, but do not assign);
c. do not lecture or expound (unless asked to do so);
d. do not evaluate and criticize (unless requested to do so);
e. do not give required examinations; and
f. do not take sole responsibility for grades (involve students in setting up exam questions and evaluating themselves).

What is being attempted with these do's and don't's, is to encourage and help the student learn to be responsibly free.

Rogers (1969, 105) expressed his feelings as follows:

The facilitation of learning - to free curiosity; to permit individuals to go charging off in new directions dictated by their own interests; to unleash the sense of inquiry; to open everything to question and exploration; to recognize that everything is in process of change - here is an experience I can never forget. Out of such a context arise true students, real learning, creative scientists and scholars and practitioners.

Rogers (1969, 164-166) summarized his major points regarding the needed qualities of the teacher or facilitator and creating an environment to facilitate learning with the ten points presented in Table 10-3.

I was fortunate to have several good teachers during my schooling years. But particularly outstanding were two high school teachers and my Ph.D. degree adviser who all practiced many of the things cited above that Rogers later recommended.

From my own experience in undergraduate and graduate classrooms, as well as on and chairing committees of all sorts over much of my more than 40 years of teaching, research, extension and administrative duties, I can attest to the importance and reality of these principles. They do help to create an open, participative atmosphere.

Table 10-3
Essentials for Facilitating a Learning Atmosphere

---

1. The facilitator has much to do with setting the initial mood or climate of the group or class experience.
2. The facilitator helps to elicit and clarify the purposes of the individuals in the class as well as the more general purposes of the group.
3. He relies upon the desire of each student to implement those purposes which have meaning for him, as the motivational force behind significant learning.
4. He endeavors to organize and make easily available the widest possible range of resources for learning.
5. He regards himself as a flexible resource to be utilized by the group.
6. In responding to expressions in the classroom group, he accepts both the intellectual content and the emotionalized attitudes, endeavoring to give each aspect the approximate degree of emphasis which it has for the individual or the group.
7. As the acceptant classroom climate becomes established, the facilitator is increasingly able to become a participant learner, a member of the group, expressing his views as those of one individual only.
8. He takes the initiative in sharing himself with the group - his feelings as well as his thoughts - in ways which do not demand nor impose but represent simply a personal sharing which students may take or leave.
9. Throughout the classroom experience, he remains alert to the expressions indicative of deep or strong feelings.
10. In his functioning as a facilitator of learning, the leader endeavors to recognize and accept his own limitations.

Constructed from text of Rogers, 1969, 164-166.

10-5 INSTITUTIONS AND ORGANIZATIONS

Individuals and teams, as well as organizations and institutions, must have a stimulating and challenging environment if the members of the separate contributing units are to become enthusiastically committed, not only to their own creative endeavors, but also to the overall productivity of their team and the organization. Institutional and governmental regulations and red tape also diminish our output. These items along with personnel problems, negative situations, and frequent less-than optimistic budgets tend to diminish our overall productivity. These will be discussed in some detail in Chapters 12 and 13, especially in conjunction with the issues of managerial blocks to creativity (12-11), and in Chapter 13, as organizational and institutional drag are considered (13-11).

10-6 CREATING AN OPEN AND SUPPORTIVE ENVIRONMENT

Much of the discussion in this chapter (and in several parts of previous chapters) has been concerned with items which relate to the atmosphere and/or environment that prevails in many situations and is detrimental or stimulatory to being creative. Many of these factors affect and relate to our morale, spirit, optimism, feeling supported or rejected, and/or being treated like a person or a thing.

When conditions or persons generate or cause the development of an environment of doubt and uncertainty, negativism, disrespect, prejudice, unbearable or other intolerant and undesirable conditions and stress, the optimum atmosphere for our creativity is likely to be impaired. Under such conditions, our motivation, spirit and morale, as well as that of our organizations are likely to suffer a severe case of the "D's" - Disappointment, Doubt, Discouragement, Degradation, Disparagement, Depression, Despondency, and Despair; the result - we are all apt to become afflicted with the "Downs."

10-6.1 Morale

Morale is variously defined as a state of our minds or attitudes in terms of confidence and courage. It involves such things as spirit, mental attitude, level of optimism, moral strength, confidence, cheerfulness, self-confidence, self-assurance, resolution, and esprit de corps (a sense of union and/or common interests and responsibilities, as developed among a group of persons associated together).

Gardner in his book on *"Morale"* (1978, 56-63) indicated:

Motivation and morale are relatively low in the U.S. today, certainly compared with what we have known through most of our history.

Gardner went on to say that we are no longer a struggling young society dreaming of its future. There is a wide element of disillusionment in the minds of many people. There is a widely shared view that our civilization exists to make everyone "happy" and to spare us problems and pain. Work has become looked upon as an unfavorable activity that we must do. We are losing sight of the good ethics and values necessary to perpetuate a nation, and finally we are showing a lack of positive views regarding the future.

Conditions seem to have improved little since then (but, hopefully, will be taking a turn for the better soon). General political, economical, and civil rights conditions in the U.S. (and even more devastating in many other parts of the world) in the past several decades have put people in stressful and restrictive positions, limiting freedoms and impairing productivity and creativity of individuals and organizations.

10-6.2 Spirit and Optimism

For creativity to thrive we must have an atmosphere alive with spirit and optimism. Spirit is defined with a host of words (vital essence, intellect, mind, psyche, will, resolve, motivation, heart, impulse, frame of mind, mood, feelings, disposition, emotions, attitude, morale, sentiment, temper, vigor, vim, zest, liveliness, animation, vitality, verve, vivacity, enthusiasm, energy, eagerness, pluck, mettle, enterprise, drive, zeal, avidity, sparkle, ardor, fire, glow, warmth, courage, bravery, audacity, dauntlessness, stoutheartedness, daring, fortitude, boldness, valor, spunk, and many others).

When used to describe people with a spirit, most of these, separately or in combinations, indicate that people are vibrantly alive, that they are showing life, activity, enthusiasm and determination. People are motivated and have faith and hope in the future. They are optimistic.

Optimism indicates a hopeful outlook, including a host of characteristics, such as: confidence, sanguineness, seeing the good side of things, hoping for the best, bright outlook, encouragement, cheerfulness, trust in the future, happy expectancy (as opposed to pessimism, cynicism, gloom, gloominess, glumness, depression, despondency).

If an atmosphere of high morale, high spirits, and optimism persist in an individual or a group, then we usually find a "can-do attitude" present too. We have pride in what we are doing; we strive for excellence; we are eager to learn new things; we are tolerant of and learn from mistakes. In groups we are fiercely supportive of one another.

Although emotional, perceptual, cultural, and relational barriers are serious deterrents to productivity and creativity, we can anticipate that they will be occurring. Appropriate preparation for such conditions can help us, other unit members, and leaders to avoid and otherwise cope with such creativity-blocking conditions and can be a great aid for general morale in the unit.

Maintaining good communications, presenting opportunities for individual growth and renewal, as well as opportunities for relief from some of the tensions are usually helpful to everyone. The unit leader can play a predominant role in helping to anticipate these adversities and encourage the group to turn them into opportunities.

10-7 DEALING WITH STRESS

In general, most stresses affect creativity negatively. Several stress effects on creativity are considered in a number of places in this book (anxiety and fear, Chapter 4-4; anger, criticism and failure, Chapter 4-5; fatigue and burnout, Chapter 11-3; management impact, Chapter 12-7; and organizational and institutional effects, Chapter 13-11). Here we shall be considering the effects of negativism, difficult persons, and physical discomforts.

10-7.1 Dealing with Negatives

We lose hours and hours of time as individuals and groups if we become dominated by negative attitudes. Negative attitudes hurt most when they are expressed between and among persons who normally have a close relationship. Negative attitudes are especially detrimental to group activities and can cost an inordinate amount of time when persons (one or more) in a committee meeting or gathering are obsessed with a negative approach. A good example (from Yunich 1958) of the kinds of things that we frequently hear in committee meetings is shown in Figure 10-2.

Oftentimes a negative attitude can be offset, at least partially, by a kind of brainstorming session in which judgement is deferred (Chapter 6-9.2). Many more constructive ideas usually come forth in a group, when critical and judgmental comments are delayed.

"It doesn't fit our program." "Why change it? It's still working OK."

"Let's shelve it for the time being."

"We don't have the time." "We're not ready for that."

"That will make our system obselete." "The executive committee would never go for it."

"It isn't in the budget."

"It won't work in our department." "That's not our problem."

**HOW TO
KILL
PROGRESS**

"Don't be ridiculous."

"We tried that before."

"It's too radical a change."

"That price is too high for us." "Let's form a committee."

"We did all right without it."

"Has anyone else tried it?" "We're too small for it."

"Not practical for operating people." "Can't teach an old dog new tricks."

"We'll be the laughing stock."

"You're two years ahead of your time."

Fig. 10-2 Negative Comments That Slow and Kill Progress
(Constructed from text of Yunich, 1958)

Dominating, negative persons may need to be reminded that with a number of persons present, they really only have a right to their proportionate percentage of the time. If that approach does not work with a particularly obnoxious, negative individual, then the group itself must unite and encourage the individual to be more positive or, as a last resort, simply ask the individual to "shut up." This can be a tough assignment for a group or committee chairperson.

It is easy for us to grow into a habit of being negative about many things. Lowered morale, fatigue and depression often cause us to lose hope and feel that nothing is going right. Think how often we have heard negative expressions which tend to kill progress. How often have we been the guilty party making that negative comment at a meeting or even to ourselves? We must practice looking for the opportunities that can be capitalized on, even in an undesirable situation.

Wilke (1986, 56) said, "We have become experts at being critical of all forms (of things)." He refers to a reply to a person who was insisting that something would not work with the statement that "I like my way of doing it better than your way of not doing it."

Practice in thinking positively and maintaining a constant vigil that we do not ourselves become the persons that are causing negativism, is not always easy. However, adhering to a practice of positive thinking can frequently aid us in turning problems and negative situations into opportunities.

10-7.2 Dealing with Difficult Persons

In almost any group we will encounter someone who tends to be or is difficult. Such persons frequently are dominant, stubborn, single minded and unwilling to bend or compromise. Sometimes such persons seem to be determined to sabotage the efforts of all of the remainder of the group. As a result the atmosphere becomes tense.

Peck (1978, 35-37) suggested that there are mainly two kinds of people in this world, namely those who have some neuroses and those with character disorders. He indicated that we all have neuroses and character disorders to some degree. As neurotics we assume too much responsibility for what happens and automatically assume we ourselves are at fault. Those with character disorders take little or no responsibility for things that happen, and they assume the world is at fault. They often "feel good about their character style, even if it bugs others to death" (Schmidt 1980, 13). They are usually extremely resistant to change. They are not a threat to society (i.e. they are not considered as having "gone off their rocker."). But, they are often difficult people to work and live with. Their presence on a team or in a group can create an especially disturbing environment.

Schmidt (1980, 38-62) discussed difficult persons who exhibit three different styles of thinking. He included the paranoid (people are out to get me) who seems threatened, hostile and bitter; the obsessive (the worrywart) who feels worried and tense most of the time; and the hysteric (the scatterbrain) who is insecure, lonely, and craves attention, approval and affection from others. In dealing with these people he suggested that we use good judgement, self-control, common sense; be gentle, kind and loving; and be easy going and loving.

He described three classes of emotional responses in difficult persons as those who are aggressive and almost constantly irritated about something; those who are apathetic and hide their resentments; and those who are temperamental and go from one extreme of hiding all feelings to an explosive outburst of rage. In working with these people he suggested we try to be calm, cheerful, avoid letting them intimidate us, and don't get caught up in their highs and lows. Be firm, fair and forgiving.

A third group of difficult persons he described as those with different styles of behavior. The compulsives drive themselves constantly and respond to tension by pressuring themselves to perform better. The impulsives respond to inner conflict by acting out one of their impulses and attempting to transfer some of their anxiety to others. He suggested we deal with them in a casual, carefree manner, but be cautious with impulsive people. Help them rechannel their energies.

His final classification was of people with varying styles of relating to others. These are the dependent style, who we should be supportive of only after they have tried to help themselves; and the manipulative style, with whom we must use wise, skeptical caution to avoid being used. Schmidt suggested with these and all the others that we should respect them, avoid looking down on them, be kind and patient, don't struggle against them, try to show them you care, and cautiously love them. Some are impossible, but in my experience a most helpful way of dealing with most is to try to find a niche for them where they can excel without requiring much interaction with others.

10-7.3 Physical Discomforts.

Physical discomforts can be distracting, stressful, and damaging to creative efforts. Whenever we are required to focus our thinking on extraneous items such as room comfort, lighting, noises, hunger, thirst, odors, etc., our attention is likely diverted away from creative endeavors. If the level of discomfort is high, we may not be able to think creatively at all. Optimal conditions for different individuals may be quite different. One of us may find music helpful, whereas another may prefer complete silence. One may like nature and the outdoors, another may prefer an indoor setting. We all should seek to place ourselves in an environment that supplies the most comfortable and creative-conducive atmospheres available and possible.

10-8 HIGHLIGHTS OF CHAPTER TEN

1. Many societal and environmental factors and practices are rigid, non-flexible, and traditional. They thus tend to standardize us, push us toward conformity, and encourage the development of restrictive laws, rules, regulations and guidelines that discourage and block our creative efforts.
2. In rearing potentially creative children during their formative years, we often overlook and consider unimportant the significance of our parental role as models and also neglect the development of our children's imagination, discipline, habits, and their desire to learn.
3. Many educational, governmental and industrial systems, all-to-frequently, fail to supply us with conditions in which imagination, learning and developing creative thinking patterns can flourish.
4. Cultural forces in the western world that hold success, productivity, rising to the top and overemphasis on competitiveness can frequently lead us to overcommitment, overwork, and anxiety that may slow output and creativity and may even bring us to burn-out.
5. We, and our organizations, need to strive to create a stimulating and relaxed atmosphere to help us reduce stress, encourage relaxation, and improve health, creativity, and productivity.
6. Developing respect for one another and living and working in an optimistic, "can-do" atmosphere where communications are good and joint efforts are made to support each other and overcome mistakes, stress and adversities can greatly stimulate our creativity.
7. The atmosphere in which we work should be one which opens the way for improvement and new ideas from everyone involved, while setting high standards and striving for quality and excellence from everyone throughout the unit.
8. For maximal creativity we need facilities and equipment that offer comfortable and pleasant physical conditions, such as temperature, lights, decor, work-space, convenience, automation, etc.

10-9 AFTERGROWTH STIMULATORS

1. In your early years what things did your parents (or caretakers) do that gave you the most encouragement to be creative?

Did they do anything that thwarted your creativity?

2. Name three things about the culture where you live that tend to push you into uniform, standardized, conforming patterns. What would be the consequences of your rebelling against these?

3. Of all the teachers you have had, how would you describe the one you consider to have been the worst ever? The best?

4. What kind of an atmosphere most encourages you to do your best work? To be most creative? To study most effectively? To get maximum relaxation? Are there similarities among all these?

5. Describe a difficult person you have had to deal with. What was the best way you found for dealing with that person?

6. Describe the group atmosphere you have experienced that was the most conducive to accomplishing the group objective.

CHAPTER 11

PERSONAL GROWTH, DEVELOPMENT, AND SELF-RENEWAL

11- 1   Introduction
11- 2   Development
11- 3   Signs of Need for Change
11- 4   Procrastination
11- 5   Willpower and Commitment
11- 6   Making Changes
11- 7   Accepting Change
11- 8   Making The Best Use of Your Time
11- 9   Health Maintenance
11-10   Outside Stimulation
11-11   Highlights of Chapter Eleven
11-12   Aftergrowth Stimulators

11-1 INTRODUCTION

We must take responsibility for the things in our lives that can be controlled. The mistake we so frequently make is to blame others when things don't go as we have planned or as we would have liked them to go. Dale (1964) said:

One reason why many persons do not feel a sense of power to control their own destiny is that they do indeed lack power. They do not think they can change themselves or society, and weak people do not make a strong society.

He went on to point out that a democratic society is one in which power and respect are shared. Vaughan (1979, 184) elaborated on this saying:

One is whole, and one is a part of a larger whole. Yet, in beginning the process of self observation one often sees only bits and pieces, seemingly fragmented and scattered. Often the necessary task is to change perception and self-image rather than changing specific contents of consciousness or circumstances of life....Awakening intuition depends on your willingness to see things as they really are, to know yourself as you really are, and to see the world as it really is, with all the beauty and all the suffering. Intuition deepens the experience of life in all its facets.

Accomplishing personal growth, development, and self-renewal can be a most difficult task for us. These processes are difficult because, as normal persons, we have a tendency to believe thoroughly in ourselves and to feel that what we have done and what we are planning to do have been right. Facing ourselves can be extremely painful at times, not only because it is difficult to honestly and thoughtfully do a self-analysis, but often we do not relish facing what a self-evaluation turns up. This is true when the self-analysis shows up desirable and good traits as well as showing up shortcomings and faults. Loomis (1960, 5) pointed out that finding good in ourselves is frequently almost as frightening as finding shortcomings. This is because we may want to avoid feeling guilty because we are not capitalizing on the capabilities where we might excel.

Even though self-evaluation may be painful and difficult because of the need for a strong self-discipline to do something about it, it is essential for all of us if growth, development, and self-renewal are to occur. The fear of rejection, whether it be self-rejection and guilt or rejection from others, is a great deterrent both to self-evaluation and to seeking opinions of others and seeking help in making changes. Basically we all must like ourselves if we are to be effective. Also, we want to be liked by others and thus we hesitate to seek external evaluations.

Once shortcomings, potential areas of growth, and opportunities for development are identified, there are lots of opportunities for help if we are willing to be mature enough to go looking for that help. However, it is not often that help will come looking for us. Thus the initiative must come from us as individuals.

Gardner (1965), in his book *Self-Renewal*, made some pertinent statements concerning renewal of individuals and societies. He said:

> The renewal of societies and organizations can go forward only if someone cares. Apathy and lowered motivation are the most widely noted characteristics of a civilization on the downward path. Apathetic men (people) accomplish nothing. Men (persons) who believe in nothing change nothing for the better. They renew nothing and heal no one, least of all themselves (p. xiii of the Introduction)....Unfortunately the commencement speakers never tell us why their advice to keep on learning is so hard to follow. People interested in adult education have struggled heroically to increase the opportunities for self-development and they have succeeded marvelously. Now they had better turn to the thing that is really blocking self-development - the individual's own intricately designed, self-constructed prison or to put it another way, the individual's incapacity for self-renewal (p. 8).

Another pertinent quote from Gardener:

> Men (persons) who have lost their adaptiveness naturally resist change. The most stubborn protector of his (her) own vested interest is the man (person) who has lost the capacity for self-renewal (p. 10).

11-2 DEVELOPMENT

Erikson (1963) published what he called the eight ages of human growth and development (see Table 11-1). He believed that individual ego strength develops over time with the growth of the person as a result of the environment and certain basic conflicts. For instance, the newborn infant soon develops a trust that feeding and care will be provided or to mistrust if they are not provided. The level of trust developed carries over into all succeeding stages of development, even though the individual has to risk trust in letting each of the next stages develop. Hope emerges as a result of developing trust. Erikson (1963, 270-271) said each of the succeeding stages, initiated at various probable ages, come as a result of:

> ...the growing person's readiness to be driven toward, to be aware of, and to interact with, a widening social radius... each item exists in some form before its critical time normally arrives....all must exist from the beginning in some form, for every act calls for an integration of all.

Table 11-1
Erikson's Eight Ages of Man

Stage (conflict)	Typical Age of Onset	Emerging Virtue or Asset	Primary Relationship
1. Trust vs. mistrust	Birth to 1 yr.	Hope and drive	Parents or caretakers
2. Autonomy vs. shame and doubt	Through 2nd yr.	Self-control, will-power	Parents and self
3. Initiative vs. guilt	3rd through 5th yrs.	Direction and purpose	Basic family
4. Industry vs. inferiority	6th to puberty	Method and competence	School
5. Identity vs. role confusion	Adolescence	Devotion and fidelity	Models and peer groups
6. Intimacy vs. isolation	Early adult	Affiliation and love	Partners and friends
7. Generativity vs. stagnation	Young and middle adult	Production and care	Children and career
8. Ego integrity vs. despair	Later adult	Renunciation and wisdom	Universe and mankind

Constructed from texts of Erikson, 1963, 247-274; Schmidt, 1980, 29-37, and Lippitt, 1982, 164-166.

Schmidt (1980, 29) and Lippitt (1982, 166) have added the typical age of onset for us, and the primary focus or relationship as a result of their interpretation of Erikson's writings. We should not take these too literally, especially regarding the age of onset which will obviously vary from one individual to the next and will carry forward at differing levels. For example, Erikson pointed out that:

> In the last stage, we would expect trust to have developed

into the most mature faith (p. 272).

When growth and development are arrested in one of the stages and the full virtue or asset is not realized earlier in life, we may have to deal with the shortcoming later in life. Some of these aspects were referred to in Chapter 10-3 and 10-4.

Bettelheim (*Love Is Not Enough*, p. 17, 1950) indicated that:

While the frequent admonition to love one's child is well-meant, it falls short of its purpose when the parent applies it without the appropriate or genuine emotions.

11-3 SIGNS OF NEED FOR CHANGE

We often do not realize that we have the need to change, develop and renew ourselves. Thus we need to constantly be on the lookout for signs of need for change. Ridenaur (1969) gave us some good suggestions for checking ourselves as to whether we have become "mission impossible" persons, and thus should seek to make changes.

11-3.1 Failure

We are not well taught how to deal with failure (see Chapter 4-4.1). From an early age we are admonished to use good judgment, to do well everything that we do. When I was young my father would say to me, "If you didn't have time to do it right in the first place, how are you going to find time to do it over." So often we are pushed to succeed and to be sure to win (unfortunately, sometimes at all costs). Many highly successful individuals have indicated that some of their greatest and most beneficial experiences came from failure. Learning to capitalize from the lessons of failing, and learning to accept these as a normal part of life can be most helpful for us. In scientific endeavors, experiment after experiment may end in failure, but each effort adds a bit in narrowing down the field and helping us to arrive ultimately to a successful resolution. We need to do the same in our lives in general. Krebs (Nobel Laureate), in an article on "The Making of a Scientist", (1968), speaks highly of the great lessons he learned from failure.

11-3.2 Fatigue

A diminution in enthusiasm on a national basis stems from a lack of enthusiasm on the part of the people of the nation and the world. The negative outlook on many fronts today is bringing people to a state of psychological fatigue, which many would say is a ridiculous statement in the face of the many great hopes and potentials existing for the future of all mankind. Tournier (1965b) edited a book on fatigue which emphasized how contagious negative attitudes can be and why there is great need for a positive outlook and hope. He emphasized that there is need for each individual to examine his/her own outlook, for therein lies the solution to the hopes for the future.

11-3.3 Burnout

In recent years considerable interest has been focused on the diminution and even complete loss of productive capacity in some previously highly productive individuals. Freudenberger (1980) focused on a number of aspects related to individual morale, exhaustion, boredom, and many other symptoms which accompany a condition now commonly referred to as "burnout." He described burnout as:

> To deplete oneself. To exhaust one's physical and mental resources. To wear oneself out by excessively striving to reach some unrealistic expectation imposed by oneself or by the values of society.

The term has been used by some to describe the cumulative effects of chronic high distress and perceived low personal growth.

Freudenberger (1980, 17-18) designed a questionnaire to help us determine whether or not recent changes are indicating potential burnout. He suggested assigning a value of one for no signs and a five to indicate considerable evidence of such a change. The essence of his questions are presented in Table 11-2. He said if our scores add up to less than 25, we are doing fine. If they are between 26 and 35, there are things we should be watching. A total score between 36 and 50 means we are candidates for burnout; between 51 and 65 indicates we are burning out; and if over 65, our physical and mental well-being are in real danger.

Common symptoms of burnout (Freudenberger, 1980, 61-111) in progressive order of severity include:

- exhaustion;
- detachment;
- boredom and cynicism;
- impatience and heightened irritability;
- a sense of omnipotence;
- a suspicion of being unappreciated;

- paranoia;
- disorientation;
- psychosomatic complaints;
- depression;
- denial of feelings;
- dulling and deadness; and
- despondency and drugs.

Table 11-2
Evaluating Your Potential Burnout Level

1. Do you find yourself feeling tired and worn out much of the time? Is it harder and harder to get up mornings?
2. Do you feel, even though you work harder and harder, that you get less done?
3. Do you have trouble meeting deadlines? Remembering appointments and people's names?
4. Do little things bother you more and more? Is it getting harder and harder to control your temper?
5. Do you find it harder and harder to get around to returning calls? Reading reports? Answering letters?
6. Have you become more and more disappointed and unhappy with things in general?
7. Do people suggest that you look worn out and are not being your usual self?
8. Do you find yourself confused and frustrated by day's end?
9. Do you often feel down and wonder why?
10. Do you have more frequent colds, headaches, and pains?
11. Are you spending less and less time with family and friends?
12. Do you find it ever more difficult to converse with people?
13. Have you lost the ability to laugh at yourself?
14. Does sex seem more like a chore than a pleasure?
15. Has it become more and more difficult to find things you really enjoy?

Constructed from text of Freudenberger, 1980.

If we are highly ambitious, hard driving, goal oriented, dynamic persons who are expecting too much of ourselves, we are likely to be the most vulnerable candidates for burnout. If we are happy-go-lucky persons, underachievers or those with modest to low aspirations, we are not nearly as likely to become victims. Trouble usually results from overdedication and overcommitment.

I have seen cases of burnout which have resulted from frustration and failure. But I have also seen near burnout from sudden and unexpected accomplishments that resulted in the person being thrust into a position of national and international interest. Unexpected controversy can also bring unexpected stress and the threat of burnout.

A list of means for us to avoid burnout problems, as suggested by participants in my workshops over a period of years, are assembled in Table 11-3. Their suggestions are many and varied, and, in general, reflect attitudes and ideas that range from quietness and aloneness to considerable physical activity, involvement with others, and therapy.

Table 11-3
Ideas of Workshop Participants on Preventing Burnout

1. Limit schedule	26. Ignore peer pressure
2. Lead your own life	27. Delegate
3. Take time for time	28. Do something new
4. Have a party	29. See a therapist
5. Try new opportunities	30. Prioritize
6. Talk	31. Be involved in a professional
7. Do something quick that is successful	organization
8. Do realistic program planning	32. Provide continual positive feedback
9. Counsel employees	33. Allow for flexibility in program
10. When uptight, leave	34. Realize you're not indispensible
11. Leave home at home, leave office at office	35. Eliminate something
12. Do something new	36. Talk to someone not in your field
13. Encourage physical fitness	37. Provide position feedback
14. Set goals for advanced studies	38. Get organized
15. Associate with enthusiastic people	39. Nurture a team approach
16. Exchange ideas at work	40. Encourage professional help
17. Learn to say no	41. Maintain enthusiasm
18. Be open to suggestions from others	42. Don't have to like everything
19. Make new acquaintances	43. Adapt an old program in a different way
20. Treasure successes	44. Develop a sounding board
21. Take a vacation	45. Make "to-do" lists
22. Go to in-service training	46. Develop a peer support system
23. Think about changing your job	47. Take your anger out in exercise
24. Get involved in outside interests	48. Change your routine
25. Say hello with enthusiasm, smile	49. Accept the fact that there will be bad days
	50. Listen to others
	51. Pray
	52. Maintain humor

What works for one of us may not work for another. Freudenberger (1980, 123) warned that:

Just as other-directedness and distance are allies of burn-out, so closeness (to others) and inner-directedness are its foes.

We can easily burn up excessive amounts of energy by being angry, vengeful, over motivated, trying too hard, wanting to impress someone, fearing criticism, fearing failure, being obsessed with perfectionism, success, and getting credit. Many of these can easily become phony gods, and as Short (1965, 61, 19) said:

There are multitudinous variations of the phony gods, ranging from the intellectually sublime to the childishly ridiculous - and vice versa. All phony gods, however, have one thing in common: it kills your soul to worship one of them....Where the center of your existence is, whatever is most important in life for you, that gives meaning, hope, order, and direction to your life, there will your heart be also (Short, p. 59).

This in effect says that wherever our life is focused, that is where our energies will be used.

11-3.4 Behavior Suggesting Change May Be Needed

We cannot say for certain when the first signs indicating the need for change mean that we should take action. However, the list in Table 11-4, as compiled from Sutherland's book on *Can an Adult Change?* (1957), presents some helpful guidelines in making the assessments of ourselves or someone else. Generally, if we are dull, uninteresting, unmoved and nonmoving, anything but dynamic, and are unwilling to change, we are likely to be our own greatest deterrent to making changes and being creative. When we notice any of these signs in ourselves, a careful look should be given as to whether or not the action means changes are necessary.

Schein (1973, 137-152), in an article on "Forces Which Undermine Management Development", listed forces which block individual change and growth from the standpoint of the person (self), the interpersonal (others), and the organization (environment). Table 11-5 is Schein's information modified.

We must be careful not to consider busyness a complete answer to the need for change. Ernest Hemingway was once reported as having said to Marlene Dietrich:

My dear, never confuse motion with action (Wilke, 1986, 32).

Table 11-4
Blocks to Personal Growth Suggesting Changes Are Needed

Persons Who Are Guilty of:

1. Resisting change - status quo seekers. "Once it was the skeptic, the critic of the status quo, who had to make a great effort. Today the skeptic is the status quo. The one who must make the effort is the man who seeks to create a new moral order." (Gardner, p. 121, 1965)
2. Oversystematizing everything, perfectionism, domination, oversupervision.
3. Being an unorganizer - disorganized, confused.
4. Resenting evaluation - resists looking back and planning ahead.
5. Mind wandering - dreams but never acts.
6. Damning things, and sometimes people. Overcritical negativism, suspicion, fear.
7. Worrying uncontrollably.
8. Sarcasm - for the sting of it; face to face and behind the back digs.
9. Nagging - authoritarian air and tenseness.
10. Procrastinating - putter offer, lacking self-discipline.
11. Making snap decisions - acting on compulsion.
12. Running for shelter - afraid to come to grips with problems, feather bedding, won't listen.
13. Overfrank - rests on honesty, the truth even if it hurts.
14. Oversensitiveness.
15. Clinging to well earned status.

Constructed from text of Sutherland, 1957.

All too often we see people extremely busy doing the same thing over and over again without stopping to think what they are trying to accomplish. I have heard such a situation referred to in a biological laboratory as:

A method or procedure looking for a problem to solve.

This, of course, is the reverse of what it should logically be, where one looks for the method or approach to solving a problem only after the problem has been clearly identified.

11-4 PROCRASTINATION

Procrastination can be a serious deterrent to our effective use of time. Poor planning, indecision, perfectionism, fear, and worry may be among the items causing us to put things off until the last possible

Table 11-5
Forces Which Block Growth

Personal - Self (our own)

1. Complacency, apathy, lack of motivation
2. Individual feeling of insecurity and inadequacy
3. Fear of the unknown and change
4. Commitment to our own self-image
5. Lack of desire and willingness to exert effort to make changes
6. Fear of responsibilities if we change and become something different

Interpersonal - Others (superior, peer, subordinate)

1. Excessive pressure and close supervision
2. Undue pressure for loyality and productivity
3. Conveying the feeling that what has been done is never enough
4. Failure of superior to recognize and reward changes in and by the individual
5. Penalty or punishment for changes not in keeping with or suggested by superior
6. Rejection by peers if changes perceived as a move to gain advantage over others

Organizational - Environment

1. Failure to recognize and reward self-initiated and self-directed changes and growth
2. Conveying the feeling that the organization is completely controlling our individual growth and development
3. Not permitting individual decision making and making the individual feel a part of the larger organizational goals
4. Over-emphasis on competitiveness between and among units within the organization
5. Conveying the feeling that opportunities and rewards are not equally available to all
6. Insisting that all decisions (large or small) must come from the top

Constructed and modified from text of Schein, 1973, 137-152.

moment or perhaps not even getting the job done at all. If we are such individuals we may then berate ourselves for being lazy, or lacking self-discipline, or otherwise feel that we are inferior or deficient. If we do a "last minute" job, we can then rationalize that the finished product is not a true representation of our ability. Thus criticism by others won't hurt as much because we feel our performance does not reflect our true ability. Setting unrealistically high standards for ourselves may be another way of attempting to salve our self-esteem because anything less than perfection is not representative of the opinion we have of ourselves.

Ferris (1977) has assembled some materials (taken in part from Lakein, 1973) which address symptoms of procrastination, some of the escapes that we use which tend to put us in the procrastination category, and make suggestions for us to overcome some of the difficulties. She emphasized that procrastination can be a major barrier to effective time management.

Ferris suggested some questions we need to address to test whether procrastination is our problem. She said the following symptoms indicate the behavior of procrastinators:
Do we:

- put things off until the last possible moment?
- live by the "better late than never" motto?
- say we work better under pressure?
- avoid doing new tasks?
- hate to start a big job?
- do what we like to do and postpone the unpleasant?
- say we haven't enough time to do it now?
- do the easy or trivial and postpone the difficult or important?
- avoid jobs where we risk failure?
- get trapped by over indulging ourselves in such activities as socializing, sleeping, playing golf, daydreaming, watching soap operas, etc.?

"Yes" answers indicate the need to take action and make changes. Ferris suggested that fear and worry often cause us to put things off. We are apt to avoid doing something important for fear of making a mistake or that we may get angry, feel guilty, or hurt someone. We may fear taking on too much responsibility. She indicated that most of these fears are usually unwarranted, and that we should ask ourselves, "What is the worst possible thing that could happen if I do it?"

According to Ferris most of us rely on one or more of the following escapes to help us procrastinate:

- Indulging ourselves - doing something we really enjoy: taking the day off to play golf, sleep, watch the "soaps".
- Socializing, visiting, telephoning, small talk.
- Reading a backlog of non-worthwhile materials.
- Doing it ourselves instead of delegating to others.
- Solving other people's problems.

- Overdoing a good thing - being overly thorough: cleaning, organizing, making lists.
- Running away - shopping, extending the lunch hour, hand carrying messages.
- Daydreaming, worrying about how we will get all our work done.

Ferris suggested that once we can admit that procrastination is a problem and can identify the escapes being used, we can find and put to work strategies that will help conquer the difficulties. The strategies she indicated that have worked for many people are presented in Table 11-6.

We must be cautious and not confuse "think time" with procrastination. "Think time" and even "daydreaming" can be valuable and productive uses of time, and when constructively used, they certainly are not procrastination.

Table 11-6
Strategies for Overcoming Procrastination

1. Admit you are wasting time. Say it out loud: "I'm not making the best use of my time!"
2. Cut off escape routes.
3. Set priorities and focus on one thing at a time.
4. Set deadlines on priorities; use reminders to keep yourself going (egg timer, alarm clock).
5. Set up a progress monitoring system with a friend, spouse, co-worker, secretary. Ask them to check at reasonable intervals to ask "how's it going?"
6. Break up the big job into smaller tasks and get started.
7. Block out a realistic amount of interruption and/or distraction free time to do a job.
8. Don't duck the unpleasant.
9. Procrastinate positively by sitting in a chair and doing absolutely nothing. Don't read, shuffle papers, knit, watch TV; just sit. Do this for 15 minutes and don't cheat. Getting started will be an appealing alternative.
10. Break the procrastination habit. Develop the habit of "Do it now."

Constructed from text of Ferris, 1977.

11-5 WILLPOWER AND COMMITMENT

The frailty of our willpower and commitment in making changes is well illustrated in this quote from Short (1965, 41):

The captivity of man's will is most often dramatized in the

comic strip *Peanuts*, just as it is most often dramatized in men's lives— by the significant change that never takes place.

Our willpower and commitment must be strong or no change will take place. Deshler (p. 16, no pub. date) said:

To become objective about ourselves involves unrelenting honesty. It is often painful, and it is not to be wondered at that we skillfully avoid coming to grips with our inner life. We believe in honesty, integrity, patience, kindness, self-control, unselfishness, purity, and all the other virtues. When we observe others violating these ideals, we are quick to condemn; but, when we ourselves violate them, we rationalize our behavior.

We may often wish that we were different, or that we could be like someone we admire for their stellar qualities. But wishing alone will not bring it about. Norman Vincent Peale (1987) said:

Wishing is usually just a form of daydreaming. It's wistful. It's weak. It's even faintly negative, because when you say "I wish," it usually means you don't believe the wish will come true.

He went on to say that we need to hope, really hope enough to be willing to do something about the situation. This then brings *expectancy* into the picture. It means then that:

This desired outcome can happen. I think it's going to happen. When you start hoping instead of just wishing, then expectation comes into power - the power that changes hopes into realities (Peale, pp.6-7).

Hoping thus can contribute a great deal to giving us the willpower to make changes and to stick with them. Deshler (p.17) went on to say:

To be objective about one's self is difficult; and, as we have already indicated, it cannot be achieved without the practice of honesty. No matter how honest we may be in our relationships, few, if any, of us are honest with ourselves. If we are honest with and about ourselves, we will destroy the self-image which we so carefully protect. Since this is distressing, we adroitly sidestep any face-to-face encounter with the real self. To sweep aside all our illusions about ourselves and to look boldly within, daring to face everything we see and calling it by its right name, requires more courage and honesty than most of us can summon without the help of others. It is here that the personal group (and close friends) brings a supporting fellowship.

If we insist on concealing our real selves from others, they are inclined to practice the same deception; but, if we say, "This is what I really am," then they, too, find courage to look within their own hearts. The escape mechanisms which we may employ are automatic, and they are not easily uncovered. Yet it is often surprising how self-revelation comes in the warm, friendly, and accepting fellowship of a personal group that practices honest sharing. We often find our own inner life revealed as we see ourselves in others (Deshler, p. 18).

Robert Schuller (1988) is another person who has written a lot about having the will power and faith to make changes. He presented a series (see Table 11-7) as a suggestion for moving from dreaming and wishing to the reality of making changes. Hopefully, then we may be set free of the doldrums and inhibitions that tend to prevent growth, slow our lives and productivity.

Table 11-7
Faith: The Force That Frees You to Succeed

FAITH starts you	is the	FORCE that leads to		FREES YOU from	to	SUCCEED by being
1. Dreaming —>		Purpose	—>	Blahs	—>	Interested
2. Desiring —>		Passion	—>	Boredom	—>	Excited
3. Praying —>		Hope	—>	Anxiety	—>	Encouraged
4. Beginning —>		Commitment	—>	Inertia	—>	Involved
5. Deciding —>		Direction	—>	Indecision	—>	Dedicated
6. Planning —>		Thinking-through	—>	Confusion	—>	Organized
7. Waiting —>		Patience	—>	Impatience —>		Consistent
8. Paying the price —>		Determination	—>	Expediency —>		Reliable
9. Managing problems—>		Control		—> Defeatism	--->	Optimistic
10. Expecting success —>		Enthusiasm	—>	Failure	—>	Successful

Modified and Adapted from Schuller, 1988, 221.

Deshler (p.16) suggested that:

The charity we show toward our own faults must be exercised toward others, and the critical appraisal we so easily make of others, we must sternly apply to ourselves.

11-6 MAKING CHANGES

Making changes is never easy for us. Understanding some of the forces which stimulate growth can encourage us to want to, and to take steps to change. Schein (1973, 150) also presented a list of forces which stimulate growth categorized in the same manner as those given for blocking growth (Table 11-5). These positive forces are presented in Table 11-8, under personal, interpersonal and organizational headings.

As we face the issue of making personal changes, Sutherland (1957) suggested that we should ask ourselves some pertinent questions which may be of help in making decisions about changing.

Table 11-8
Forces Which Stimulate Growth

Personal - Self (our own)

1. Individual desire for self-fulfillment and doing something that counts
2. Ability and willingness to self-evaluate and be evaluated
3. Recognition of our capabilities to change, grow and improve
4. Desire to fulfill our responsibilities and commitment to ourselves and to our organization
5. Feeling accepted and trusted by our superiors and peers

Interpersonal - Others

1. Encouragement from superiors and peers to change and grow
2. Regular performance evaluation and joint agreement on ways for improvement
3. Encouragement to continuously participate with new ideas and involvement in decisions
4. Treatment conveying openness and trust by superiors, peers, and subordinates
5. Regular acknowledgement of our accomplishments by superiors and peers

Organizational - Environment

1. General recognition and respect for all members of the organization
2. Strong support for and encouragement of interaction and teamwork throughout the organization
3. Regular practice of recognition and rewards for individual growth and development
4. Policy of encouraging and supporting self-development efforts at all levels
5. Regular in-house and external training and development programs

Constructed and modified from text of Schein, 1973, 137-152.

Modified and paraphrased, here they are:

- Isn't insight into the need a necessary first step?
- Will accentuating the positive be an aid or an illusion for us?
- Can a more satisfying way be found?
- What are the alternatives?
- Will new skills or tools help?
- How about if we associate with individuals who are already moving in the direction we want to go?
- Why not help others in their development (maybe we can learn from their approach and experience)?
- Would more self-reliance and independence aid us in making the change?
- Would more open-mindedness be helpful?
- Could a belief in the goodness of human nature be of use?
- Might a faith in the future give us confidence?
- Would developing a confident relationship to the more lasting, rather than the superficial, things of life be helpful?

11-7 ACCEPTING CHANGE

Accepting the suggestions and/or criticisms which indicate our need for personal change is not easy. Our first reaction is that we are being unjustly attacked. Short (1965, 34) cited a "Snoopy" quote which is fitting here:

It never fails. Just hint that some of their troubles might be with themselves, and they get mad at you!

A number of factors such as reacting and adjusting to burnout, criticism, and health problems, dealing with stress, adversity, and difficult persons (see 10-7.2), making difficult decisions, and managing tight time schedules can all cause us difficulty in accepting change.

11-7.1 Willingness to Accept Criticism

Learning how to give and accept criticism is an art that usually takes real effort and careful attention on our part (see Chapter 4-5.5, Fear of Criticism). Weisinger and Lobsenz (1981, 98) made a number of suggestions on how we can learn to give and accept criticism, so that both will help us to change and grow. They suggested that accepting criticism in a constructive way means we should:

- Think of criticism as a source of new information to be evaluated objectively.
- Channel the emotional energy aroused by criticism into fruitful avenues.
- Take the necessary steps to put behavioral changes into action.

Following criticism we usually need to first cool down from the natural reaction that we are being attacked. We need to decide whether there is a personal attack or is it really the issue in question? Does the critic really understand the issue or the circumstances? If there is a misunderstanding or if the critic is focusing on an irrelevant aspect, the situation should be clarified. Often when this is done the criticism is defused.However, if the criticism is warranted, we need to try to put ourselves in the critic's shoes and visualize what our own reaction would be in assessing the validity of the criticism. It is amazing how often this will make us realize that the critic is actually doing us a favor.

It is also frequently helpful for us to try to visualize where the critic is coming from. Is the person an expert in the area that is being criticized, or is it someone who is in the "difficult person" class? We may have to give some ground and accept the fact that the critic has not learned to give criticism in a graceful manner. Weisinger and Lobsenz (pp. 95-96) presented the following checklist for giving constructive criticism:

1. Target the behavior (or issue) you want to criticize.
2. Make your criticism as specific as possible.
3. Be sure the behavior (issue) you are criticizing can be changed. If it cannot, then stop.
4. Use "I-statements" and avoid threats and/or accusations.
5. Make sure the other person understands your criticism and the reason for it.
6. Don't belabor the point.
7. Offer incentives for changed behavior, and commit yourself to share in resolving the situation.
8. Don't allow your own negative feelings to color your words and actions.
9. Show that you empathize with the other person's problem or feelings.
10. Hold criticism for an appropriate time and place.
11. Consider trying to defuse a hostile response by "predict-

ing" the other person's reaction: "I know I can say this to you because I know you will take it well."

12. If your criticism produces positive results, give verbal recognition and appreciation.

In giving consideration to these suggestions, both in giving and accepting criticism, we must adjust to meet each individual situation. Hopefully they should be helpful to us in bringing about the most good for change and improvement in creativity and productivity.

11-7.2 Dealing with Stress, Adversity and Difficult Persons

The tendency to impose unrealistic goals on ourselves - the drive for betterment, to be more than what we are, to accomplish more than time will permit, and the emphasis on excellence and success - drives many of us to impose unrealistic goals upon ourselves. We may not be able to realistically assess our need to change. This can result in stress and anxiety. To avoid this stress we should set realistic goals which are compatible with our capabilities and are reasonable from the standpoint of time. In addition we must be willing to deal with the impatience which we cause ourselves through improper management of time, reluctance to seek advice, neglect of careful planning, procrastination, lack of support, and many other personal idiosyncrasies.

We must also keep in mind that stress, hardship, and sometimes suffering often are beneficial in the long-run. As is indicated in the Charlie Brown quote published by Short (1965, 82):

But adversity is what makes you mature. The growing soul is watered best by tears of sadness.

11-8 MAKING THE BEST USE OF YOUR TIME

Each Day is a New Account. If you had a bank that credited your account each morning with $86,400 - That carried over no balance from day to day - Allowed you to keep no cash in your account - And every evening cancelled whatever part of the amount you had failed to use during the day - What would you do? Draw out every cent every day, of course, and use it to your advantage. Well, you have such a bank - and its name is "TIME."

Every morning, it credits you with 86,400 seconds. Every night, it rules off as lost whatever of this you have failed to invest to good purpose. It carries no balances. It allows no overdrafts. Each day, it opens a new account with you. Each night, it burns the records of the day. If you fail to use the day's deposits, the loss is yours. There is no going back. There is no drawing against the "Tomorrow."

It is up to each of us to invest this precious fund of hours, minutes and seconds in order to get from it the utmost in health, happiness and success. (Taken from *The Ag Student*, Ohio State University, Columbus, Ohio. Vol 79(4):2. 1973. Credited with having appeared in *Rotary Bulletin*, date not given).

Every day has 24 hours or 86,400 seconds, every week 168 hours or 604,800 seconds. In a year, if we sleep 8 hours a day, we use 121 days or 17.3 weeks. If we use 30 minutes a day for bathing, grooming and/or shaving, we use over another week, and we most likely use about 2 weeks a year in eating. Altogether, nearly 40% of our total available time is used in what might be classed as "routine essentials" (roughly 3,500 hours). This still leaves over 5,200 hours of time to be used at our discretion. Thus it would appear that making the best use of our time is not so much a matter of having more time as it is a matter of making maximum use of the time that is available.

An excellent movie based on Lakein's (1973) book, *How to Get Control of Your Time and Your Life*, suggested the following guidelines for better use of time:

1. List goals and set priorities.
2. Make a daily "to do" list and rate each item A, B, or C, according to its importance to you.
3. Start with A's (your highest priorities for the day), not with C's.
4. Handle each piece of paper (each item) only once.
5. Do it now!
6. Ask yourself "What is the best use of my time right now?"

If we expand on these suggestions a bit, we may come up with the following "Ten time tips":

1. Assess how you have been using your time.
2. Plan ahead.
3. Do your high priorities first.
4. Avoid procrastination.
5. Don't get stalled by "indecision."

6. Don't waste time worrying about things you can't change.
7. Make maximum use of your help by delegating.
8. Become an effective communicator.
9. Watch out for negative attitudes (yours and others).
10. Be realistic in your commitments.

The discussion that follows explores several of these 10 items in more detail. They may help you in "Making the best use of your time."

11-8.1 Analyze the Use of Your Time

Make an analysis of your time over a period of two or three days. Where did you spend the most time? Was it spent doing your highest priority? Where and when did you waste the most time? How much time did you spend doing things of low priority? Did you suffer many interruptions? Could some of these (or many) have been avoided? What could you cut out altogether? How could you arrange your day so you could spend more time on your highest priorities?

After answering these and other pertinent questions, see if you can determine your own effectiveness in using time.

- Are you a procrastinator?
- Do you use up a lot of time because you can't make a decision?
- Is your problem one of poor planning?
- Are you trying to do the impossible - more than is humanly possible in the time allowed?
- Are you wasting time in dealing with things that cannot be changed, or are you failing to delegate items which could be easily done by those available to assist you?
- Could your means of communication be improved by shorter telephone conversations, by writing short notes, cutting down on unnecessary chit-chat, or writing things out when you could be dictating them?
- Or are you a victim of your own self-negativism or the negativism of others?

11-8.2 Make Decisions and Delegate

Refer again to Chapter 5-5, which deals with choice and decision-making, and review the response grid shown in Figure 5-1. Do you concentrate on making decisions and changing those things where you have some flexibility and some chance of bringing about a change? Can you eliminate (or at least put on the back burner) and quit worrying about those things you can't change.

Refer also to Chapter 12-6 for suggestions on delegating as a means of making the best use of your own time. All too often we repeatedly do simple tasks that we could delegate because we do not take the time to teach another to do it, or we feel no one can do that task well enough to suit us.

11-8.3 Communicate

Much time is lost because of poor communications. In some cases this may be caused by excessive small talk such as on the telephone, at refreshment time, or even in conferences in which side issues or unimportant issues are discussed at length rather than sticking to the major reason for the get-together. Sometimes we write when a quick telephone conversation would settle the issue. At other times we waste time by repeatedly trying to call when writing a brief note would better serve the purpose. Experts suggest a brief hand-written reply on the original letter we have received as being a fully adequate means of responding in many cases.

If we can become a dictator (using a recording machine) instead of typing or writing out by hand we can save an immense amount of time. It takes some practice and some skill to become a good dictator, but in the long run, it pays off greatly for us. We need to be fully prepared before we start talking. We need to avoid excessively wordy and lengthy dictations, and we must overcome the fear of dictation, particularly in the initial stages. However, it is well to remember that in these days of the word processor it is easy to edit as compared to rewriting by hand. With the prospects of voice recording and transcribing equipment being available in the near future, we all, young and old, should give serious thought to becoming dictators or using our own desk word processor.

We cannot leave the issue of communication time-wasting without discussing a most serious time consumer, particularly in educational circles and in many industries and government. This involves the many meetings that we hold. Too many meetings are held without adequate preparation, without clearly stated objectives, with too many long conversations that do not pertain to the issues of the meeting, without clearly reaching and stating conclusions that can be drawn, and without making arrangements for follow-up so that something happens as a result of the meeting that has taken so much time.

Some suggestions for a successful meeting are contained in

Chapter 9-10. A more extensive list, which resulted from the Hughes Aircraft studies, is contained in the Ranftl R & D Productivity Report (1978, 66).

11-8.4 Avoid Overcommitment

No discussion of time utilization would be complete without considering the issue of overcommitment. All of us would like to accomplish a great deal more than we can. We all have trouble saying no. We all have trouble being all that we would like to be. It is foolish to take on tasks when we know that someone else could handle a job much more efficiently and with less effort than would be required of us. This issue is well illustrated in the article "Who Killed Cock Robin?" (see Dragstedt, 1962). This article illustrates vividly what happens to many persons in academic circles, and parallels can be seen in industry and the home as well. An outstanding scientist is lured into more and more extraneous tasks until he is eventually spread so thin that he no longer excels as a scientist. The cessation of scientific research to the scientist is a form of death. The cessation of our own major likes and capabilities, whatever our field is also like death. We must be alert and cautious in taking on more and more things just because we are capable and vulnerable to praise and flattery.

11-8.5 How to Beat the Time Trap

Avoiding the pitfalls in time utilization can help us to avoid the feeling of being pressured, hurried, and stressed to meet deadlines. In turn, our feelings of well-being will likely be improved. Using the extra time that is made available can be used in any way we choose. We may find time for more "think time," being more creative, enjoying relaxation and refreshment, or finally getting at that long-dreamed of hobby, project or vacation we have been planning for so long.

Lock (1977, 6-77) has assembled a rather lengthy list of ways to beat the time trap. These are presented in Table 11-9.

We may need to modify some of these suggestions, depending on the nature of the position we hold. Much more could be said with regards to managing time, but a great deal of help can be obtained by referring to suggestions like those of Lakein (1973), Lock (1977) and in many other volumes of written materials.

11-9 HEALTH MAINTENANCE

Our physical well-being is very important to our mental well-

Table 11-9
How to Beat the Time Trap

1. Write daily "To-Do" lists, highlighting top priorities.
2. On Mondays, plan a whole week's work.
3. Have your secretary screen your mail and phone calls.
4. Delegate routine chores.
5. Set deadlines for subordinates when you delegate projects to them. (But be reasonable. Rushed, or arbitrary deadlines kill creativity and cause burnout).
6. Set deadlines for yourself. Again; be reasonable.
7. Use waiting time to plan projects for the rest of your day.
8. Carry blank 3 x 5 cards to jot down spontaneous ideas.
9. When you procrastinate, ask yourself what you're avoiding.
10. Cut off nonproductive activities, phone calls, rambling conversations.
11. Put up reminder signs to keep yourself on task. Example: Are you daydreaming? Keep phone calls brief!
12. Handle every piece of paper only once. Immediately throw away what you don't need; don't mull over it.
13. Answer mail by writing comments on each letter. Have your secretary complete correspondence.
14. Keep desk cleared and ready for action. Items waiting for attention should be in the middle of the desk.
15. Have a place for everything so you know immediately where to find it.
16. Schedule meetings only when they inform, solve a problem or sell an idea. Replace meetings with memos.
17. When you read, skim for important words, headlines.
18. Listen carefully. Ask direct questions to obtain needed information quickly.
19. Do your thinking on paper. It helps you organize and motivates you to continue because you can see progress.
20. Set aside your most productive time period each day for creative work.
21. Ask help from specialists (engineers, accountants, artists, marketing executives, etc.).
22. Write letters to people who regularly talk too long on the phone.
23. Face your desk away from your office door to avoid looking up every time someone passes by and others from stopping in.
24. Make it clear that unannounced "drop-ins" aren't welcome.
25. Try to arrive at your office a half hour early each day to take advantage of the quiet time before other employees arrive.

Constructed from text of Lock, 1977, 6-7.

being. Frequently, as enthusiastic, dedicated and goal-oriented persons, we become so enmeshed in our endeavors that we begin to abuse and disregard our physical well-being. We must take care to eat properly, eat regularly, exercise at least minimally, sleep regularly and sufficiently and to get some type of relaxation in order to continue to perform maximally mentally. Refraining from other detrimental practices such as smoking, excessive drinking (both alcoholic and caffeine containing substances) and the use of drugs are also important aspects in maintaining our good health.

11-10 OUTSIDE STIMULATION

For growth and development we need intellectual challenge, refreshment, and renewal both from within the organization and from the outside. Self-challenge may be needed almost constantly. Appropriate periods of relaxation and refreshment are also essential.

11-10.1 Inside and Outside Contacts with People

Frequent contacts with our peers as well as outstanding people in specialized fields at home, in seminars, conferences, and lectures, as well as maintaining a regular schedule of attending professional meetings and conferences away from home, can be especially helpful in supplying us with intellectual stimulation. We can even use our daily refreshment breaks or lunch period to make contacts with individuals who provide mental stimulation as well as a relaxed environment. Taking regular sabbatic leaves and travel, making contacts and visits to other laboratories, places of business and with other professional workers, can help to keep us aware that there are challenging and interesting discoveries and progress being made on many fronts. These contacts usually help to keep us humble about our own progress, but at times will also give us and other employees a boost to know that the local efforts are out in front.

Taking sabbatic or other work leaves on a regular basis can contribute heavily to the opportunities of looking at new areas, becoming aware of what is going on at other places, and give us the opportunity of breaking the routines of committees and other activities which tend to cut into our "think-time."

11-10.2 Relaxation

We need to be very concerned for the workaholic; the over-committed, overstimulated, intensely dedicated individual who has time for nothing but work. Work should be fun, but it sometimes can reach a point of addiction. We refer to such persons as workaholics. Oates (1977, 57-60) described the workaholic as being:

1. truly professionals, whatever they do is done exceptionally well;
2. real perfectionists, merciless in their demands on themselves for peak performance and mastery of the tasks they are involved in;
3. vigorous intolerants of incompetence;
4. usually over-committed to themselves and the business, organization, or institution for which they work; and
5. persons with skills that are in much demand because they can do things well, but because of constant overcommitment often do not do as well as could be done with a little more time.

Some indications of the workaholic syndrome, gleaned from a number of places as well as personal observations suggest workaholic tendencies. If our answer is "yes" to a number of the following questions, look out, for we may already be an addict:

- Do we often let our minds wander when we are talking to someone?
- Do we interrupt people when they are talking to us before they are finished?
- Do we take phone calls even when we are in the midst of a conference with someone?
- Do we check back two or more times a day when we are away from our office or work place?
- Is being admired by our friends and colleagues more important to us than being liked?
- Do we consider the midmorning and midafternoon refreshment time a waste of time?
- Do we routinely spend nights and weekends back at the work place or on work we have taken home from our job?
- Are we annoyed when drivers are slow in responding in traffic?
- Do we feel that repetitive recreation such as golf, tennis, or table games are a waste of time?

Breaking the workaholic pattern is not easy. Oates (p. 109) said that the workaholic must "work at not working." If we are caught in this trap, the development of hobbies and extraneous interests may

PERSONAL NEEDS FULFILLED

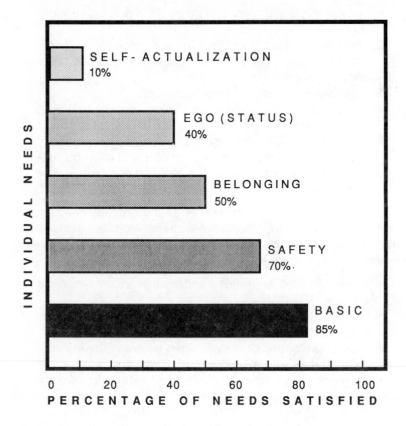

Fig.11-1 Average Percentage of Basic and Growth Needs of the Individual That Are Actually Met
(Adapted from Patten, 1981, 45)

be very beneficial to us and help us to let our intuition play a more significant role as we attempt to solve problems.

As workaholics we may be vacation skippers too. However, vacations aren't a guaranteed cure-all for our emotional problems or fatigue. However, the value of time off, whether for several short vacations, perhaps three-day weekends taken a half-dozen times a year, or one fairly long vacation, can be immensely helpful for rest, recuperation, and refreshment.

Much benefit can be gained by incorporating several relaxation periods - short 10 minute periods with a change of pace, or moving around - into the daily schedule. These can be helpful in breaking the monotony of the tasks involved. Giving our bodies some stimulation from exercise, from a refreshing (non-caffeine) drink, or conversation at these break times can be beneficial even when one talks with colleagues about business or other things.

Another great help for us in relaxation is to practice relaxation exercises. A number of such techniques are proposed by Benson (1975) in his book entitled *The Relaxation Response.* Keeping the mind and body relaxed can greatly aid our creative capabilities. However, disciplining ourselves to do the things that are necessary to keep the body and mind functioning at their best takes an unusual amount of personal commitment and dedication. A number of suggestions that will aid us in developing improved creative abilities are summarized in Chapter 14. Incorporating these and many of the other suggestions in this book should help us to acquire a higher percentage of our growth and being needs than the general average of 10 percent for self-actualization and 40 percent for ego (status) needs acquired by the average person (cited by Patten 1981 [see Figure 11-1]).

11-11 HIGHLIGHTS OF CHAPTER ELEVEN

1. Accomplishing personal growth, development and self-renewal can be a most difficult task, for it is not easy to accurately assess our own shortcomings and needs.
2. A high self-esteem, a strong self-discipline, and an almost continuous self-evaluation are required for us to make self-improvements.
3. We need to constantly watch for signs of fatigue, failure, fear, burn-out, depression, etc., that indicate the need for us to change, and then have the courage to make the change.
4. We can not overcome procrastination (especially putting things off until the last moment) until we carefully assess the possible disasters that may result if sickness or accident prevents us from meeting a deadline.
5. Learning to accept criticism is difficult, but may be required if we are to make appropriate, timely changes.
6. Effectively managing our time can greatly increase our productivity and can help us make way for more "think time" and greater creativity.

7. Proper health maintenance, including good nutrition, adequate exercise, avoiding the use of alcohol and drugs, and proper rest, can greatly enhance our mental performance.
8. Guarding against falling into a workaholic pattern may be important, especially if we are over-enthusiastic persons.
9. It is extremely important that we learn to get away from our usual routines by taking short breaks and relaxing during the day, by periodically attending lectures or symposia, visiting workers in similar or different fields than our own, and regularly taking vacations.

11-12 AFTERGROWTH STIMULATORS

1. What is the most important thing you have done in the last six months that has or will contribute to your growth and development and self-renewal? What caused you to realize the need for change?
2. Would you consider yourself a mild, average, or severe procrastinator? What has been the most embarrassing or detrimental result of procrastinating in your life?
3. Do you find it easy to discipline yourself to stick to making changes in your living patterns that you feel will be really beneficial for you? Why or why not?
4. Would you rate yourself as poor, fair, good, or very good at managing your time? What could you do to improve?
5. What changes should you make that would be most beneficial to your physical and/or mental well-being? Can you muster the courage to do it?
6. What have you done in the last six months that has brought good outside, digressing stimulation from your usual activities in connection with your job? Recreation? Spiritual enrichment?

CHAPTER 12

LEADING AND MANAGING TO FOSTER CREATIVITY

12- 1   Introduction
12- 2   Leadership
12- 3   Motivating
12- 4   Morale Building
12- 5   Managing Other's Time
12- 6   Delegating
12- 7   Minimizing Stress
12- 8   Planning
12- 9   Goal Setting
12-10   Evaluation
12-11   Managerial Blocks to Creativity
12-12   Highlights of Chapter Twelve
12-13   Aftergrowth Stimulators

12-1 INTRODUCTION

No organization, institution, or unit can function smoothly nor be productive without good leadership and management. Without dynamic leaders, the members of a unit are likely to each go in different and isolated directions or fail to be real contributors to any kind of a unified effort. The more capable individuals are, the greater the need and challenge we have in molding them into a team. Different situations call for different leadership approaches. Some situations call for a definite democratic approach and others require us to exercise a more authoritarian response.

All too frequently, especially in academic circles and industries where completely independent action and decision-making are required of many persons, we find there is a strong feeling that complete (academic) freedom should prevail to such an extent that all should be permitted to go in their own separate directions. In fact, sometimes the impression exists among a group of outstanding employees (researchers, teachers, etc.) that there is no particular need for outstanding leadership. In such a unit, the reputation of the different components will supposedly sustain the reputation of the organization and its leaders. Such an attitude tends to develop a strong adversary relationship among employees, supervisors, and other leadership (academic faculty, staff, and administrators). Siu (1957, 146) in his book, *The Tao of Science*, said:

> The more expert the men in the organized effort, the more valuable are their skills, the more significant are their potential contributions, and the more exacting is their need for wise management.

Some of the challenges we face as leaders and managers in an organization include:

- Assuming major responsibilities for finding, attracting, and keeping creative individuals.
- Supplying dynamic and effective leadership.
- Providing a stimulating environment.
- Developing an effective organization.
- Managing time, change, stress, and conflict judiciously.
- Carefully evaluating and rewarding personnel.
- Maintaining effective communications.
- Keeping individuals and the organization refreshed and renewed.

- Responding to all sorts of unexpected situations.
- Understanding and executing all these personnel management and administrative roles and responsibilities.

If the organization and the individuals in it are to stay alive and productive, we need to pay special attention to keeping channels open for all employees to contribute new and creative ideas. If we accept only the ideas that are generated from above in the organization we are likely to miss many potentially valuable ideas. Furthermore, the existence of openness and acceptance of communications throughout the organization is not only valuable to the organization, but is stimulating and rewarding to the morale of all individuals. This is a practice considered by Peters and Waterman (1982, 14), in their book, *In Search of Excellence*, to be of prime importance in companies they classed as "Excellent." Such an atmosphere can only be created in an organization where as leaders, we not only condone, but foster and practice openness and respect for persons at all levels. Personnel throughout must be aware of the policy and see that those who risk openness are affirmed and rewarded, not punished.

12-2 LEADERSHIP

Becoming a unit leader offers the opportunity for great rewards for us, if we are interested and capable of working with people at all levels. To be able to perform such a function, we must possess a considerable sensitivity to the needs and emotions of people and the skills to deal, in many cases, with complicated interpersonal relationships. The rewards come for us from aiding and witnessing the accomplishment of others, with rewards to us being primarily a humble realization that we have played a role in stimulating and facilitating those accomplishments of others. We might say that:

We, as leaders, have nothing more to brag about than what the members of our unit accomplish.

Being the leader of a highly productive unit can be an unbelievably rewarding experience.

12-2.1 Being Drawn into a New and Unexpected Role

Frequently we are picked to become unit leaders because we have shown outstanding performance in the job and capacity we have been fulfilling. Often we may have limited experience in broad fields (although we may be outstanding experts in our own specialty), and may be relatively unaware that the rewards for our new

BOMBARDED from all DIRECTIONS

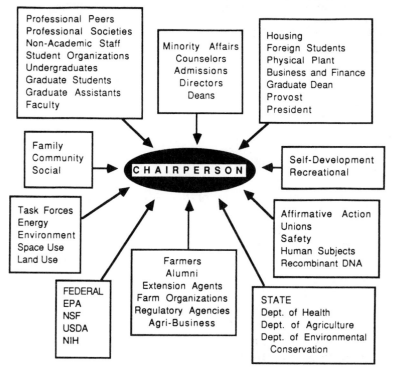

Fig. 12-1 Example of the Many Programs, Persons and Other Items Which a Leader Can Expect to Demand Attention

activities must come from a set of entirely different accomplishments than has been true in the past. Expectations for the role we are to play are likely to be the traditional ones that suggest a manager organizes, coordinates, plans, and controls. A number of years ago Mintzberg (1975, 49-61) pointed out that these roles had changed and, in fact, had become more:

- interpersonal roles (as figurehead, leader, liaison);
- informational (as monitor, disseminator, spokesman); and
- decisional (as entrepreneur, disturbance handler, resource allocator, negotiator).

All too often we are placed in leadership roles with little expectation or training and education for the interpersonal tasks. Not only are we surprised at the interpersonal contacts within the organization, but also, we are not expecting to be bombarded from all directions (superiors, peers, subordinates, and outside sources). An example of the bombardment from my experience in an academic setting in an agricultural department is presented in Figure 12-1.

These contacts meant that I, as head of a department, had a real responsibility to be a figurehead and liaison person, as well as playing the all important informational role as monitor, information disseminator and spokesman in many different ways. Mintzberg (1975, 55) cited several studies which showed that top managers found they were spending roughly 45 percent of their time with outsiders, about the same within their units with subordinates and peers and only about 10 percent of their time with superiors.

In our roles as unit leaders, we may also be surprised at the many situations in which we must deal with a budget which is largely committed to the support of personnel (not a lot of funds to support new and creative program approaches). While as new unit leaders we can usually get help in handling financial matters, facilities, and many of the other routines involving things, most of the load for managing personnel falls directly on our shoulders with limited outside help. Since productivity is the major focus for a unit, we are faced with real challenges in selecting personnel, encouraging productivity throughout the individual members' careers, and bringing about and encouraging team effort. Also, dealing with such troubling issues as ineptness, burnout, and personal conflicts constantly require considerable attention from us as unit leaders.

Comment - To avoid such surprises for new unit leaders, and to supply refresher information for those who have been in such positions, orientation and information workshops can be extremely valuable. As a result of my concern and that of others for this issue, such five-day workshops for department chairpersons in the Agricultural Experiment Stations of the 12 Northeastern States were organized, offered, and met with considerable favor.

To be successful, the unit of the future must have creative individuals, effective teams, dynamic leadership, a stimulating environment, and be a part of an effective organization.

12-2.2 General Responsibilities

As unit leaders we must see that responsibilities are done well, promptly and efficiently. (To accomplish this we become leaders, facilitators, managers). To be able to do this we must know what is going on and must keep the members of the unit informed (monitor, disseminator, spokesman). It has been said that good leadership is the art of getting average people to do superior work. To this point are some appropriate quotes:

The leaders cannot lead until first they know what is happening (Wilke, 1986, 48).

Leaders focus the attention of everyone in the organization on the issues that are important. Leaders remind the people what the collective goals are....The task of leadership is to center in on that which is vital (Wilke, p. 63).

This (The) new leadership (for today) has to create a positive, productive, and ethically grounded environment. (They pointed out that a senior board chairman in Japan said his role was): "To model love. I am the soul of this company. It is through me that our organization's values pass." (Blanchard and Peale, 1988, 87)

Leadership *should be* the soul of an organization, the place:

... where you house your values, your purpose in life, including the picture of the kind of person (organization) you want to be (Blanchard and Peale, 1988, 91).

The leader must play a role in helping to provide an opportunity for everyone to develop to the maximum of their ability (motivator, encourager). One of the most important roles is for us to master the skills required in dealing with interpersonal relationships (communicator, negotiator, disturbance handler, counselor). In this latter role, being fair and decisive in allocating and managing resources is very important (organizer, evaluator) for us. All these combined mean that we must be willing to devote much time to fostering the well-being of the unit, often at a cost and sacrifice of our own time. This means we must be patient, determined, have a great reserve of strength, and possess the discipline and desire to be an outstanding role model.

12-2.3 Skills and Personal Attributes Needed

Ends and Page (1977) surveyed 266 top and middle managers in business, government, and nonprofit organizations for their opinion on what skills and personal attributes they considered most important for us in becoming successful managers. Skills suggested as needed, in the order of their importance, were:

1. leadership and motivation;
2. information systems;
3. communication;
4. understanding human behavior;
5. finance;
6. an awareness of environment; and
7. planning.

Personal attributes in order were:

1. ability to work with others;
2. drive and energy;
3. adaptability to change;
4. ability to communicate; and
5. integrity.

Peter (1987) suggested inner characteristics we need for leadership to be: honesty, loyalty, courage, naturalness, courtesy, self-respect, tolerance, and modesty. His list of what he called outer characteristics needed for good leadership included: ambition, quickness of perception, judgement, self-confidence, resourcefulness, promptness of action, tenacity of purpose, thoroughness of method, and audacity. According to Blanchard and Peale (p. 86, 1988), a recent survey naming the most desirable leadership qualities mentioned integrity most often.

12-2.4 Do's and Don'ts for an Effective Leader

In listing some do's, if we want to become effective leaders, Peter (1987) suggested:

1. Do become inspired with ourselves before we can expect to inspire others.
2. Do maintain our standards of life on a high moral plane so that we will merit the respect and admiration of others.
3. Do strive to perfect ourselves in the art of our duty so that others will have faith in our professional judgment and confidence in our decisions.
4. Do make our motives clear and above suspicion so as to earn trust.
5. Do be jealous of our reputation with our superiors, our contemporaries and our subordinates.
6. Do be able to tell the difference between error and offense.

Don't punish for punishment sake but correct for the sake of humanity.

His list of don'ts to consider in leadership included:

1. Don't be a driver - the nagging, harsh and relentless type. This form of command, through brute force, lacks the human touch and is command by bullying. It may get immediate results for us but can never inspire the loyalty needed to build morale for the long haul.
2. Don't be a nagger - nothing is ever right; fault finding is continuous.
3. Don't be a snooper - using underhanded means.
4. Don't be peevish, fretful, fussy.
5. Don't be the untrustful type. Be able to delegate authority. Give subordinates initiative. Develop a team concept.
6. Don't be a jellyfish - no backbone, can't make a decision; won't back up subordinates.
7. Don't be the dumb-type, not knowledgeable about our jobs.

We need to concentrate on motivating, encouraging, communicating effectively, knowing when and how to delegate, utilizing time efficiently, planning effectively, helping to alleviate stresses, as well as a number of other competencies which can help to make us effective leaders. Without attention to a number of these items, we may find it difficult to keep the efforts of a unit from becoming too diffuse, or otherwise causing a loss of interest by the members and a decrease in effectiveness of the unit as a whole.

Our constant efforts are imperative to keep the unit renewed, enthusiastic, and moving toward unit and institutional goals. To this end we should periodically do a self-evaluation in order not to be surprised by our peers, subordinates, or by our superiors when periodic evaluations are called for. A constant effort at self-renewal, seeking feedback from subordinates, and working smarter should improve our leadership performance and our feeling of accomplishment and well-being.

12-3 MOTIVATING

We saw back in Chapter 7-5 that self-preservation is a primary motivating force. The opportunity to gain the highest reward of actually becoming what we are capable of becoming is a most useful motivating force, because all of us have some spark of that innermost drive to provide the thrust to do our best, or at least do better. We all want to count for something.

Many of us, as leaders, managers, supervisors and nonsupervisors, would like to have a magic formula or cookbook approach to motivating people. People and environments are much too complex to hope for a simple formula. However, there are some things which have been found to be helpful for us in many situations.

We need to let people know where they fit into the organization. They need to know that their jobs are important. They need to be told what their contributions will be to the overall objectives. They need to know what is expected of them. Failures often occur because we have not made clear what they are expected to do. It is important that we eliminate as much role ambiguity as possible. We should constantly be aware of the challenge of matching responsibilities to individual capabilities and desires.

If individuals accept the challenge of certain responsibilities, then they will be more motivated to meet them. Early small successes should be within their reach, and we should be sure to recognize, give credit and, at least verbally, reward them for their accomplishments. Formal recognition and reward should be given at an appropriate time and in conjunction with letting the person know where they stand.

We should delegate responsibilities to individuals in keeping with their capabilities, and then hold them accountable for fulfilling them. It is important that we open the way for individuals to participate in decision-making, not only in things which affect their own day-to-day activities, but also in larger goals and objectives of the unit.

Communications are of the utmost importance. One of the basic rules of communication is that we don't dare not communicate. We are always communicating, whether we mean to or not. Even silence sends a message. Thus those of us in management need to make sure that our messages are clearly conveyed upward, downward and sideways. One of the greatest demotivators in a unit is to have people wondering what is going on. When people reach this state, they begin to speculate, rumors run rampant, and misinformation spreads rapidly.

Another important motivating force, which we should utilize, is offering the opportunity for individual growth and advancement within the unit. Such opportunities convey to the members of the unit that they, as individuals, are worth something to the organization, and betterment of them means betterment of the unit.

As leaders, managers, or supervisors we must familiarize our-

CHALLENGES FACED in MAKING CHANGES

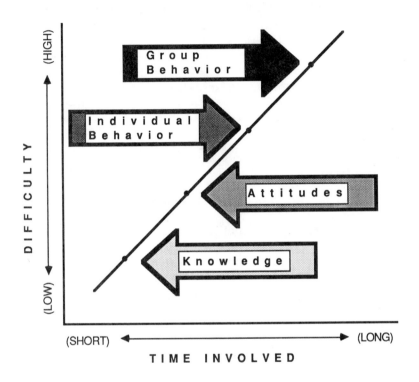

Fig. 12-2 Comparative Time and Difficulty in Making Various Changes (Adapted from Hersey and Blanchard, 1982, 2)

selves and learn, at least to some extent, what the persons with various roles under our control are and should be doing. Then we should learn and apply appropriate leadership and management practices which will bring out the best in everyone. The response of personnel to evolving management techniques and procedures needs to be understood in order to develop an efficient working organization. When we need to make changes, it is well to remember that behavior patterns are far more difficult to alter than are simply altering attitudes and obtaining new knowledge to perform certain tasks. This has been well illustrated by Hersey and Blanchard (1982,

2; see Figure 12-2). Note from this figure that individual behavior is more rapidly and more easily changed than group behavior. If individuals are to be creative, we must give them freedom.

Table 12-1
Historical Patterns of Leadership Attitudes

- **The Traditional Model - Early Models**

Since work was assumed to be disliked by most people, the manager's principal task was to supervise and control subordinates. Since what people did was considered less important than what they earned, the supervisor usually set up tasks in a simple, repetitive, easily learned format so that people could be controlled to produce up to set strandards. It was believed that few want or could do self-directed, creative work on their own. Thus the manager had to establish and carefully control work procedures.

- **The Human Relations Model - Started in the 1930's**

Since it began to be understood that people need to feel useful and important, the manager's role changed to trying to make the workers feel that what they were doing was important. It was thought that sharing information with them and involving them in routine decisions would satisfy these workers' needs. It was learned that people want to feel that they belong and are treated as individuals. Thus, managers found they also needed to listen to workers' objections. The workers' needs were also found to be more important than money for motivation. When allowed some self-direction and self-control, morale was improved, and there was more cooperation and less resistance to authority.

- **The Human Resources Model - Came into Being in the 1960's**

It was gradually recognized that work is not distasteful and that people want to help establish and contribute to goals. Thus, the managers' tasks were seen as utilizing human resources. To do this they needed to permit more self-direction, self-control, and more involvement in helping coordinate operating procedures. It was learned that most people can handle far more creative responsibility than their jobs demand. Thus, managers become challenged to create an environment where individuals can contribute more nearly to their limits. This entails participation of workers in more and more decision-making on important matters. As a result of involvement, worker satisfaction becomes a by-product of their greater output and involvement.

Constructed from materials of Miles, et al., 1973, 63-67.

LEADER BEHAVIOR AND DECISION MAKING

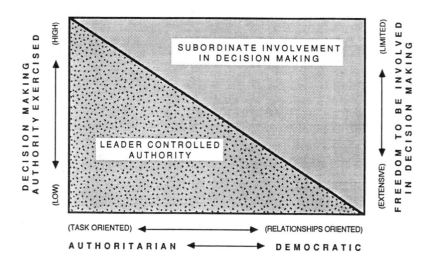

Fig. 12-3 Leader Behavior Can Either Enhance or Restrict the Freedom of Subordinates
(Adapted from Hersey and Blanchard, 1982, 86)

Much depends on the pattern of leadership that we are imposing on our subordinates. If we are autocratic, we are apt to be inclined or even insist on making all the decisions independently, and then expect that these decisions will be carried out. Under such a leadership pattern we will allow subordinates little freedom in decision-making, and thus little opportunity for creativity. Hersey and Blanchard (1982, 86) have depicted graphically the impact on freedom for subordinates when control ranges from autocratic, boss-centered control to democratic, subordinate-centered involvement and control (see Figure 12-3). With freedom to participate and contribute in decision-making we give much more opportunity for creative ideas to be voiced by everyone throughout the unit.

A number of years ago Miles, et al. (1973, 63-67) summarized how changes in leadership patterns and thinking have occurred over several decades (see Table 12-1). Note they started with the traditional model, which was based on assumptions that people considered work as distasteful and only as a source of income, and gave subordinates little opportunity to contribute or to affect productivity and work satisfaction. This changed to where people were found to be desirous of belonging and being recognized as individuals in the human relations model. Then came the human resources model where at last it was found that people want to contribute to meaningful goals, and are far more responsible and creative than previously believed. More recently Peters and Waterman (1982, 14) reported that companies, in which they found "excellence," were encouraging idea contributions and decision-making participation from all employees.

If we involve and allow persons to participate in decisions which affect their work, they will improve in their performance and productivity. French and Caplan (1978, 328) tallied a number of positive results from employee participation in decision-making (see Figure 12-4). From their report it is obvious that health was improved, work attitudes were much better, and people must have been much happier and more creative.

12-4 MORALE BUILDING

Our management and leadership patterns play a significant role in the degree of satisfaction people get from their jobs. One of the most effective ways for our leadership to foster building morale is to help individuals find satisfaction in meeting their own needs. (Refer back to Chapter 10-6 for information on creating an open and supportive atmosphere relating to morale, spirit and optimism). Patten (p. 45, 1981) showed that, while from 50 to 85 percent of people's basic physiological, safety, and belonging needs are satisfied, only 40 percent of their ego needs and 10 percent of their self-actualization needs are fulfilled (see Figure 11-1).

If we give praise, when appropriate, it can be an important element in building morale. Blanchard and Johnson (1982, 44) have emphasized the importance of praise as soon as possible when something has been done right. They indicated that we should look for things that people do right, not for what they do wrong. Blanchard and Peale (1988, 93) have indicated that there is "psychic income" from praise from management. The effectiveness of this is readily understood when we remember that people usually get attention only when they do something wrong. If we recognize what people's reactions to being ignored, criticized or verbally abused are, we can understand them better. We need to treat people with respect. All

PARTICIPATION in DECISION-MAKING

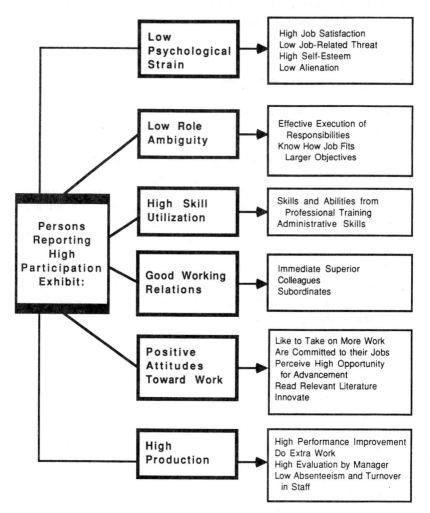

Fig. 12-4 Characteristic Responses of Persons Who Participate in Decisions Which Affect Their Work

(Constructed from text and figure of French and Caplan, 1978, 324-330)

too often we treat persons like things. Nothing is more destructive of morale in a unit than when we follow procedures which disregard people's feelings and insult the dignity of them as individuals. Freeh (1981) said:

As a leader, praise, not criticism is our most useful tool. Most people need periodic indications that their work is acceptable and appreciated. The pleasure of reward motivates people much more than the pain of punishment.

12-5 MANAGING OTHER'S TIME

It is extremely important to remember that as leaders, managers, or supervisors, poor use of time and poor planning can result in not only our own loss of time, but that of many of those under our jurisdiction. All of the items suggested for making the best use of time discussed in Chapter 11-8 apply to us, as leaders, as well as others in our unit. These include our assessing time use, planning ahead, doing high priorities first, avoiding indecision, being realistic in commitments, avoiding negative attitudes, and communicating clearly - up and down. It is critical that we not become the bottleneck in a unit's operation by indecision and delay, nor to have others wasting time by sending them off in a wrong direction because of a bad or hasty decision. In my years of coming up through the ranks in academia, I experienced several kinds of superiors. They ranged from the kind that never seems to be there when you need them and take forever or essentially make no decisions, to the kind who "shoot from the hip," appear to want to make all the decisions, or constantly need to be upstaging everyone. Most of these are frustrating to work with.

In scheduling other's time it is important for us to be considerate at all times. Remember both our superiors and our subordinates are human beings, although we, and they, may at times question that from our, and their, actions. We must use reasonable deadlines. If a "rush job" is not needed, don't ask for it. It is best if we save that request for a time when we are really in a jam and a "rush job" is the only way out.

Role ambiguity can be a big cause of confusion and discontent in many units. As mentioned in Chapter 12-3, we need to make sure individuals know what their job is. We need to be sure we give clear instructions on what it is we want done and when and how we expect it. If we give careless and sloppy instructions, we may encourage sloppy responses. Many times we need to put our instructions in writing, and have the recipient verify that they are understood. We should give reasonable advance notice of task requests and of meetings. If we are arranging for a meeting, we need to confirm dates and times in writing, indicate what we will want from each individual, and supply background information the participants will need to be most capable of contributing when they get there. We should set up systematized procedures where possible to avoid the necessity for repeated detailed instructions.

In working with our superiors, we need to keep them informed of what is happening, and get to know their patterns and idiosyncrasies. We should inform them of the important items, but spare them the trivia. When problems occur, we should propose solutions and go with alternative possible solutions. We should be selective in timing our requests, remind and offer to help when possible, and make it easy for them to reply ("Unless you disagree, I will start working on this next week.").

All too often we delay and avoid facing an unpleasant or difficult task. It is important that we not put off doing the distasteful. It likely will never go away nor get any easier. It will likely disrupt our thinking and consume valuable "free-thought time." Rarely should the distasteful be delegated. However, we shouldn't confuse the distasteful with the difficult. Difficult tasks call for help. We need to take time and think them through carefully. Outline a possible plan and establish a schedule for tackling the difficult task. Do small parts of it at a time. Round up help and delegate parts of it. Broken into pieces the parts may not seem so difficult. One of the important challenges for us, as leaders, is effective delegation.

12-6 DELEGATING

If we are fulfilling our responsibilities as leaders, managers, or supervisors, we will be expected, sooner or later, to face up to the problem of delegating tasks. Delegation goes beyond just making the decision to get or assign help. Even though we could do some routine things, such as drawing, typing, cleaning, routine analysis, etc., the question is, "Would it be better use of our time if we delegated a particular activity or farmed the activity out or hired it done rather than taking the time to do it ourselves?" A number of symptoms that signal that we should be delegating certain tasks include:

1. working longer hours than our subordinates;
2. taking work home routinely;
3. skipping vacations;
4. continuously rushing to meet deadlines;
5. rarely if ever feeling like there is time to relax a bit and think;
6. making most or all of the decisions;
7. doing routine or technical tasks;
8. frequently checking the work of many others;
9. finding ourselves the bottle neck to many operations;
10. often bothered for advice;
11. frequently overruling other's decisions; and
12. often finding that there is no one available to fill in for us when our presence is required elsewhere (based in part on McConkey 1977, 10-11).

In an administrative workshop in the early 1980's at the University of Minnesota, Hoyt (1977) made some suggestions concerning the how, what, whom, and when of delegation. He suggested the following:

1. Delegate only what someone else can do in less time than it takes us to do ourselves UNLESS:

   a. it is a repetitive chore;
   b. we can train someone to do it for us; or
   c. we are training our successor.

   (Perhaps it should be - delegate only to people better able than we are to do the job, and this may be capability or simply a matter of available time.)

2. Remember, when we delegate we are giving authority, but retaining ultimate responsibility.
3. Lose our pride of authorship - if we ask someone to do it for us, don't rewrite to our style (It has always provoked me to have my writing redone, if my words clearly conveyed the desired thoughts).
4. Delegate up in writing with background materials or down by note or verbally.
5. Finally, we should always back up the delegatee in public and reproach privately.

Some common mistakes we make in delegating have been suggested by Baker and Holmberg (1981, 19-20). Their list has included:

1. delegating only trivial or unappealing tasks;
2. dumping tasks;
3. creating responsibility without authority;
4. exerting too little or too much control; and
5. delegating too much.

For most of us there is a great tendency to underestimate the capabilities of our subordinates. That fact, combined with our experiences of earlier days when supplementary help was not available, tends to cause us to do too many things ourselves rather than utilizing the capabilities of our help. Effective delegation is an art and a skill which we must work at constantly if, as a team, we are to be most effective.

Learning to carefully and appropriately delegate responsibility can increase effectiveness and productivity. Freeh (1981) has said:

No one is truly a leader until he has learned the art of delegating responsibility to others. This includes getting out of the way to let them do it - and yet following up to see that it has been done. A good leader lets people alone to do a job. But having delegated a job or responsibility, he doesn't simply fade out of the picture. He stays in touch - and keeps control - by following the process.

12-7 MINIMIZING STRESS

If we as leaders, managers, and supervisors understand stresses and create an encouraging climate we often can help reduce stress and other potentially adverse effects and make both the individual and the unit more productive. We need to be aware of stressful situations and signs in individuals. Some actions that may help include:

- avoid underemployment;
- relieve individuals from overload, overanxiety, and over-commitment;
- offer training and opportunity for maintaining health, nutrition, exercise, relaxation and rest;
- deal with conflict promptly; and
- counsel individuals where things aren't going well.

12-7.1 Getting the New Person Started

Role ambiguity, role conflict and limits to participation can cause considerable stress for new individuals in our groups. Special attention needs to be given to getting new members started effectively in their new roles. As indicated earlier, we must be sure that individuals' roles, and where they fit in the unit, have been clearly defined. Make sure specific work objectives and responsibilities have been made clear, and both employees and employers see these the same way and agree upon them. Also, be sure there is agreement on immediate and future expectations and opportunities.

We need to keep a close watch and give guidance even after individuals have gotten started. All too frequently, especially in situations where individuals are expected to work on their own, new persons are left without guidance. Sometimes a policy of having an experienced employee help guide a newcomer in a kind of big brother - big sister arrangement can work well, and is often an assist to us as managers. We should give appropriate constructive criticism early when deserved (and done in a considerate manner).

12-7.2 Avoiding and Managing Conflict

In his discussion of conflict, Lippitt (1982, 150-156) indicated that corporate executives and managers devote 24 percent of their time to conflict management. School and hospital administrators, mayors and city managers, and leaders and managers in similar fields reported 49 percent of their time consumed by conflict. Causes reported included: misunderstanding (communication failure), personality clashes, value and goal differences, substandard performance, differences over method, responsibility issues, lack of cooperation, authority issues, frustration and irritability, competition for limited resources, and noncompliance with rules and policies.

Some of the factors in the work place which predispose people to unnecessary conflict, which we should be alert for, as summarized by Lippitt (p.154) included:

- poorly defined responsibilities and ranges of authority;
- interunit goals which place members at cross purposes;
- unreasonable pressure and pace in the organization;
- conditions which jeopardize job security;
- overly competitive climate fostered by management;
- favoritism;
- punitive, accusative, or threatening style of treatment by a unit manager;

- unclear and arbitrary standards for advancement and promotion;
- overly secretive and competitive organizational politics;
- great confusion or uncertainty about upcoming major changes or upheavals in the organization; and
- inability of employees to define their future roles and interactions.

There can be a real challenge for us as leaders, managers and supervisors to keep the above conditions from developing and thus diminish the frequency with which conflict is likely to occur. But, it is better for us to spend time in developing conditions that help to avoid conflict rather than spending an inordinate amount of time dealing with conflict. As a result all will likely be much happier, more creative, and more productive.

12-7-3 General Management Practices

Paying close attention to those things that will help avoid conflict, maintaining good communications, presenting opportunities for individual growth and renewal, as well as opportunities for relief from some of the tensions, are usually helpful to everyone and usually will diminish the frequency and severity of stress. As unit leaders, we can play a predominant role in helping to anticipate these adversities and encourage unit members to turn them into opportunities.

We also need to give attention to encouraging cooperation among members internally, as well as with those in other units and disciplines. Mid-career and late-career members may also need help in staying productive.

Time stresses and numerous factors which can lead to "burnout" strike people at all ages. Good time management practices, minimizing stresses, and an awareness of factors that lead to burnout usually prove helpful, especially if we make efforts to cope with them before conditions become too serious.

Fear is a major stressing factor. Therefore it behooves us, as leaders, to keep in mind what Dale (1969) put so aptly:

Justice diminishes fear; injustice creates and nourishes it. And the searing memories of injustice far outlast the correction of the injustice. The good society replaces fear with courage.

As good leaders, we can play a key role in minimizing the development of fear among members of a unit by making sure that justice prevails as completely as possible within our unit.

12-8 PLANNING

Lippitt (1982, 63) has defined planning as "...a description of what we want to accomplish in the future and the means for achieving these objectives." Lippitt has suggested that:

> ...planning must include good data collection, appropriate involvement, consequence assessment, action taking, evaluation, and provision of flexibility for change and replanning.

Many managers feel uncomfortable with planning or do it haphazardly. It may be that such managers want to make most of the decisions themselves and feel they have the plan in their own heads. Lippitt reported that goal setting by non-organizational development oriented companies was done largely by top or top and middle management. However, in organizational development oriented companies, goal setting was done with all management levels, and even work groups involved in many instances. This is similar to what Peters and Waterman (1982, 16) indicated for excellent companies and their commitment to people.

If, as leaders, we choose to make all planning decisions ourselves, we are likely not only to miss good ideas, but we will also likely get less interest and response from our employees in implementing plans. Because of this, if we insist, we may become the "bottleneck" to operations and productivity. This may be especially true for us if we fail to gather the appropriate information and make a habit of "shooting from the hip."

Careful planning can help us in avoiding a lot of wasted time. Blanchard and Peale (1988, 118) have said:

> If we take care in the beginning, the end will take care of itself.

This suggests that we need to make planning a constant endeavor. But other activities should not come to a halt for planning to get under way. In my experience a five-year plan with an annual update proved to work well. We can be fairly specific for one year in advance, less so for two and subsequent years. Of course we must plan for some things with a longer lead time. With an annual update priorities may have changed and some activity originally planned for three or four years hence may need to be moved up to an earlier year.

It thus appears that important items in developing plans should include taking time to plan, setting clearly defined goals, developing specific objectives, doing it on a regular basis, involving those affected, following through on implementation, and evaluating the results.

Although we have emphasized much regarding frequent and careful planning, there can be a danger in over-planning and in too much rigidity and sticking too closely to previous plans. There needs to be flexibility enough so that we can seize unforeseen opportunities, and change plans in light of new or unexpected developments. However, over-planning should not be carried to an extreme which can result in "paralysis by analysis." In essence this means we need to "get on with implementation," and don't go on planning forever. A balance between planning and implementation should be sought.

Lippitt (1982, 67-68) has suggested that managers need to be aware that effective planning:

1. Is based on clear goals.
2. Is based upon an image of the future.
3. Requires continuous input of reliable information.
4. Needs intelligent, appropriate, and enthusiastic participation.
5. Must be kept simple, practical, flexible, measurable, and comprehensible.
6. Should minimize paperwork.
7. Should make use of professional help.
8. Should assess consequences.
9. Should result in taking appropriate action.
10. Should include evaluation of results.
11. Should serve as a basis for further planning.

12-9 GOAL SETTING

Organizations and units within them are usually established to accomplish certain general purposes. We should have some general intent and focus in setting up a unit. This is called the objective of the overall unit or specific parts of it. To meet the general aims (objectives) of the unit, we usually set up goals. This involves our defining what specifically has to be done, setting priorities and some kind of time frame in which it is to be done, who will be responsible, how progress is to be evaluated, and what the controls will be. This is the goal setting process.

If we give all levels within the organization an opportunity to express their views in setting up goals for a unit, we then will have better chances of coming up with clear goals that all will understand and be willing to pursue. It is important to pay attention to those who will benefit from the output of the unit that is doing the goal setting. The process comes down to attempting to satisfy those involved in producing a product or service, those who manage and control the effort, and perhaps most important of all, those who will be the users, consumers or benefactors of what has been done.

Implementation, control and evaluation of the goals that have been set become the responsibility of management, especially. However, much is to be gained if all levels of employees realize that each individual has a responsibility for turning out a quality product or service. Each must take pride in what has been done in order to feel that what has been done is of value and they have contributed.

12-10 EVALUATION

Leaders, managers and supervisors all must shoulder the responsibilities for evaluating, not only the program, but the personnel who are involved. Performance appraisals can help to promote job understanding, aid employee development, provide factual information for employee raises and promotions, and maintain congruency between job expectation and job description.

Blanchard and Peale (1988, 98) have emphasized the value of and need for good, solid performance reviews and evaluations. Properly designed and properly used they can encourage feedback, encourage individual growth, and help build self-esteem. For the results to be motivational and increase pride in the organization, emphasis in the review needs to be placed on what people are doing right. When improperly used and people are attacked or are not dealt with in a truthful manner, they lose their respect for and pride in the organization.

It is important, if we are at the management level, that we look for and reward creative, positive, and productive individuals. Such an evaluation needs to be done on a regular basis and the results communicated to each individual. While at least an annual, thorough review should be conducted, we should make much more frequent contact. It helps if we become acquainted, hear how things are going, and give praise or constructive criticism to the employee so that there are no big surprises at the annual review. At the annual review we should have a more complete two-way discussion. It is important for us to face up to and communicate the need for change, making sure an open dialogue occurs with both sides staying receptive to:

1. seek constructive criticism;
2. listen to feedback;
3. jointly set goals for individual accomplishment;
4 stay aware of personnel needs and wishes; and
5. offer opportunities for growth and development.

During the review, as managers, we may want to assess (depending on the person's responsibilities) such things as the employee's abilities to communicate, analyze, make decisions, work independently, understand instructions, plan, organize work, initiate ideas, meet objectives, evaluate, follow through, work well with others, supervise others, and train others. These should give us some indication of such general characteristics as job knowledge, dependability, decisiveness, judgement, quality and quantity of work, pride of work, performance under pressure, ability to deal with varying situations, readiness to assume responsibility, response to criticism and suggestions, and level of creativity.

We can make evaluations orally or written, but if written they should be discussed in an open, free exchange. It is valuable if we give individuals an opportunity for self-evaluation with the same instrument used by the official evaluator. Then the opinions of both can be discussed. People usually realize their strengths and weaknesses before being told about them. Sometimes peer evaluations are valuable, for managers may not have had an opportunity to get to know the persons as well as others who have worked closer to them.

Fairness and objectivity in reviewing and evaluating every individual is extremely important. It is most destructive (as I have experienced) when personnel people require managers or unit leaders to rate people on a normal curve, as though there is a problem if no one gets a poor rating. Under such conditions unit leaders who have helped to develop a group of outstanding persons, are forced to rate some persons down. This is a gross injustice to some of the outstanding members of the unit, and, in a sense, is punishment for personnel and leaders who have succeeded in building units with a high proportion of outstanding personnel.

12-11 MANAGERIAL BLOCKS TO CREATIVITY

Superiors, especially persons in managerial roles, probably affect creativity more than any other factor, except for individuals themselves. All too many who serve in leadership, managerial, or supervisory roles are firmly convinced that they must guide, direct, control and/or manipulate those under their jurisdiction to get them to be creative. In fact, attempting too hard to do just that may cause the end result to be just the opposite. This may actually cause individual creative capabilities to be lessened.

12-11.1 Failing to Supply an Encouraging Atmosphere

Freeh (1981) pointed out that as administrators (leaders, managers, etc.) we create three atmospheres in conjunction with our requests and activities which influence how subordinates will react to those requests. The first he called a:

• *"Discourage" Atmosphere* - This one may often be inadvertent. It signals "Don't bother" or "It's not really important." Among our actions which signal discouragement to the recipient are such things as:

1. I'll do it myself ("I don't think you can do this to suit me.").
2. Setting unrealistic goals.
3. Making contradictory and conflicting policies.
4. Showing a lack of interest.
5. Failing to reward or reinforce.
6. Issuing unclear directions.
7. Giving promotions for reasons other than performance.
8. Telling the person, "Forget that stuff."
9. Killing their ideas.
10. Failing to provide the necessary support funds, policies, directives.
11. Setting up impossible procedures or structures.

All too often, if we are leaders of this type we may become, as Blanchard and Peale (1988, 108) have labelled them:

Sea gull managers - they fly in, make a lot of noise, dump on everyone, and then fly out.

A most devastating action which causes a discouraging atmosphere is implying that others' opinions or actions are worthless. There are a number of ways in which we can convey this kind of a message. All of the following ways of "How to kill and idea" fit that category:

1. Agree to it, but don't do it.

2. Insist it go through channels.
3. Be a foot dragger.
4. Insist on a full analysis.
5. Wait for more information.
6. Insist on sticking to protocol.
7. Avoid any sense of urgency.
8. Be sure everybody approves.
9. Call lots of meetings.
10. Never follow up.
11. Don't spend time or money if things are going well.
12. If the idea didn't originate with you, don't waste time on it.

- An "Allow" atmosphere - This atmosphere is created by our actions which tend to signal "It's OK, in fact I encourage time and attention to this area," but actions speak louder than words. Actions may include such things as:

1. Sending a memo or letter (without any follow up).
2. Holding a staff meeting (without follow up).
3. Providing some resources, but not enough to properly do the task.
4. Holding some training sessions and seminars (without follow up).
5. Setting some deadlines (without follow up).
6. Promising a reward or punishment (without follow up).

All actions lead other people to believe we didn't want the effort to succeed after all.

- The "Causal" Atmosphere - This is an atmosphere in which we are so enthusiastic that it practically forces all members to perform. This kind of an atmosphere is characterized by such things as:

1. Discussing specific aspects of program planning and implementation with unit members periodically.
2. Giving recognition and rewards to members on a continuing basis including negative recognition (on a one-to-one basis) when necessary.
3. Getting personally involved in program planning and implementation (but not to the extent of doing it for the members).
4. Setting reasonable deadlines and holding people to them.
5. Talking to subordinates informally between scheduled reviews.

6. Asking specific questions.
7. Developing a structured counseling and performance evaluation procedure.

The causal atmosphere results when we constantly apply gentle pressure without giving the impression of trying to force.

If administrators, leaders, managers, and supervisors create an atmosphere of discouragement we will likely get a negative response from the members of the unit. They will be likely to feel uncooperative, be anti-administration, lack interest in what they are doing, and morale will likely be low. The results over all will probably be a lower level of productivity, and a lower level of creativity than the potential for the unit. An allow atmosphere will be somewhat better in that there are apt to be less anti-leader feelings expressed, but potential productivity and creativity will still likely be below par. Usually, if we create a causal atmosphere, creativity will come out, opportunities will be seized, productivity will increase, and morale will be raised. If we fail to recognize the impact we have on members of our unit and miss out on developing a causal atmosphere we are probably missing an opportunity for a more productive, higher morale unit that will be more progressive, make changes more easily, and will have happier group members.

12-11.2 Failing to Keep Personnel Involved

As leaders at all levels, we must be people-oriented to be most effective. We must practice "interpersonal relational power" methods (see Chapter 8-6), listen to feedback, and keep people involved in order to get maximum performance.

Freeh (1981) advised us that several ways to help keep people involved include:

1. Believing in people and showing it.
2. Giving them all the responsibility and authority they can handle.
3. Including them in what's going on.
4. Assigning them responsibilities which are important in their eyes - and which they can take pride in doing.
5. Letting them share the spotlight.
6. Taking a sincere interest in them as individuals and in the programs for which they are responsible.
7. Never belittling or ridiculing them.
8. Asking for and listening to their advice.
9. Confiding in them whenever possible.

10. Letting them know how much we appreciate their work.
11. Counseling and assisting them when they need help or aren't performing as well as they should.
12. Telling them if we are dissatisfied with their performance - and taking any necessary action as needed.

Freeh emphasized that too many of us shirk our responsibilities in the latter two areas - and it isn't fair to the person who isn't performing up to standard or to the people who are.

When we fail to recognize the potential effectiveness of the above suggestions and insist on using our unilateral power tactics (see Chapter 8-5) we will likely find that we do not develop many potentially independent leaders within the membership of our units, and the tactics we have been using must always be applied to get action. If members of the unit do not learn to act independently, they can never be expected to be effective independent actors. On the other hand, as people-oriented leaders, probabilities are high that we will develop many potentially capable leaders.

12-11.3 Failing to Communicate Effectively

Our behavior as leaders in a group can affect communications positively or negatively. If we are open and communicative, members of our group will likely be also. If we are not communicative, neither will our unit members be so. Failure to communicate can be a most destructive situation in a unit. Considerable discussion of various aspects of communication were covered in Chapter 8-10. If we are non-communicative leaders we tend to keep our unit members in the dark concerning what is happening and what they are supposed to do and will be doing. This is sometimes called the "mushroom" technique, "Keep them in the dark and feed them a lot of barnyard fertilizer." Such a management practice is likely to require a lot of our time in cleaning up the messes that are thus created. This is also apt to be true if we are "shoot-from-the-hip" managers. Without regular clear directions and information, none of our members can be very effective. If we are non-communicative unit leaders, we will likely not be nearly as effective as we might be.

Even as communicative unit leaders we can negatively affect communications by arousing members to too high a level of competitiveness. As Johnson and Johnson (1987, 193) have indicated, when we generate too competitive an atmosphere, people are threatened or anticipate a threat and become defensive. Defensive persons spend a lot of energy to defend themselves. They worry about how they can outdo others, how they are perceived by others, how to impress their leaders, how to protect themselves, etc., and as a result they become less communicative. Johnson and Johnson have cited evidence that defensive behavior has been shown to be correlated with losses in efficiency and effectiveness in communication. Under such conditions, ideas are not proposed or conveyed, directions may not be given clearly, and competitiveness in one member of a group breeds competitiveness in others. If we convey disinterest, this also arouses defensive behavior.

Whether through a simple lack of communication, or inciting behavior that leads to defensiveness and the resultant impairment of communication, we need to be aware that good communications are essential for productivity and creativity.

12-11.4 Failing to Use Effective Administrative Practices

One of the most detrimental factors for a unit is to be saddled with leaders who do not know what they should be doing. This includes not only the technical aspects of the task that is to be performed, but equally, and maybe even more importantly, how to implement effective administrative practices to help the unit members accomplish the task.

It is most devastating if we lack respect for ourselves and for others. With such an attitude we are apt to be dominating, making decisions that should be made by others and over-riding decisions of subordinates to whom we have given authority to act. We will frequently criticize in public, show favoritism, be unfair in our practices, apply double standards (one set for ourselves and another set for unit members), and may even be unethical in what we do. We may claim credit for other's ideas, be dishonest, lie often, and cover up or blame others for our own mistakes. Usually, as such individuals, we fail to set standards (especially for ourselves) and uphold them. We seldom recognize, praise and reward good work and new ideas. We fail miserably as far as serving as a model for the group, but think we are excelling. Few unit members approve of our actions, and a majority are unhappy with their unit and the job they are able to do under the circumstances.

Such leaders are obviously misfits and do much to impair individual creativity and productivity. They could gain much from learning from Hoyt's (1977) list of needed managerial competencies:

1. He considered listening actively, giving clear and effective

instructions, accepting one's share of responsibilities for problems, and identifying real problems as super-critical needs.

2. He said managing time, setting priorities, giving recognition for excellent performance, communicating effectively, obtaining and providing feedback in two-way communication sessions, and being able to shift priorities if necessary, as highly critical.

3. A third level of competencies he called critical. These included: writing effectively, preparing action plans, defining job qualifications, effectively implementing unit changes, explaining and using cost reduction methods, preparing and operating within a budget, developing written goals, justifying new personnel and equipment, participating in meetings and seminars, and reading.

Hoyt's list is demanding, but certainly can increase considerably our chances of success as leaders at most levels.

12-11.5 Failing to Keep Individuals and the Unit Renewed and Growing

If our management styles fall short of giving the individuals of a unit the opportunity for renewal and growth, we are ultimately likely to lose many of our better and more capable members. Such units are not likely to develop many leaders within the unit. Furthermore, many members of such a unit are apt to grow restless and become unhappy. Those who stay will likely be those with lower ambitions. Thus maximum creativity and productivity will likely be stalemated. Unit members and leaders should be urged to participate in training "on-the-job," and developing new and extended capabilities through workshops, and enrichment programs.

12-12 HIGHLIGHTS OF CHAPTER TWELVE

1. No organization, institution, or unit can function smoothly nor be productive without effective leadership and management.

2. Without dynamic leaders (managers, coordinators, supervisors), as members of a unit, we are likely to be confused, squabbling, and going in different directions or failing to be real contributors to a unified effort.

3. As unit leaders we should constantly strive to keep the unit informed, renewed, enthusiastic, and moving toward the unit

and organizational goals.
4. As leaders we should show great respect for all individuals and be able to bring out the best in them. We should set and be exemplary role models for others.
5. Some desirable inner characteristics for us as leaders are: honesty, loyalty, courtesy, courage, tolerance, modesty, and self-respect.
6.. Other characteristics we need as leaders include: quick perception, good judgement, promptness, tenacity of purpose, resourcefulness, ambition, thoroughness, and high standards.
7. As leaders or managers we should possess good skills and effectiveness in communicating, delegating, planning, evaluating, and an ability to motivate (ourselves and others) and follow through.
8. In leading we should encourage and help every member of the unit to contribute new and creative ways of doing things to improve unit effectiveness.

12-13 AFTERGROWTH STIMULATORS

1. List three ways that your own creativity has been enhanced by the actions of a superior or leader at your workplace. On a committee. In a recreational club or group.
2. List three ways that your creativity has been impaired by a superior, leader or supervisor.
3. What actions by a leader or superior give your morale the greatest boost?
4. How do you react when jobs or responsibilities are delegated to you? What makes the assignment pleasant and easy? What makes it difficult or irritating?
5. Do you enjoy being in on the overall planning and goal setting for a project even if your responsibility will only be for a part of the total effort? Why or why not?
6. Do you think evaluations of your performance are valuable? What conditions can make them most valuable to you? What might make them most detrimental?

CHAPTER 13

ORGANIZATIONAL AND INSTITUTIONAL GROWTH, CHANGE, AND IMPACT

13- 1 Introduction
13- 2 Profile of a Creative, Productive
      Organization
13- 3 Selecting Creative Personnel
13- 4 Developing Balanced, Dynamic
      Leadership
13- 5 Organizational Values and Principles
13- 6 Treatment of Persons
13- 7 Developing a Creative Environment
13- 8 Recognizing the Need for and
      Implementing Change
13- 9 Guidelines for Managing Change
13-10 Encouraging Creativity Through
      Management and Organization
13-11 Minimizing Organizational
      and Institutional Drag
13-12 Preventing Organizational Dry Rot
13-13 Highlights of Chapter Thirteen
13-14 Aftergrowth Stimulators

13-1 INTRODUCTION

Organizations and institutions in their infancy are usually open, flexible, innovative and largely free of rigid rules, regulations and practices. As they grow and age they tend to become more rigid, less flexible, and more bureaucratic. This does, in fact, seem to be the situation in a high proportion of most organizations. Senge (1984) has said that:

> In most organizations people see themselves as trapped within a "system" that is too large, too complex, and too indifferent for them to have any meaningful impact.

Yet in recent years things seem to be changing as also noted by Senge:

> In the organizations we see emerging, people come to believe that they can determine their destiny. They believe that through responsible participation they can empower themselves and others to create the type of organization and life they truly want.

Peters and Waterman (1982), in their extensive search for excellent companies, found that excellence and involvement of personnel at all levels seemed to go together.

An effective organization must be made up of creative individuals, leaders and groups or units that clearly understand the overall goals and objectives of the organization as a whole. Each individual, each team, and each unit must clearly understand the role that each should be playing in order for the overall effort to be most productive.

Throughout the organization, there must be dynamic leadership, with the skills and determination to mold each individual and group into productive and contributing units. This means, as a whole, that the organization must be people-oriented and effective in communicating and rewarding individuals and groups. Careful planning and establishing clear cut goals is a must. But a looseness and flexibility to accept new ideas and accommodate rapid changes are essential.

The organization must provide a stimulating and challenging environment for the members of the separate contributing units so that they become enthusiastically committed, not only to their own creative endeavors but also to the overall productivity of their team and the organization.

No individual or organization should attempt to operate without serious thinking and planning for what they wish to accomplish or for what changes must be made to continue effectively. Change is often painful and thus is avoided or purposefully neglected. We all resist change. Thus changes for us as individuals and for our organizations must be carefully planned, the objectives clearly communicated to those affected, and our moves judicially managed if the goals are to be reached. Continuous evaluation of individuals and programs should be integrated parts of our planning efforts. Planning enables us and our unit to better understand where we are and what must be done to move toward a productive and satisfying future. However planning should be a continuing part of our normal operations and should not become the cause of continuing "paralysis by analysis."

Organizations that have a high "can do attitude," usually, not only foster creativity, but also are effective in many ways. Controlling members of such organizations strive to succeed in:

- staffing with creative individuals and dynamic leaders;
- developing effective teams;
- communicating organizational goals;
- pushing for excellence;
- offering opportunity for advancement and reward;
- avoiding becoming an institutional "dead hand on discovery"; and
- making changes and avoiding organizational dry rot.

Achievement of these aims usually result in a high probability that the organization will become creative and productive.

13-2 PROFILE OF A CREATIVE, PRODUCTIVE ORGANIZATION

Many things stated or alluded to above are critical to the development of a productive and creative organization. Steiner (1965) identified the following characteristics of creative organizations, they:

- include unusual types of people;
- have open channels of communication;
- encourage contacts with outside sources;
- experiment with new ideas rather than prejudging on "rational" grounds - everything gets a chance;
- are not run as a "tight-ship";
- let employees have fun;
- reward people who have ideas;
- evaluate ideas on merits, not according to the status of the originator;

- allow new, ad hoc approaches to emerge; and,
- have risk-taking ethos - tolerate and expect taking chances.

In highlighting the characteristics of companies that they found were "excelling," Peters and Waterman (1982, 13-15) echoed the Steiner list and cited eight characteristics that seemed to predominate. The first that they cited was "A bias for action." They said that:

What is striking is the host of practical devices the excellent companies employ, to maintain corporate fleetness of foot and counter the stultification that almost inevitably comes with size.

This is similar to what Ranftl (1978, 103-105) also listed as a common indicator in his profile of a productive organization as "The organization has a 'can-do' attitude." They are quick to get things done. A strong team spirit prevails and small groups are quickly pulled together to suggest action when a problem occurs. There is a genuine sense of commitment and loyalty, and a confidence and trust between administration and workers that enables the group to come up with a possible solution and implement it.

The second characteristic Peters and Waterman listed was "Close to the customer." This is essentially what Ranftl indicated as "The organization operates in a sound, competitive manner." There is commitment to producing a product (service) that is consistent with user (audience, student, population) needs and demands and to delivering a product of "unparalleled quality, service, and reliability" in a timely fashion and at a reasonable cost. The producer listens, stays in touch, up-todate, accountable, and sensitive to the user's changing needs and desires. This also encompasses the item that Ranftl referred to as "The organization has high standards."

The next item Ranftl mentioned was "The organization has a creative and productive atmosphere." Peters and Waterman called their third item "Autonomy and entrepreneurship." Creativity is encouraged and rewarded throughout the organization. Practical risk taking is encouraged. Making mistakes is anticipated, for an atmosphere prevails which implies "nothing ventured, nothing gained." Open and effective communication exchange is encouraged among the various disciplines and technologies involved in the operations. Idea swapping is commonplace.

Peters and Waterman listed the fourth item as "Productivity through people." Ranftl stated this as "The organization is effectively staffed and is people-oriented." Essentially this means respect for every individual. Effective and outstanding management leadership respects the employees and vice versa. All personnel are kept informed by effective "up, down, and sideways" internal communication methods. Individual responsibilities are carefully matched to individual capabilities. Individual differences are aired, honored, listened to, and given consideration. This also encompasses the fifth Peters and Waterman item of "Hands-on, value driven." Those controlling operations in the organization make a special effort to stay in touch with employees at all levels. Bosses know the people, the people see and know the bosses.

The sixth characteristic listed for excelling companies was "Stick to the knitting." Those controlling excellent organizations are cautious about diversifying too widely or spreading too thin. They stick to doing the thing(s) they do well. This helps them insure living up to "high standards," as Ranftl mentioned. The seventh item, "Simple form, lean staff," helps the organization avoid having too many bosses compared to the number of workers involved. It is far better to have the members of separate units organized so that they are making many of the decisions and are largely regulating themselves.

The Peters and Waterman eighth characteristic of "Excellent" companies was their "Simultaneous loose-tight properties." They decentralize by relegating a lot of the decision making to the teams and subgroups, while holding vigorously to the central values and principles that make for quality service and products that fulfill and fit user needs and demands. Thus it is obvious that many factors go to make up a creative and productive organization (see Table 13-1).

Because of the importance of the individuals involved and the impact they have on what any organization or institution becomes, we must consider personnel, the individuals and leaders, the most critical component of any organization. Thus creative individuals, dynamic leaders, and effective teams must form the personnel base. They must possess the knowledge, talents, and technical know-how for the task at hand. They must be skilled in promoting interpersonal relationships which allow and promote maximum performance and cooperation with and among the other members of the unit. There should be an optimal and maximal utilization of individual abilities, and full commitment to the task, unit and organization.

Fran Tarkenton, in one of his video presentations, said that three major things are important if we want to get productivity. These are:

1. Keep everyone involved - share their ideas, reinforce

Table 13-1
Characteristics of the Good Organization

1. Is, above all else, a learning organization, growing, moving forward and improving.
2. Makes peace (and peace is more than the absence of war), and avoids actions causing fear.
3. Replaces fear with courage.
4. Honors all its members, not just a chosen few.
5. Is sensitive and gentle, not harsh and rough, not rigid, but flexible, pliant, generous and courteous.
6. Is a thinking organization, one which not only tolerates ambiguity, but welcomes it.
7. Constantly puts before its members the models of good men and good women.
8. Counts its costs - the cost of desired action and of negligence, socially as well as economically.
9. Sets up a time table for evaluation and needed changes and reforms.
10. Is a disciplined organization.
11. Arranges quiet times and places for its members.

Constructed from text of Dale, 1969, 1-4.

them. He suggested that we think of the successful organizations - Boy Scouts, Service Clubs, etc.
2. Have everyone be accountable - if we don't there is sure to be waste. Each should be willing to accept accountability, for it is the means of rewarding people (those who produce).
3. Maintain constant feed-back related to specific performance. Reinforcement that is too general misses the mark and is not nearly as effective. Be positive (teachers who were most effective were found to be positive four times to one negative). Make the negative constructively corrective.

13-3 SELECTING CREATIVE PERSONNEL

Many segments of the previous discussions in this book have focused on developing creative individuals and dynamic leaders and finding ways to bring out untapped creative resources in ourselves and in others. Organizations and institutions must find creative individuals, those with creative - mental capacities, attitudes, expertise, self-discipline, interpersonal relational interacting capacities, ambition, and balance. Attracting such persons to the organization does not just happen by accident. We must vigorously recruit and convince them that they are going to become part of an organization that is going places and offers a future for them.

13-3.1 Finding and Attracting Creative Individuals

As creative individuals we usually seek to become part of an active, productive unit. The reputation and past record of the organization or unit plays an important role in attracting us. We are usually looking for what the opportunities will be to contribute and excel in the new position. We ought to find out what the possibilities are for recognition and advancement. We need to know where and just how we can relate and fit in. We should be assured that we will be treated with dignity and respect. Our opportunities of being heard when we have new and constructive ideas will be highly important to us. We also need assurance that there will be strong administrative support for what we will be doing. Of course, we should ultimately discuss the appropriateness and adequacy of the salary, and the opportunity and potential for earned increases.

At the time of the interview for the position it is important to be sure that, as applicants, we match reasonably well what the organization wants. As candidates we should have the opportunity to visit with potential co-workers as well as future bosses. Openness is important. It is far better for us, as well as for the organization, to learn of a possible mismatch before the hiring than have either be disappointed and unhappy afterwards. Some well worded, open ended questions can reveal a great deal about our capabilities to relate to realities within the organization, as well as the dreams and visions of those managing the organization. Our hopes for the future should match those of the organization. What would we like to be doing five years from now? In 10 years? What life-time goals can we envision? What are those of the organization?

It may be wise if we are controlling the organization to remember that with the focus on individual rights and affirmative action in recent years, and the frequent difficulties in dismissing a person, especially in many government and public funded areas, a careless hiring may be locking the unit into the presence of a new and undesirable individual for a considerable period of time. Likewise, the individual risks losing a great deal and suffering considerable anxiety if a mismatch is made. Whereas, both may profit greatly from a proper match.

13-3.2 Developing Effective Teams

Another important aspect that we need to keep in mind in selecting personnel for an organization is that of finding individuals who are willing to become team members. Many organizations find that team and small group subdivisions are the most effective way of organizing for creative and productive challenges. In fact, Peters and Waterman (1982, 125-130) found that one of the characteristics of organizations that excelled, was their reliance on small groups for carrying out many of the more important tasks. They said:

Small groups are, quite simply, the basic organizational building blocks of excellent companies. There is an underlying principle here, an important trait of the action orientation that we call "chunking." That simply means breaking things up to facilitate organizational fluidity and to encourage action. The action-oriented bits and pieces come under many labels - champions, teams, task forces, czars, project centers, skunk works, and quality circles - but they seldom show up on the formal organization chart or the corporate phone directory.

They indicated that, "The true power of the small group lies in its flexibility."

Characteristics of these small groups are that they usually consist of ten or fewer members, their reporting level and the seniority of the members are usually proportional to the importance of the problem, their duration is usually limited, membership is usually voluntary, they are pulled together rapidly and as needed, follow up is quick, no staff are assigned, and documentation is usually informal and often scant. Communications are underscored and contacts between and among members are intense. They are usually encouraged to experiment. They are truly action groups. Peters and Waterman (1982, 145) indicated that:

These ad hoc devices won't work unless the environment supports fluidity and informality, experimenting won't work if the context is wrong. Management has to be tolerant of leaky systems; it has to accept mistakes, support bootlegging, roll with unexpected changes, and encourage champions.

If, as part of the organizational leadership and management, we are not in favor of this kind of an approach to encourage creativity, these procedures, used by many excellent organizations, simply will not work.

13-4   DEVELOPING BALANCED, DYNAMIC LEADERSHIP

Success of an organization or institution is first and foremost dependent upon balanced, dynamic leadership. Many and varied leadership styles can and do work, depending upon many circumstances and influencing factors. In practically every situation the leaders need to be creative, imaginative, dedicated and dynamic. They must be capable of making things happen, and this means they must be able to motivate others to do things.

In his study of organizations in industry, government, and education (involving some 2,350 managers and senior technical personnel), Ranftl (1978, 100-102) characterized "ideal" outstanding leaders. He found they were described as those individuals who *set a particularly positive example* as a person. They were unusually competent, had quality and quickness of mind, and were particularly creative, innovative, and non-traditional. They were highly self-motivated, self-confident, and self-directing, and had a high level of deserved self-respect and self-esteem. They had extremely high integrity, values, and standards, and usually stood above organizational politics and gamesmanship. They were dedicated, hard working, high vitality persons with a firm sense of purpose and commitment (never self-serving). They were strongly positive and displayed total self-command. They were continually searching, learning, developing, evolving and expanding. They were winners.

He also found that they were characterized as persons who *take a dynamic approach to activities.* They were action oriented with a compelling drive to accomplish and achieve. They had persuasive personalities and were tenacious and willing to stand up and be counted. They were visionary, quick to size up the merit of people, ideas, and opportunities, continually seeking new and better ways, and were constantly seeking and seeing new challenges and new fields to conquer.

He found further that they *bring out the best in people.* They are strongly people-oriented, have great respect for human dignity, and are especially skillful in motivating people. They have well defined goals and are able to clearly communicate them to their subordinates. They instill confidence and generate enthusiasm and a can-do attitude in all actions. They are especially skilled in helping subordinates achieve their full potential. They *demonstrate great skill in directing day-to-day operations.* They are able to integrate various facets of the action, have a strong sense of timing, and an uncanny knack of cutting through complexities. They develop and control workable plans in an "elegantly" simplistic way. We need to pay attention also to an individual potential leader's particular skills. In picking potential assistant leaders we have a great tendency to pick persons who will largely agree with the decisions and actions we would make. Most of us are likely to think that we could do the job best, if we just had the time. Thus we seek to duplicate ourselves. However, in picking another to help us most effectively, we should likely pick a person who will complement and supplement, rather than duplicate, our own abilities, likes and dislikes. If we are adventurous, fluent idea persons, we may need most a methodical person who is good at management and follow through. If we are methodical top administrators, we may need most of all an idea person. Together we will become a more potent team than if we both tend to think and act alike. If we are technical, science-oriented persons, we may be best helped by being joined by a more practical person. The ideas person may need someone to help with marketing, public relations and advertising, etc. Judicious use of personality profile tests may be helpful in identifying the presence or absence of needed skills.

Good administrators soon find that respect for their authority must be earned. As Freeh (1981) said:

> Authority, to be effective, must be earned. The more able your subordinates feel you are, the more willingly they will follow your directions. Competent leaders rarely feel the need to "pull rank." People who are confident they can handle their jobs find no necessity to impress everyone that they are the boss. They get better results and are better liked by relying on reason and persuasion rather than by ordering people to do things.

He concluded by suggesting that if we are informed and competent we will usually be allowed to exercise all the authority we need to get the job done.

All too frequently we are placed in leadership and administrative roles with minimal understanding of the role we will be facing and with little or no training for dealing with administrative challenges. Most organizations need to be more aware of the needs of new leaders and administrators. Not only should preparatory orientation and training be offered, but also follow-up and later refresher and broadening training should be made available to us. Help in developing leadership skills, organizing abilities, relating to subordinates and superiors, and communicating, as well as many other aspects can be especially helpful to us as new leaders (see Chapter 12-2.1).

13-5 ORGANIZATIONAL VALUES AND PRINCIPLES

People in an organization operate under a set of written or unwritten organizational values, principles, objectives, policies, guidelines, goals, directions and focus (stated or unstated). These then are major factors in establishing the environment in which we all will work and operate. Much of how we treat and react with one another, as well as the general overall atmosphere, is governed by how these values, principles, guidelines, and policies are implemented, demonstrated and administered.

For an organization to be successfully productive over an extended period of time, the organization itself and its members must be ethical in their procedures and practices. Blanchard and Peale (1988, 125) have suggested five essential principles as guidelines for an organization that wishes to make its ethics program work to the best advantage of all. All of these principles support creative individuals well. They all help us to bolster our self-esteem, and if continuously followed, contribute to our commitment, growth, and outlook. These Blanchard and Peale ethical principles are given in Table 13-2.

If we are unhappy and feel negative toward our organization, Blanchard and Peale (p.84, 1988) indicated that we are likely to seek revenge. We are apt to feel that the organization owes us something and, in the attempt to even things out, we may resort to the unethical practices of stealing, cheating, calling in sick, etc. In essence they were convinced that people's negative feelings about their organization are at the root of unethical behavior.

The organization, just as indicated for the individual (see Chapter 7-3), can help to diminish unethical behavior by applying the three criteria suggested by Blanchard and Peale (1988, 27) in making decisions and in taking actions. You will recall that these were: "Is it legal?" (Will it violate criminal or civil law or company policy?) "Is it balanced?" (Will it be fair to all concerned?) "How will it make you feel about yourself?" (Will you be proud or will it hurt you and the organization if others learn of your action?)

Table 13-2
The Five Principles of Ethical Power for Organizations

1. **Purpose:** The mission of our organization is communicated from the top. Our organization is guided by the values, hopes, and a vision that helps us to determine what is acceptable and unacceptable behavior.
2. **Pride:** We feel proud of ourselves and of our organization. We know that when we feel this way, we can resist temptations to behave unethically.
3. **Patience:** We believe that holding to our ethical values will lead us to success in the long term. This involves maintaining a balance between obtaining results and caring how we achieve these results.
4. **Persistence:** We have a commitment to live by ethical principles. We are committed to our commitment. We make sure our actions are consistent with our purpose.
5. **Perspective:** Our managers and employees take time to pause and reflect, take stock of where we are, evaluate where we are going and determine how we are going to get there.

From Blanchard and Peale, 1988, 125 (by permission)

13-6 TREATMENT OF PERSONS

Throughout this book, and especially as first discussed in Chapter 8, respect for and treatment of each individual as a person is critical in encouraging performance. Peters and Waterman (1982, 234-238) presented an excellent discussion of the devastating effects of labelling and treating people as immature, unintelligent, disinterested, and incapable. They cited the impact and change that ex-Chief of Naval Operations, Elmo Zumwalt, got in a few short months in the U.S. Navy by ensuring that every officer and sailor on a ship was treated as an adult. He made sure that they not only knew what they were trying to do, but understood why and how they hoped to accomplish it. This was a dramatic change from some of the older military practices which attempted in many cases to simply force blind obedience with many of the participants knowing little of what was going on. The Zumwalt experience parallels what has been found in "Excellent" companies. In relation to performance in industry Peters and Waterman said:

> Treat people as adults. Treat them as partners; treat them with dignity; treat them with respect. Treat them - not capital spending and automation - as the primary source of produc-

tivity gains. These are fundamental lessons from the excellent companies research. In other words, if you want productivity and the financial reward that goes with it, you must treat your workers as your most important asset.

Freedom, openness, autonomy, entrepreneurship, respect, trust, cooperation, consistency, communication (inform them, let them speak, hear them), tolerance of mistakes, not do to them what you would not have them do to you, are all a part of bringing out the best in people. Institutions and organizations all too frequently fail in carrying through with these. Many of us give lip service to the principle that "people are the most important elements for success, productivity, and creativity," but we don't live up to that claim. As a result few employees can reach their potential in making contributions to our organizations.

We need to have in our organizations, effective systems of evaluating personnel and recognizing the talents and capabilities of each individual; thus looking for and rewarding the positive, dedicated person on a regular basis. We need to help each member face up to and recognize the need for change, for setting goals for individual and organizational accomplishment, for becoming aware of personnel needs and wishes, and then offer them opportunities for growth and development. We also need to be aware of stressful signs in individuals, avoid underemployment, relieve the individual from overload-overanxiety, overcommitment, offer training and opportunity for maintaining health, nutrition, exercise, relaxation and rest, and counsel individuals where things aren't going well. We also need to deal with conflict promptly and fairly.

If we keep our members of the organization informed and let them inform us and their superiors, peers and subordinates, fewer members of the organization will be wondering what is happening or is about to happen. There will be much less confusion and far fewer rumors. All will stay more interested and excited about what is happening and will be more aware of how what they are doing is contributing to the overall efforts of the organization.

13-7 DEVELOPING A CREATIVE ENVIRONMENT

Organizational climate is dependent on a set of values, attitudes, and traditions, all of which affect the way people in the organization behave and work together. Ends and Page (1977, 101-102) have identified five major factors as determinants of organizational climate. These are:

- value systems;
- patterns of authority and power;
- cohesiveness;
- openness of communication; and
- the cooperation or conflict between individuals and groups.

If our organization consists of creative and valued individuals, leaders, and teams who are free to be themselves, are action oriented, live with and in a can-do-atmosphere, have high standards, strive for excellence and quality, participate in setting ethical guidelines and making plans and decisions, and are appropriately recognized and rewarded, we are probably providing a creative environment.

We can either be helpful or harmful to people within the organization being creative, depending on the climate that is developed by those doing the supervising (see Chapters 10-6 and 12-11). Supervision for the creative organization (as suggested and adapted from Mangrum, 1981, 34-40) should be:

1. Confrontive - Squarely face the problems, issues, and differences that arise.
2. Responsive - Recognize both the needs of employees and the demands of the task and organization.
3. Enabling - Allow individuals to become what they are capable of becoming.
4. Appreciative - Those doing well are told so.
5. Timely - Reactions and responses are not delayed.
6. Innovative - New ways are constantly looked for to enable individuals to be creative in their roles.
7. Vigorous - All are enthusiastically involved in making things happen.
8. Equitable - Fairness to all is essential.

The intentional acronym (or acrostic) formed by these eight items is CREATIVE. We should look for the presence of these indicators (and those mentioned in the second paragraph of this section) when there is an opportunity to choose a potential position or organization in which to work and live.

13-8 RECOGNIZING THE NEED FOR AND IMPLEMENTING CHANGE

Organizations, just as individuals (see Chapter 11-3), need to be continuously on the alert for signs that suggest the need for change.

History, tradition, habit, and the smug feeling that the organization (or the individual) "has it made" are great deterrents to seeing the need for change. No individual or organization should attempt to operate without serious thinking and planning for what they wish to accomplish or for what changes must be made to keep up with the times and continue to be effective. Change is often painful and thus is avoided or purposefully neglected. We all resist change. Thus changes for individuals or for organizations must be carefully planned, the objectives clearly communicated to those affected, and moves judicially managed if the goals are to be reached. Continuous evaluation of individuals and programs should be integral parts of planning efforts. Planning enables an individual or a unit to better understand where they are and what must be done to move toward a productive and satisfying future.

We often take the attitude that the need for a change is too small to bother with. We say, "Well, some day we need to change that." However, we dare not lose sight of the fact that often large changes can only result from carrying out a number of small changes. Dale (1967) said:

> We should realize that we create futures, not the future. The future is a collective term, the combined futures of all individuals. If you change one individual, you change the future.

A small change may be the first step toward understanding and larger changes, for a more productive and happier future.

Wilke (1986; 64) suggested a good reason for taking things bit by bit. He said:

> A person can keep only so many problems and concerns in his or her head and heart at any one time. Organizational experts agree that if you want to move a company or some other kind of institution in a new direction, people within that institution must share a sense of that direction.

This emphasizes the importance of having those involved informed, whether the change is big or little.

13-8.1 Resistance to Change

We all naturally resist change, for we need stability, and we apparently anticipate something worse than we are currently experiencing. We fear the unknown. Ends and Page (1977, 100) suggested five major sources of resistance to change:

- inertia;

- past experience;
- personal self-concept;
- risk of failure; and
- perception of psychological disadvantage.

For these reasons (and probably many others too) we fight change, often without good reason or alternate plans. It is important that we, as leaders, keep these things in mind both in considering the people in the organization and the organization itself. As Ends and Page have said:

> Adults tend to accept change only when it is presented as a series of small safe steps.

13-8.2 Planning and Making Change

From the above discussion of the probabilities of resistance to change, it is obvious that we must take care in planning and implementing change. We must solicit suggestions from those who will be affected to get the best evaluation of the impact of the change at that level. It is often helpful if we have experience in the area that the change will affect most. Organizational planning, just as individual and leader planning (see Chapters 11-6 and 12-8), requires special attention. Goals, procedures, consequences, timing, frequency, and ultimate evaluation would obviously be somewhat different than for individuals or smaller units, but the principles and concerns for members of the organization would be similar.

Lippitt (1982, 368-372) suggested some important issues to consider in planning for changes, if the changes are going to be accepted by the members and cooperation is to be attained in accomplishing the desired results. His suggestions are recorded in Table 13-3.

Table 13-3
Necessities in Order to Accomplish Group Changes

- Recognition of the worth of each individual in the group.
- Group relationships must be authentic and satisfy the yearning for acceptance.
- Members must be able to influence group decisions.
- The search for truth and the use of the mind must be based on an objective search for the right answers (not on likes or dislikes, friendships, hunches, etc.).
- The group leader should be sure that all members are free to dissent, stand alone, and differ with the leader(s) and the rest of the group without fear of reprisal.
- There should be tolerance of diverse behavior and an avoidance of sitting in judgement of others.

Constructed from text of Lippitt, 1982, 368-372.

The importance of these suggested guidelines was also voiced by Blanchard and Peale (1988, 83), who pointed out that lofty goals set only by those at the top may often take on the appearance of threats by the time they reach the lower levels. Whether and how our suggestions are accepted will depend greatly on how others in the organization perceive the way we are treating them.

13-8.3 Changing Others

We need to recognize that changing others is usually a slow and difficult process. We can only accomplish it by fear tactics or by gaining the confidence and trust of those involved. If we do it by fear, the change will be made reluctantly and will likely be reversed as soon as the threat over them is no longer present. If we accomplish change by building trust and appealing to members' desires to better themselves and gain praise, we will likely get lasting change and will also gain the cooperation and good will of those involved.

We must help individuals make changes by building up their self-esteem, which can be done by accentuating positive experiences. The latter can be accomplished, as Blanchard and Johnson (1981, 39) said if an attempt is made to:

Help people reach their full potential - catch them doing something right.

13-9 GUIDELINES FOR MANAGING CHANGE

Beyond diagnosing the difficulties and identifying what changes must be made to correct and improve the situation comes the more difficult task of implementing the change. It is important that, as organizational leaders, we not only understand change and plan for it, but we must also develop the approaches and skills to implement change so that acceptance and cooperation are obtained. Lippitt (1982, 68-69) developed several guidelines to aid in making and managing change. These are presented in abbreviated form in Table 13-4.

Table 13-4
Guidelines for Managing Change

1. Involve individuals affected in planning for change.
2. Provide accurate and complete information.
3. Give employees a chance to air their objections.
4. Always take group norms and habits into account.
5. Make only essential changes.
6. Provide adequate motivation.
7. Develop a trusting work climate.
8. Learn to use the problem-solving approach.

Constructed from text of Lippitt, 1982, 68-69.

Along with using the above guidelines, it is important that we make clear to all involved and affected what our expectations are from making the changes. We need to point out how the changes will help in meeting these expectations.

13-10 ENCOURAGING CREATIVITY THROUGH MANAGEMENT AND ORGANIZATION

If our members are trying to decide whether the organization is "creativity encouraging" or not, Dyer (1977, 108-109) presented a useful check list (he credits it to P. B. Daniels and himself). We can use this list to determine to what extent the type of leadership and management and the organizational conditions supply, support and encourage us to be creative. His form is reproduced in Table 13-5.

Table 13-5
Encouraging Creativity through Management and Organization

1.	My ideas or suggestions never get a fair hearing.	1 2 3 4 5 6 7	My ideas or suggestions get a fair hearing.
2.	I feel like my boss is not interested in my ideas.	1 2 3 4 5 6 7	I feel like my boss is very interested in my ideas.
3.	I receive no encouragement to innovate on my job.	1 2 3 4 5 6 7	I am encouraged to innovate on my job.
4.	There is no reward for innovating or improving things on my job.	1 2 3 4 5 6 7	I am rewarded for innovating and improving on my job.
5.	There is no encouragement for diverse opinions among subordinates.	1 2 3 4 5 6 7	There is encouragement of diversity of opinion among subordinates.
6.	I'm very reluctant to tell the boss about mistakes I make.	1 2 3 4 5 6 7	I feel comfortable enough with my boss to tell about mistakes I make.
7.	I'm not given enough responsibility to do my job right.	1 2 3 4 5 6 7	I am given enough responsibility to do my job right.
8.	To succeed in this organization, one needs to be a friend or a relative of the boss.	1 2 3 4 5 6 7	There is no favoritism in the organization.

Table 13-5 (continued)

9.	There are other jobs in this organization I would prefer to have.	1 2 3 4 5 6 7	I have the job in this organization that I think I do best.
10.	They keep close watch over me too much of the time.	1 2 3 4 5 6 7	They trust me to do my job without always checking on me.
11.	They would not let me try other jobs in the organization.	1 2 3 4 5 6 7	I could try other kinds of jobs in the organization if I wanted to.
12.	The management is made very uptight by confusion, disorder, and chaos.	1 2 3 4 5 6 7	The management deals easily with confusion, disorder, and chaos.
13.	There is a low standard of excellence on the job.	1 2 3 4 5 6 7	There is a high standard of excellence on the job.
14.	My boss is not open to receive my opinion of how he/she might improve his/her performance on the job.	1 2 3 4 5 6 7	My boss is very open to suggestions on how he/she might improve his/her own performance.
15.	My boss has a very low standard for judging his/her own performance.	1 2 3 4 5 6 7	My boss has a very high standard of excellence for judging his/her own performance.
16.	I am not asked for suggestions on how to improve service to the customers.	1 2 3 4 5 6 7	The management actively solicits my suggestions and ideas on how to improve service to the customers.
17.	My boss shows no enthusiasm for the work we are engaged in.	1 2 3 4 5 6 7	My boss exhibits lots of enthusiasm for the work we are engaged in.
18.	Mistakes get you in trouble; they aren't to learn from.	1 2 3 4 5 6 7	Around here mistakes are to learn from and not to penalize you.
19.	Someone else dictates how much I should accomplish on my job.	1 2 3 4 5 6 7	I'm allowed to set my own goals for my job.
20.	The organization has too many rules and regulations for me.	1 2 3 4 5 6 7	The organization has adequate rules and regulations for me.

Taken by permission from Dyer, 1977, 108-109.

13-11 MINIMIZING ORGANIZATIONAL AND INSTITUTIONAL DRAG

Many organizations, institutions and governments deter creativity and innovation in many ways. Many were set up in the first place to control and regulate certain things and to guard against unwanted changes. As a result they became more and more rigid and entrenched in rules, regulations, and traditions. Aging can affect both organizations and individuals this way if a special effort is not made to avoid letting it happen. Years ago Darlington (1949-50, 7-11) discussed the devastating effects that organizations, institutions, and governments have on creativity, innovation, and discovery (because of their rules, regulations, and red-tape) in an article entitled, "The Dead Hand on Discovery."

Shepard (1973, 179-186) illustrated the older defensive and restrictive attitude when he said:

> To insure reliable repetition of prescribed operations, the organization requires strong defenses against innovation. Efforts to innovate must be relegated to the categories of error, irresponsibility, and insubordination and appropriate corrective action taken to bring the would-be innovators "back in line." Any change is likely to run counter to vested interests and to violate certain territorial rights. Sentiments of vested interest and territorial rights are sanctified as delegation of legitimate authority in traditional organizations, thus guaranteeing quick and effective counteraction against disturbances.

Leaders in most organizations give lip service to the need for creativity and giving people freedom to experiment. And they proclaim and thoroughly believe that they do. They are likely to be unaware that many of their actions, policies, rules and regulations are counterforces to creativity. Even if some of the inhibiting conditions are pointed out to them, they usually declare that in their organization the creative and innovative people are free to try new things, and are not slowed down by these kinds of deterrents. A number of these conditions have been discussed earlier; more of them are discussed below.

13-11.1 Topheavy Organizations

Most organizations, especially those that have been operating for some time, tend to become "topheavy". Those running the organization gradually begin to feel they are overloaded and need more and more second line administrators. Each added layer goes through the same thing and adds another layer. This process goes on and on because of the big mistake of not realizing that those at the operating level are likely quite capable (and probably much more efficient because they are working near the point of action) of controlling themselves and pulling the working team together and proceeding toward the goals of the organization. Peters and Waterman (1982, 313) have pointed out the contrast between Toyota, where there were five levels between the chairman and first-line supervisors, and Ford, where there were over 15.

The more layers of middle management, the more demands and pressures will get passed along to those at the working front. In my own experience in academia in a middle level administrative post over a 10-year period, the number of higher level officers and staff added resulted in a doubling of the number of persons who had the authority to demand some kind of action from me. It is easy to see how, the "not-so-funny" joking about an organization becoming so big and so administratively "topheavy" that it would create enough paper work and other activities to keep all top people completely occupied, could happen. To get relief from too much pressure from superiors, the working force in many instances may reach the point where they are secretly hoping for this, so they would no longer be bothered and could finally concentrate and get on with doing the job the organization was originally created to do.

Peters and Waterman (p. 311) believed the maximum number of persons at the corporate level of management, even with companies of several thousands of employees, is approximately 100.

Central staffs can always seem to find reasons to show that something won't work. As Peters and Waterman (1982, 31) said:

> The central staff plays it safe by taking the negative view; and as it gains power, it stamps all verve, life, and initiative out of the company.

Management calls for risk-taking, but then turns around and penalizes and punishes even the smallest of mistakes.

Another factor that can come into play, especially in the older (and others too, even the relatively young) organization, is the promotion of people into positions beyond their capabilities. This is known as the Peter Principle, which is:

> In a hierarchy every employee tends to rise to his level of incompetence (Peter and Hull, 1969).

If people are not capable of handling the role that their job demands, they may contribute devastatingly against the fostering of creativity and innovation. And, the more people there are in the top and middle level management group, the greater the probabilities that there will be such persons exerting their negative forces. Often academia and some industrial organizations use a rotating system which places people in upper management roles for a period of three to five years, and then they go back to middle management or to the work force (usually they are evaluated at that time, and may be given a second short term in management). Such a plan thus brings the experience of "having been there" on the working front, and more consideration is then given to the impact of decisions on those affected by them. If administrators know that they will be back at the working front in the next year or so, they are more careful to not implement practices that are detrimental to the people at the production front. By the same token, working front persons often visualize the management role as a soft job. Many are surprised when they get into administration and management to find how wrong they were in believing that management would be easy. Usually they are most surprised at the amount of time and difficulty encountered in dealing with personnel. The net result of the "short-term" exchange is better understanding on the part of both levels in the organization.

13-11.2 Rules, Regulations, Reports and Red Tape (the 4 R's)

One of the reasons that bigness may result in increasing institutional drag is that more management brings with it the need to implement more rules, regulations, reports and red tape. Each new administrative person added must continuously show that they are important (to protect, justify and preserve their own positions), and so they busy themselves by burdening the people at the working front with more and more reports, surveys, planning projections, etc. This is true when additional administrative levels are added - whatever the organization. Government is especially prone to expansion and adding rules and regulations. During and following World War II, the U.S. government went through tremendous growth and enlargement. By the mid seventies, for example in the making of steel, companies had to comply with more than 5000 regulations issued by 27 different federal agencies (Abelson, 1978). This kind of enlargement and implementation of rules, regulations and restrictions prevail throughout the government.

Concern over the curtailment of innovation and productivity in the U.S. prompted the formation of a "Domestic Policy Review of Industrial Innovation" committee with representatives from 15 federal agencies and departments. As a result of a year-long study, started in 1978, this committee reported that:

> There is widespread sentiment that government could help most if it stopped hindering. The blame is put squarely on "disincentives" built up in federal regulatory rules, tax policy, and patent and antitrust laws (Walsh 1979, 378-380).

The reports from this committee also sent, "A powerful admonition to government to get out of the way." The regulatory agencies were also "scored for mandating how industry was to meet environmental standards - rather than allowing industry to be innovative in meeting the standards." The report also indicated that while there was no known causal relationship between research and development, there was a correlation between total research and development effort and the rate of innovation.

As individuals (and institutions) we face similar hurdles in our efforts to qualify for grants and contracts from the federal government for doing research and other educational and social efforts. Creativity and innovation are hindered for such reasons as:

1. In many instances guidelines and procedures are under strict and limited bureaucratic control and central administration.
2. Priorities are often set by one or a few top level administrators with limited vision of the needs of state and local conditions.
3. Planning and preparation requirements are excessive.
4. In many instances preliminary results attesting to the potential success of the proposed effort are required before funds will be made available (in other words the proof to the proposed question practically has to be in hand).
5. The review and award process is long and uncertain and by the time an award is made an average time input of the proposer and reviewers is likely to be equivalent to one half a person-year (or more) before the opportunity to do any part of the proposed research.
6. Funding duration is usually short and little or no notion of continuation is provided.
7. Time delays often result in "on-off" funding (in the meantime research teams and support personnel may have to be disbanded, then reformed, if funding does come through).

8. Excessive report writing and accountability are demanded on how funds are spent; how time was used and doing what; and writing quarterly, annual and final reports.
9. Civil rights compliance in working with human subjects, following appropriate affirmative action policies in searches, hiring and firing, and dealing with unionization.
10. Dealing with clearance, compliance and permits for animal care, new chemicals, hazardous substances, radiation, and care in working with recombinant DNA, etc.
11. Providing environmental impact statements.
12. Dealing with criticism from groups and "watch dogs" (like animal rights groups and the Golden Fleece Awards) who often do not understand basic research, or are biased against certain areas of research.

There is some logic for the implementation of nearly every one of the items listed as costing a researcher time if federal funds are used. Many of the items have become necessary to protect the health and well-being of people and guard against fraud. Comparable lists of deterrents could be developed for practically all funding where government is involved. Unfortunately, many of the guidelines and rules often get developed by people who are unfamiliar with the areas being regulated. In many cases safeguards could be developed with far less impact on those who are expected to be responsible for the new developments.

Unfortunately many leaders in organizations, institutions, and government go into their roles and remain convinced that their role should be that of control and coercion. Creative and innovative talents do not thrive under such conditions. Coercive leadership, instead of bringing out the best in people, sets up an adversary situation, workers against managers, faculty versus higher administration, students against teachers, middle management versus top bosses, wives against husbands, and children against parents. As a result, instead of getting cooperative team efforts on whatever the objectives might be, a competitive, defensive atmosphere is developed. Then a large amount of energy that could be going to finding solutions to the major aims is dissipated in trying to force, outwit, bypass, avoid, do as little as possible to get by, protect one's position, or back the opponents into a corner. The result is far less productivity than potentially possible if all were to work together as a cohesive team. A major challenge to the organization is that of developing and fostering an attitude and atmosphere where togetherness can and will flourish.

13-12 PREVENTING ORGANIZATIONAL DRY ROT

As an old saying goes, "As long as you think you are green, you are growing. As soon as you think you are ripe, you have begun to rot." Both individuals and organizations are subject to this danger. Gardner (1965, 20-26) suggested several items to help organizations avoid dryrot and implement organizational renewal. His rules suggest that to stay effective the organization must:

1. Have an effective program for the recruitment and development of talent.
2. Be a hospitable environment for the individual.
3. Have built-in provisions for self-criticism.
4. Have fluidity of internal structure.
5. Have an adequate system of internal communication.
6. Have some means of combating the process by which people become prisoners of their procedures.
7. Have found some means of combating the vested interests that grow up in every human institution.
8. Be interested in what it is going to become and not what it has been.
9. Promote motivation, conviction and morale, people must believe that it makes a difference whether they do well or badly. They have to care.
10. Maintain high motivation in order to break through the rigidness of the aging organization.

One major mistake many organizations make (especially in academia) is that they reach the point where they think they are the only ones capable of "properly educating and training new personnel," or they are the only ones who can make such a good product, and they see no danger of ever losing their advantage. Because of this they fall into a smug pattern of not continuing to strive for excellence, and hiring only their own graduates or trained people. Over time this then often results in a kind of "inbreeding" and a "hardening of the categories (and arteries)," thus developing restricted patterns of thinking and approaching problems. A new person from within is likely to carry for some time the image of "student, trainee, or underling," whether it is deserved or not. Many times really capable individuals can soon change that image, but there are times when organizational renewal can only be accomplished by an influx of new blood via new leadership and other new personnel. There certainly is nothing wrong with moving people up within the organization. In fact, the possibility of this opportunity is extremely important to the members of an organization. As Gardner (1963-64, 76) said:

Nothing is more vital to the renewal of an organization (or society) than the system by which able people are nurtured and moved into positions where they can make their contribution.

All too often, as top administrators, we fail to get out among the other members of the organization and outside the organization as well. We don't or won't listen to criticism, become isolated, and surround ourselves with people who won't argue with us. As a result we hear only the things we want to hear. Peters and Waterman (1983, 209) have quoted Ed Carson of United Airlines as having said, "When that happens you are on the way to developing what I call corporate cancer."

An organization or institution can only hope to reach its greatest potential if it constantly tries to avoid developing disincentives, encourages experimentation, maintains a tolerance for and avoids punishment for mistakes, and pays attention to all members no matter what their role. Only in such an environment can the potential creative, innovative capabilities of the members throughout the unit be set free.

13-13 HIGHLIGHTS OF CHAPTER THIRTEEN

1. To be effective, organizations (institutions) must be staffed with competent, creative, people-oriented members with balanced leadership, and with individuals and groups that clearly understand the goals and objectives of the organization.
2. The effective organization holds to high standards, has a can-do attitude, keeps two-way channels of communication open, and involves people at all levels in evolving plans and maintaining a creative atmosphere.
3. Risk-taking is encouraged, new approaches are allowed to emerge, mistakes are tolerated, outside contacts are encouraged, and people at all levels are rewarded for new and usable ideas in the most effective organizations.
4. There are regular performance evaluations and appraisals, and on-the-job training and broadening learning "at-home" and "away" are encouraged.
5. There are effective mechanisms for hearing suggestions, evaluating complaints, fairly adjudicating disagreements,

and helping people avoid becoming prisoners of their own procedures or becoming victims of vested interest groups.

6. Need for organizational change must be continuously and carefully evaluated on the basis of reliable information, effect on future hopes, visualization of the consequences, clarification with all involved, and then courageously implemented.

7. We can expect resistance to organizational change if our purposes are not made clear, vested interests are threatened, job security is at risk, the cost is too high, past practices and traditions are in jeopardy, and when those affected are not involved in the planning.

8. We may encounter difficulties in changing organizations when there are differences of opinion, change is for personal reasons, there are fears of failure, there is lack of respect and trust in the initiators, or when the change is too rapid.

9. Plans for change should be kept simple, flexible, practical and understandable and should provide for an appropriate evaluation of the results of the plan.

10. We should always implement plans and changes with the objective of reducing the chances of the organization or institution being or becoming the "dead hand on discovery," and to avoid the rigidness of an aging organization.

11. The progressive organization lets its personnel know they are valued by providing, in so far as possible, an effective health plan, an "in-house" recreational program, a well-thought-out leave plan, and a fair vacation plan.

13-14 AFTERGROWTH STIMULATORS

1. What organizational characteristics would you consider to be most important in attracting you to become an employee?

2. What would you want to know about the organization's policies regarding forming small teams to accomplish specific tasks?

3. List five of the most important qualities you would like to see in the leaders of the organization you are about to join?

4. Describe what constitutes a creative environment for you in the workplace. In the community. In a committee meeting.

5. Describe a procedure, regulation, or condition in your schooling or workplace that needs to be changed. Suggest a trial way of implementing such a change.

6. List three ways your school, your workplace, or your government impedes your productivity and creativity. Suggest a plan for correcting or removing one of them.

CHAPTER 14

PUTTING IT ALL TOGETHER

14- 1   Introduction
14- 2   Put Things into Action
14- 3   Maintain Faith, Hope and Discipline
14- 4   Mature as You Grow
14- 5   Be Committed, Determined
            and Persevering
14- 6   Learn to Deal with Disappointment
14- 7   Let Go, Let Intuition and Freedom Work
14- 8   Make It Fun
14- 9   Strive to Maximize Your Creativity
14-10   Help Others to Be More Creative
14-11   Highlights of Chapter Fourteen
14-12   Aftergrowth Stimulators

14-1 INTRODUCTION

We began this book by pointing out the complexity of the world and universe in which we live. We recognized that each of us is limited in our capacity to learn of and understand these enormous complexities. We have seen and discussed many of the complexities of the creative and innovative processes. Yet our knowledge and understanding of the processes are still limited. Even with what we know, there is great variation in our own capabilities to apply our talents in bringing creativity to fruition. Unfortunately there is no simple, standard formula for developing creativity and innovativeness.

The making of a creative person is more than just being born, more than just being educated, more than just being curious and imaginative, more than sensing needs and opportunities, more than associating the unusual, more than caring for and appreciating others, and more than just hard work. Creative persons are the result of many inherent characteristics and their interactions with hundreds of factors learned and imposed on us by society and the environment. It is also apparent that making us creative persons is a continuing process that extends over our entire life.

How far the development of our creativity goes is dependent on how each of us deals with our own intellect, emotions and feelings. It also depends on how we each deal with the world and the persons around us. We can choose to acknowledge, learn and try to understand our individual makeup; accept it as is; do nothing to change or better it; or we can decide we want to alter our makeup and the circumstances surrounding us and help those changes to occur. Without action and determination on our part little change is apt to occur, other than the way the surrounding forces succeed in pushing us. Only by our own decisions, determination and action can we help to create the future we would like. We must be prepared to not only try to control the changes, but also to be ready to respond to unexpected changes and events and turn them into opportunities.

14-2 PUT THINGS INTO ACTION

In his book on *The Adventure of Living*, Tournier (1965, 5) said:

Instinct of adventure is one of the most obvious explanations for the characteristic behavior of man, one of the great driving forces behind his actions, as important as the instinct of self-preservation, which has so often been described as the mainspring of civilization and its technical progress.

But he went on to point out that this initial great drive for adventure, action and discovery, with its difficulties and challenges, gradually becomes more familiar, more organized and then standardized. After a time the adventure becomes common-place, routine, and no longer a challenge. Thus the thrills are gone and our impulse to action wanes. As a result the exciting fever of adventure and discovery can scarcely ever last. If we are to continue to be creative this search for adventure must be constantly renewed. The impetus for renewal must come mainly from us, but the environment in which we live tends to constantly push us toward standardization and compliance. Thus there is little wonder that continuing to push ourselves into action and creativity requires so much effort.

There is nothing that we can do to change the environment into which we are born. We can only try later to make changes into which future generations may be born. If we find ourselves in an environment of mediocrity, apparent hopelessness, and among persons who are low achievers, it may be extremely difficult to visualize that we have any possibility of ever getting out of that situation or changing it for future generations. Even when being born into an environment of excellence and among high achievers we may feel that there is no way for us to ever achieve those levels of excellence and perfection. We have a great tendency in such a situation to give up without trying. In either of these situations we must constantly remind ourselves that altering the situation depends largely on taking individual action.

All of us must know and believe that we are unique. We each must realize that, of the billions of people on earth, no one ever before, or ever to appear after us, had or will have the same genetic and environmental makeup that we are experiencing. From this we must try to visualize the enormous potential locked within us. We will likely be amazed at what we find we can do, especially if we find support for our actions from others.

We need to pattern our lives after the positive and good qualities of outstanding models and mentors, being careful to sort out and discard their faults. It is, however, extremely important that we work the good aspects into our own being. It can be disastrous for us to try to copy exactly the patterns of an admired mentor and ignore our own individuality. If we are special-made, unduplicated individuals, surely we must be expected to manifest our own unique potentials. It is equally important for us to observe the many undesirable characteristics in those we would never want to serve as mentors. Becoming what we would like to become is as dependent on avoiding the faults and shortcomings of others as it is on mimicking and developing their good qualities.

We need to stretch and challenge ourselves in order to find what our potential is. We need to learn that failures will occur, but realize that a bigger failure is not to try at all. We can learn from failures, and the more of them we experience; the more we should learn. If we analyze what went wrong and use our creativity in planning the next venture, success will come eventually. Soon we are no longer novices, but experienced in many things. We can find great thrills in overcoming adversity and experiencing achievement. We also get great satisfactions from knowing that we have served and helped others by our efforts. One of life's great challenges is that of keeping hope alive and continuing to take action. Accepting things just as they are is one sure way of never improving the circumstances in which we live. And what usually happens is that things get worse for us because the world and our environment keep changing and we may begin to feel we are running but getting nowhere. Our motto for life must be, "If you don't like it, do something." Don't let hope die.

Action is not just busyness. Our actions need to be directed. Day (1977) quoted Simone Weil as having said:

> One quarter of an hour of attention is worth any quantity of good works....After months of inner darkness, I suddenly and irrevocably acquired the certitude that all human beings, even if their natural faculties are almost nil, can penetrate into the realm of truth reserved to genius, if only they desire the truth and are willing to make an unceasing effort to achieve it....the quantity of creative genius in any epoch is strictly proportionate to the quantity of extreme attention....consciousness can develop habits. Repeated attention to any subject makes it certain that that subject will attain a dominant position in consciousness.

This says a great deal to us about the value of concentrated effort. Action that is well thought out and put into action can bring us amazing results. Even if we are mediocre persons, we may reach great heights and achievements by proper concentrated efforts.

As pointed out in Chapter 13-2, the companies that Peters and Waterman (1982, 119-155) classed as "Excellent" were companies with a bias for action. Excellent companies saw the needs, the problems, the opportunities, and acted promptly to deal with them, using personnel from all levels of the organization. They did not allow any level of their personnel to "grow stale," become standardized, or get in a rut. They made a conscious and continuous effort to avoid those things that cause a company to regress to mediocrity. They devised ways of keeping the employees involved and enthusiastic by letting them know they were needed, valued and appreciated by the company and making them a part of the force to help keep things moving.

14-3 MAINTAIN FAITH, HOPE AND DISCIPLINE

Today's dreams of success, security, pleasure, satisfaction, happiness, companionship, harmony, adjustment, maturity and peace are held by many of us. But it is difficult for us to hang on to faith and hope, and stay optimistic in the face of many of today's trying problems. In fact pessimism and hopelessness can be devastating to our creativity and innovativeness. It is easy for us to become discouraged and let ourselves be defeated before we even give an issue a careful thought or an honest try.

If we lose hope, we lose confidence in ourselves. We become afraid to "stick our necks out". We become afraid to take the risks of facing everyday life. When people lose hope and self-confidence, Howe (1959, 44) said:

> Instead of being able to use their originality and energy for living, they have had to use it to defend and hide themselves.

It is easy for us to fall into a habit of cautiousness and become afraid to take risks. It is also easy for us to reach an overconfident state in which we think we have something mastered. We think we know all about what will work and what won't work. We must take this kind of a feeling as a warning. It should signal to us that we may be developing restricted vision and getting ourselves into a rut. Frequently, if we are new to a field we may make amazing new discoveries and breakthroughs. We come into a field free of most of the notions of what can and what can't be done. Being free of such deterrents we try things that those familiar with the field think impossible, and we succeed in doing them. The following Edgar A. Guest (1927) poem says it well:

IT COULDN'T BE DONE
Somebody said that it couldn't be done.
　　But he, with a chuckle replied,
　"Well, maybe it couldn't but he would be one
　　who wouldn't say so until he tried."

So he buckled right in with a trace of a grin
    on his face. If he worried he hid it.

He started to sing as he tackled the thing
    that couldn't be done, and he did it.
Somebody scoffed and said, "You'll never do that.
    At least no one has ever done it."
And he took off his coat, and he took off his hat
    and the first thing we knew he begun it.

With a lift of his chin and a bit of a grin,
    without any doubting or quitting,
He started to sing as he tackled the thing
    that couldn't be done, and he did it.

There are thousands to process the failure.
There are thousands to point out to you one by one
    the dangers that wait to assail you.
But just buckle right in with a bit of a grin.
    Just take off your coat and go to it.
Just start to sing as you tackle the thing that
    cannot be done, and you'll do it.

It is important for us to keep faith in ourselves, in others and in whatever supreme being fits our beliefs. Many of us fail to realize that developing faith takes real discipline, practiced constantly (see Chapter 5-3). Benson (1987, 189-190) said:

It's a fact that people who improve their health, frame of mind, physical fitness or intellectual capacities may simultaneously experience a broadening and deepening of their personal value system and world view.

The same is true as we hope to be more creative. To attain any or all of these hoped for items, we need real discipline. If we continue to discipline ourselves, grow in faith, and stay hopeful, our chances that solutions to our problems and opportunities will be found are greatly increased.

Our ultimate objective, however, should not be discipline, but rather attaining at least a piece of the dreams. As Day (1977, 14) said so well:

Discipline must not be practiced for its own sake. It is only the means to an end; it is not the end in itself....Discipline must never be conceived as denial or destruction of your own uniqueness....Discipline must fit the person, not destroy but preserve individuality, not create a copy but an authentic character.

He pointed out that discipline dare not be repressive, rather it should confront and master reality. When that occurs, we generate hope and optimism.

Staying optimistic and thinking positively is important if we are to maintain a high level of commitment and determination. Optimist International has a creed that advises well to staying optimistic:

THE OPTIMIST'S CREED

To be so strong that nothing can disturb your peace of mind.

To talk health, happiness and prosperity to every person you meet.

To make all your friends feel that there is something in them.

To look at the sunny side of everything and make your optimism come true.

To think only of the best, to work only for the best and to expect only the best.

To be just as enthusiastic about the success of others as you are about your own.

To forget the mistakes of the past and press on to the greater achievements of the future.

To wear a cheerful countenance at all times and give every living creature you meet a smile.

To give so much time to the improvement of yourself that you have no time to criticize others.

To be too large for worry, too noble for anger, too strong for fear, and too happy to permit the presence of trouble.

Although some of us may see some of these as over-optimistic and somewhat unrealistic (and perhaps missing the point of needing to learn from our mistakes rather than forgetting them), the creed offers much good advice.

14-4 MATURE AS YOU GROW

We maturate as a result of continuous learning, growth, and experience throughout life. We also must develop and use common sense and wisdom. This whole process is a complicated one and does not come easy. Yet if we can establish certain disciplines, it will come gradually; and we may not even be aware that it is occurring. However, we may have to sacrifice some of our own selfish beliefs, and we are likely to suffer a number of hardships along the way.

Gardner (1963-64, 94-96) illustrated this in his comments on maturity and commitment:

> In the process of growing up the young person frees himself from the utter dependence on others. As the process of maturing continues he must also free himself from the prison of utter self-preoccupation....In short, he must recognize the hazard of having no commitments beyond the self and the hazard of commitments that imperil the self....The mature individual, then, makes commitments of something larger than the service of his "convulsive little ego"....

Gardner also pointed out that we make it more difficult for the young person to mature and understand commitment when we continue to use the juvenile interpretation of the "pursuit of happiness". He said:

> The plain truth is that man is not capable of achieving the vegetative state implied in the current conception of happiness. Despite almost universal belief to the contrary, gratification, ease, comfort, diversion and a state of having achieved all one's goals do not constitute happiness for man. The reason Americans have not trapped the bluebird of happiness... is that happiness as total gratification is not a state to which man can aspire....The storybook conception tells of desires fulfilled; the truer version involves striving toward meaningful goals ....Storybook happiness involves a bland idleness; the truer conception involves seeking and purposeful effort. Storybook happiness involves every form of pleasant thumb-twiddling; true happiness involves the full use of one's powers and talents....the storybook version puts great emphasis on being loved, the truer version more emphasis on the capacity to give love.

Gardner concluded that the more mature and meaningful view of achieving happiness likely lies in our "striving toward meaningful goals rather than in attaining those goals."

Maturing is certainly more than just aging. It includes the total of the physical, mental and emotional aspects of our being. Howe (1959, 198-208) suggested several measures of maturity (see Table 14-1). We often ignore the great need for emotional maturation which is so essential for true wisdom to be reached. Dale (1966) posed an interesting question, "Why aren't we smarter than we are?" which speaks to some of both the mental and emotional aspects. He then suggested some answers. Here they are:

We aren't smarter than we are because:

1. We don't know our own strengths and weaknesses.
2. We have not organized our knowledge to create more knowledge.
3. Our life goals may not be realistic.
4. We don't associate with people who know more than we do.
5. We may tend to avoid the kind of conflict that educates.
6. We have not learned how to learn nor developed a taste for learning.
7. We haven't learned to read or listen at a mature level.
8. There is too little rigorous challenge and confrontation in school, college, or in life itself.
9. We may have chosen, deliberately or unwittingly, to be uninvolved, unimmersed, disengaged.
10. Far too much of our schooling has required memorizing answers to questions we never asked.

Table 14-1
Some Measures of Maturity

1. We are mature to the extent that we are guided by our long-term purposes, rather than by our immediate desires.
2. Mature persons are able to accept things and people the way they are, rather than pretend they are the way they want them to be.
3. Mature persons are able to accept the authority of others without rebellion or without the self-abdication that we call "folding-up."
4. Mature persons are able to accept themselves as an authority without either a sense of bravado or a sense of guilt.
5. Mature persons are able to defend themselves, both from their own unacceptable impulses and from attacks from the outside.
6. Mature persons are able to work without being slaves, and to play without feeling that they ought to be working.
7. Mature persons are able to accept their own, and the opposite, sex and a relation between the two in ways that are appropriately fulfilling.
8. Mature persons are able to love others so satisfyingly that they become less dependent upon being loved.
9. Mature persons are able to accept their significant place and role in the larger scheme of things.

Constructed from text of Howe, 1959, 198-208.

Dale concluded his discussion of the issue of being smarter than we are with the question, "Isn't the answer that we aren't smarter than we are because we don't want to be?" He concluded, "It's all a matter of motivation."

Gardner (1963-64, xiii) suggested:

Apathy and lowered motivation are the most widely noted characteristics of a civilization on the downward path. Apathetic men accomplish nothing. Men who believe in nothing change nothing for the better. They renew nothing and heal no one, least of all themselves.

14-5 BE COMMITTED, DETERMINED, AND PERSEVERING

In order to be committed, determined and perseverant we have to believe in ourselves. We have to be confident that we will have the ability (or can learn what is necessary) to handle a task.

When I was young and growing up on the farm, my father often would say to me that the talents I was born with were enough to enable me to "do just about anything I set my mind to, if I had the courage and 'stick-to-itiveness' to keep at it long enough." As I mentioned earlier in Chapter 10-3, Parental Influence, he would often tell me when I showed doubt about being old enough to handle certain tasks that "I would never learn any younger." What he was saying in his wise and experienced way was that I should learn and try things as soon in life as I could and was willing to try. He was saying I wouldn't know if I didn't try. What a lesson in learning determination, commitment and persevering. I am sure he had learned well from the old adage, "Try, if you don't succeed, try, try again."

14-6 LEARN TO DEAL WITH DISAPPOINTMENT

One of the most difficult things that we have to guard against in life is to keep from letting disappointment lead us to discouragement. We often do not realize how valuable some of life's disappointments and sufferings can be for us. Strange as it may seem, my full realization of this fact did not become completely clear to me until I was in my sixties. I was asked on the spur of the moment in front of a crowd of some 200 or more students and faculty how I had gotten to where I was in my career and what were the important factors along the way. Suddenly I realized that the major strengthening events in my life had come almost entirely from times and events when I had wondered, worried and suffered. Growing up on the farm in the drought and depression days of the '30's, scraping up a measly 200 dollars to start college in the late '30's, and then working part time for 20 cents an hour just to have enough to buy food, were early experiences. Then married and in graduate school on 60 to 100 dollars a month, and being turned back by my prelim committee to study another six months before coming up again were some of the greatest lessons of my life. Then having my Ph. D. studies and other life's dreams interrupted by World War II and struggling through service as an infantryman, Counter Intelligence Corp Officer, and overseas service after the shooting had stopped, taught me more about working with people and how not to treat others, domestic and foreign, than any schooling could have done.

But I suffered and, as it was happening, I thought it was the worst (and sometimes I thought near the end of my hopes and dreams), for part of the time I was separated from my wife and child. Disappointment was maximal many times during those years, and discouragement crept in time and time again. I wouldn't want to go through it all again, but neither would I be willing to give up the great lessons I learned.

Hanging on to hope, keeping faith that things would work out, being committed and determined to do the best I could, kept me trying (and sometimes crying). Lessons learned the hard way are never forgotten. But there is no simple way of conveying these thoughts and lessons to someone else just by words. So, it seems to me that hanging in there and trusting that things will work out can be extremely satisfying when you know you have given your best at the time of the greatest testing.

14-7   LET GO, LET INTUITION AND FREEDOM WORK

As we are attempting to work through tough problems or facing extremely challenging opportunities, we frequently fall into a pattern of attempting to force our thinking processes. One of the early lessons I learned about not trying to force things came through clearly when my father was teaching me to use hand tools on the farm. In particular two events that stand out related to his advice on using a hand saw on a board or a cross-cut saw on a tree. He would always say, "You are trying to push the saw through the board (or tree), relax, pull the saw back and forth and let the teeth of the saw do the work." Today the same principle applies on the golf course.

I have trouble letting the golf club do the work. I try to force the club through the ball, and I can seldom hit the ball straight unless I relax and let the club do the work.

This same principle applies to our thinking. When we try to force thoughts, they are apt to be slower in coming. But if we feed our brain and memory with bits and pieces, and then relax and let intuition go to work, we often come up with much more than we think we are capable of producing.

Over the years I have repeatedly been amazed, when I thought I had a thing well thought out or had done all I could do, to find that further (even better) thoughts, ideas or solutions often came to me "out of the blue," when I relaxed the intentional effort to push my thinking. The same often happens when we get stalled in trying to come up with an idea or reach a suggested approach to a knotty problem. It seems that what is important is to avoid thinking that we have arrived at the best or only answer and thus we turn off all thoughts related to the issue. It is extremely important that we keep an open mind and let intuition and freewheeling have a chance to work. It is equally important not to consciously keep reviewing the issue to the point that the solution reached becomes a worry.

It seems that when we try to completely force, cajole and control the conscious mind by planning, calculating and steering, some of the best and most creative ideas don't surface. But, when we allow our thinking to shift into freewheeling of its own accord, the intuitive process is more far-reaching, and more varied ideas come out.

We need to cultivate and improve our alertness to what is going on around us. I have often referred to this alertness as an "index of suggestibility." This is kind of an arbitrary way of rating how keen we are in picking up ideas, hints, and suggestions from the literature, other persons, disciplines, or fields (related or unrelated) which may be placed into our thinking and associated in new and varied ways into our array of concepts. Getting facts into our thought patterns, and then letting go can often free the way for the "voice from within" to steer our conscious minds in the right direction.

I have been amazed how greatly this "index of suggestibility" can vary from person to person. I was frequently watching for it in my students to get some assessment of their potential creative abilities. Some would pick up on minimal suggestions and be back in a day or two wanting to explore the idea further, or they would even come in with literature or laboratory data pertinent to the issue. Others often required more forthright and repeated suggestions after which they might eventually catch on (some never did rise to the bait).

Their eventual creativity and productivity confirmed my belief that such an evaluation was a good indicator of future performance.

14-8 MAKE IT FUN

Life's challenges are often disappointing and trying. Humor can help us to face those trials and tribulations, if we can laugh at ourselves in all our frailties and weaknesses. Once I heard a Nobel Laureate (Sir Bernard Katz) reply to a question on what he considered the most important thing a young scientist needed to succeed in his job. His reply was, "Like what you are doing." It seems to me this applies equally well to practically any person in any job. If we do not like what we are doing, there is little chance of the job being fun. Going to that kind of a job every day can make life seem endless. I have enjoyed the following set of humorous recommendations on "How to Have a Long Life":

1. Marry a person who takes pride in never getting anywhere on time. You can live several lifetimes while waiting.
2. Don't take a job that is fresh, exciting, or challenging. A dull, routine, and safe job will make every day crawl by.
3. Borrow money. Buy everything on installment. A person in debt can't afford to die.
4. Avoid friends, make enemies. Friends' deaths leave you mournful, but enemies spur you on with a desire to outlive them.
5. Engage in lawsuits as a means of seeking justice. It takes a long time to get justice in this world.
6. Be afraid of everything you can. Every minute of fear seems like an eternity.
7. Do something wrong everyday to build up your sense of guilt. Feeling guilty makes each day seem longer.
8. Avoid joy, seek boredom. Time always weighs heaviest with the bored.

Anyone who conscientiously follows these rules is bound to come as close to a feeling of personal immortality as human nature allows. They may not live forever, but they will feel their dreary existence is endless. (Abbreviated from an article by Boyle, 1957).

14-9 STRIVE TO MAXIMIZE
YOUR CREATIVITY

Throughout this book I have emphasized that productivity and self-fulfillment are highly dependent upon the opportunity of individuals to fulfill their basic and self-actualizing needs. I have also indicated that creative people must have at least a reasonable intelligence and an inherent drive for work and adventure. One of the really challenging aspects for us is to find ways of helping others find an environment where this potential productivity and self-fulfillment mix can flourish. We must each take a large part of the responsibility to self-stimulate ourselves and also in finding and/or creating situations and groups where our abilities can be exercised. We need to make special efforts to avoid conditions which block or impede our potential creativity.

14-9.1 To Be More Creative

In summary, if we are to be more creative, we should:

- Think - broadly, differently.
- Seek several answers to a problem or an opportunity, then choose the best alternative.
- Interact with others, they can help us develop ideas.
- Refuse to accept the negative (our own or that of others).
- Seek a stimulating climate, generate it ourselves if we must.
- Be self-starters, self-challengers, and self-finishers.

We should:

1. Have a creative but pragmatic imagination.
2. Develop a psychological security and an autonomous nature.
3. Learn to trust others, and develop the sensitivity and skills to earn trust in return.
4. Possess a great amount of energy and determination.
5. Master skills in organizing ourselves and others.
6. Be willing and learn to be clever, cunning and crafty in an honorable and humble manner.
7. Change things we can change. Accept things we cannot change. Learn to differentiate between the two.

14-9.2 We Dare Not Get Hung Up on:

1. Status.
2. Controlling others.
3. Getting a larger slice of the pie.

14-9.3 Some Ways to Help to Maximize Your Creativity

1. Like what you are doing, but don't become so narrow that you miss the rest of life.
2. Pick good models and mentors to follow - but be critical. Don't mimic their shortcomings.
3. Be confident that you have the ability. Develop the skill if you need to. Think.
4. Be curious. Be aware of what is going on around you. Try to understand what is happening.
5. Be a constant doubter. Even if you think you have the right answer, test it. Check it.
6. Widen your circle, but don't overextend. Borrow from other disciplines.
7. Take advantage of what others already know. But don't be afraid to differ.
8. Be open, risk it. (Little given - little gained.) Don't be afraid to share. Be flexible.
9. Don't let the negatives get you down - your own or those of others. Think positively.
10. Be honest with yourself and others.
11. Be committed, determined and optimistic.
12. Let tradition guide you, but don't let it blind you or bind you.
13. Challenge yourself. Be a self-starter. Persevere and be a strong finisher.
14. Look for several possible solutions to problems. Then choose the best. The first one you think of may not be the best. A closer look may prove the problem to be an opportunity.
15. Develop your own ways to increase your own creativity.
16. Life is short. Enjoy it. Have fun. Follow the above and you will end up contributing more than you think possible.

14-10 HELP OTHERS TO BE MORE CREATIVE

Clearly all of us must work together to create the future because, as inventor Charles Kettering once pointed out, "We all will have to spend the rest of our lives there." (Cited by Dale, 1969)

There has been a lot of advice giving in this book. In many respects Ehrnmann's (1927) "Desiderata" gives us a good summary to follow in our lives and living. He suggested that we should appreciate peace and quiet in this noisy, troubled world. We are advised to learn to relate and respect nature and all sorts of persons without abusing or looking down on them, or overly admiring anyone. This means we should beware of those who would do us in, but appreciate the good that exists everywhere. He said we should speak the truth and listen carefully, even to those we might consider dull or ignorant. He warned that we should not become victims of fear, fatigue, and misfortune, but be disciplined and wise in growing older. We need to learn to love and keep up our spirits. We are as much a part of the universe as are the things of nature, the earth and the skies, all of which are beautiful when we get to know them. He suggested that we should be at peace with ourselves and with that higher power that put us here, whatever we perceive that power to be. He also said we need to learn to be thankful that things do go wrong. I heartily agree with his advice, as I hope you have detected throughout this book.

As much as we might hope to be able to discipline ourselves to accomplish many of the suggestions in this book to become more creative, we must remember that no one can be perfect. There are, no doubt, many, many aspects that I have missed in compiling these suggestions. Yet participants in my workshops have frequently indicated that they were intimidated by the wide array of things that have been mentioned. Certainly no one should think or feel that they must overcome or master all of the items to be creative. Each creative person is made up of a different mix of what it takes to be creative. The mix that was appropriate for someone else may not be at all right for you. And it may never be known just what mix is the most likely to be most productive for everyone in general. It is important to remember that it is not enough just to recognize and remove the barriers to our own creativity. We must be aware of and help others overcome the deterrents that we ourselves, and the environment create for them. We should try not to become one of the everyday barriers to someone else's creativity.

It is my hope that the words recorded in this book, mine and those of the many from whom I have borrowed so profusely, will give you encouragement to make every effort to be youself and help you to unleash those creative urgings that have perhaps laid hidden or untapped for so long. May they also help you encourage others to break through the multitude of things which have hindered them from bringing forth the creative ideas that lay smoldering within them.

May we all expand our creative horizons and reach more of our full potential.

14-11 HIGHLIGHTS OF CHAPTER FOURTEEN

1. Creativity is influenced by so many factors that there seem to be no simple ways to guarantee that we can increase these abilities. However, with some effort all of us should be able to make considerable improvement and tap creative resources that we did not realize lay buried within us.

2. Understanding how many factors become barriers to creativity can help us avoid, diminish or negate the severity of their impact.

3. Once we understand the barriers and hindrances to creativity, the great challenge to us is developing the will to take action in removing or diminishing their effects.

4. Many of life's experiences cause us to wonder, worry, and suffer. Dealing with these often requires us to be committed and perseverant. We must be aware that these difficulties often cause us pain.

5. Continuing to learn, grow, and mature mentally and emotionally throughout life can help us cope with life's problems.

6. Hanging on to faith, hope and optimism can help us direct our energies toward positive productivity and creativity; whereas, loss of them forces us to devote most of our energies to trying to escape the negative effects.

7. We dare not let disappointment push us into discouragement. Valuable lessons from disappointments and failures can guide us and help improve our chances of later successes.

8. Developing ways to relax and avoid trying to force our thinking should help us bring intuition and free thinking into play.

9. Humor, having fun and enjoying our work can help us loosen up and let our creative abilities come forth.

10. The knowledge that we have helped another person to be creative can give us great pleasure and satisfaction.

11. While none of us can hope to surmount all the barriers to creativity, with determined effort, we should be able to realize a lot of our creative potential.

14-12 AFTERGROWTH STIMULATORS

1. Think of three things you could do you to put more of your dreams into action.
2. On a scale of one (low) to ten (high), where would rate your own commitment and determination? Can they be increased?
3. On the same kind of scale, how do you compare to others you know in level of hope and optimism? Can these be raised?
4. List some ways you could be more mature. Play more. Have more fun. Are these compatible in the same person?
5. List five ways you could use to help yourself become more creative. Five ways to help others be more creative. What kind of a timetable do you need to help you accomplish these?
6. Are you now more aware of the hundreds of barriers to your creativity than you were when you first picked up this book?

REFERENCES AND SUGGESTED READINGS

Abelson, P.H. The Federal Government and Innovation. (Editorial) *Science* Vol. 201, 11 Aug. 1978.

Adams, J.L. *Conceptual Blockbusting - A Guide to Better Ideas.* (3rd ed.) Addison - Wesley Publishing Co. Inc. Reading, MA. 1986.

Amabile, T.M. *The Social Psychology of Creativity.* Springer-Verlag New York Inc. 1983.

Anderson, B.F. *The Complete Thinker.* Prentice-Hall, Inc. Englewood Cliffs, NJ. 1980.

Andrews, F.M. Creative Process. In D. C. Pelz and F. M. Andrews. *Scientists in Organizations.* Institute for Social Research, University of Michigan. Ann Arbor, 1976.

Baker, H.K., and S.H. Holmberg. Stepping Up to Supervision: Mastering Delegation. *Supervisory Management* 26: 20-21. 1981.

Benson, H. *The Relaxation Response.* Avon Books. New York. 1975.

Benson, H. *Your Maximum Mind.* Times Books. New York. 1987.

Bettelheim, B. *Love Is Not Enough.* Avon Books. New York. 1950.

Bettelheim, B. *The Uses of Enchantment.* Vintage Books. New York. 1977.

Beveridge,W.I.B. *The Art of Scientific Investigation.* (3rd ed.) Vintage Books. New York. 1957.

Bible, Holy (Possibility Thinkers Edition) New King James Version. Thomas Nelson Publishers. Nashville, TN. 1984.

Bible, The Living. Tyndale House Publishers, Inc. Wheaton, IL. 1971.

Black, M. Principles of Really Sound Thinking. *Scientific Monthly* 66 (3): 232-234, 1948.

Blanchard, K., and S. Johnson. *The One Minute Manager.* William Morrow & Co. New York. 1981-82.

Blanchard, K., and N.V. Peale. *The Power of Ethical Management.* William Morrow & Co. New York. 1988.

Block, J.D. *Friendship: How to Give it, How to Get it.* Macmillan Publishing Co., Inc. New York. 1980.

Boyle, H. Here's How to Have a Long Life. *A.I. Digest.* p.28, Sept. 1957.

Branden, N. *The Psychology of Self-Esteem.* Bantam Books. New York. 1969.

Burns, D.D. *Feeling Good.* William Morrow & Co. New York. 1980.

Buscaglia, L.F. *Loving Each Other.* Fawcett Columbine. NY. 1984.

Buzan, T. *Use Both Sides of Your Brain.* Dutton. New York. 1974.

Capener, H.R., and R.J. Young. Interdisciplinary Research in the University. In *Nitrogen and Phosphorus: Food Production, Waste and the Environment,* by K.S. Porter (ed.) Ann Arbor Science Publishing, Inc. pp. 345-357, 1975.

335

Clark, C.H. *Idea Management: How to Motivate Creativity and Innovation.* American Management Assoc. New York. 1980. (AMACOM, 135 West 50th St., New York, NY 10020) pages 53, 54, 55.

Cotman, C. How We Age. *AARP News Bulletin.* 28: No.8, 1987.

Cousins, N. *Anatomy of an Illness.* W.W. Norton & Co. New York. 1979.

Crick, F.H.C. Thinking About the Brain. In *The Brain.* Scientific American Book. 1979.

Dale, E. Who Has the Power. *The News Letter* 30:(1), October, 1964. College of Education, Ohio State University. Columbus, OH.

Dale, E. Why Aren't We Smarter Than We Are? *The News Letter* 31:(6), March, 1966. College of Education, Ohio State University. Columbus, OH.

Dale, E. Creating the Future. *The News Letter* 32:(8), May, 1967. College of Education, Ohio State University. Columbus, OH.

Dale, E. The Good Society. *The News Letter* 34: (8), May, 1969. College of Education, Ohio State University. Columbus, OH.

Dale, E. Writing for Nearly Everybody. *The News Letter* 35:(2) November, 1969. College of Education, Ohio State University. Columbus, OH.

Dale, E. Everything Is Related. *The News Letter* 36: (1), October, 1970. College of Education, Ohio State University. Columbus, OH.

Dale, E. Communication as Participation. *The News Letter* 36: (3), December, 1970. College of Education, Ohio State University. Columbus, OH.

Darlington, C.D. The Dead Hand on Discovery. *Discovery* 9:(2), pp. 358-362; and 10:(1), pp. 7-11, 1949-50. (Reprinted in *The Graduate Journal* 4:(1), pp. 64-81, 1961, University of Texas. Austin.)

Day, A.E. *Discipline and Discovery.* The Upper Room. Nashville, TN 37202. 1947, 1961, 1977.

Day, R.A. *How to Write and Publish a Scientific Paper.* ISI Press. Philadelphia. 1979.

Deshler, G.B. *The Power of the Personal Group.* Tidings. Nashville, TN. (No publication date given).

Doyle, M., and D. Straus. *How to Make Meetings Work.* Playboy Press. Chicago, IL. 1976.

Dragstedt, C.A. Who Killed Cock Robin? The Martyred Scientist. *Perspectives in Biology and Medicine* 5:364-376, 1962.

Dyer, W.G. *Team Building: Issues and Alternatives.* Addison-Wesley Co. Reading, MA. 1977.

DuBois, E.F. On the Reading of Scientific Papers. *Science* 95 (2463):273-274, 1942.

Educational Policy Commission. *The Central Purpose of American Education.* National Education Assoc. of the U.S. Washington, D.C. 1961.

Ehrnmann, M. *Desiderata/1692.* 1927. (Reprinted by Crescendo Publishing Co. Boston, MA).

Eliot, T. S. Religion and Literature, in *Selected Essays of T.S. Eliot.* Harcourt, Brace & Co. New York. p. 348. 1950. Cited by Short, 1965, p. 32.

Emmet, E.R. *101 Brain Puzzlers.* Harper & Row, Publishers. New York. 1970.

Ends, E.J., and C.W. Page. *Organizational Team Building.* Winthrop Publishing, Inc. Cambridge, MA. 1977.

Engstrom, T.W., and R.A. MacKenzie. *Managing Your Time.* Zondervan Books. Grand Rapids, MI. 1967.

Erikson, E.H. *Childhood and Society.* Norton & Co., Inc. New York. 1963.

Evans, L.H. *Covenant To Care.* Victor Books. Wheaton, IL. 1982.

Evans, R.I. *Carl Rogers: The Man and His Ideas.* E.P. Dutton & Co. Inc. 1975.

Executive Digest. Be a Decision Maker. April 1975.

Fast, J. *The Body Language of Sex, Power and Aggression.* M. Evans and Co., Inc. New York. 1977.

Fast, J. Excuse Me, But Your Eyes Are Talking. *Family Health,* pp. 22-25, Sept. 1978.

Ferris, M. *Time Management: A Tool to Improve Effectiveness.* Agriculture and Natural Resources Education Institute Michigan State University. 1977.

Fincher, J. *The Human Body: The Brain.* U.S. News Books. Washington, D.C. pp. 81-89, 1981.

Freeh, L.A. *Praise As a Motivator.* (Workshop for administrators) Kansas State University. June 8-19, 1981.

French, J.R.P., and R.D. Caplan. Organizational Stress and Individual Strain. In *The Applied Psychology of Work Behavior* by D.W. Organ. Business Publications, Inc. Dallas Texas, pp. 307-340, 1978.

Freudenberger, H.J. *Burnout.* Anchor Press/Doubleday and Co. New York. 1980.

Fries, J.F., and L.M. Crapo. *Vitality and Aging.* W.H. Freeman & Co. San Francisco, CA. 1981.

Fromm, E. *Man for Himself.* (Originally published by Rinehart. New York, 1947) Reprinted by Henry Holt and Co., Inc. New York. 1990.

Fromm, E. *The Art of Loving.* Bantam Books. New York. 1956.

Fromm, E. *The Heart of Man - Its Genius for Good and Evil.* Harper & Row. New York. 1964.

Gardner, J.W. *Excellence: Can We Be Equal and Excellent too?* Harper & Row Publishers, Inc. New York. 1961.

Gardner, J.W. *Self-Renewal: The Individual and the Innovative Society.* Harper & Row Publishers, Inc. New York. 1963-64.

Gardner, J.W. How to Prevent Organizational Dry Rot. *Harpers Magazine,* pp. 20-26, October, 1965.

Gardner, J.W. *Morale.* W.W. Norton & Co., Inc. New York. 1978.

Garfield, E. On Style in Scientific Writing. *Current Contents.* No. 2, Jan. 10, p. 5-15, 1977.

Gaylin, W. *Feelings: Our Vital Signs.* Harper and Row Publishers, Inc. New York. 1979.

Goble, F.G. *The Third Force - The Psychology of Abraham Maslow.* Pocket Books. New York. 1970.

Gowin, D.B. *Educating*. Cornell University Press. Ithaca, NY. 1981.

Guest, E.A. It Couldn't Be Done. In *You*, The Reilly & Lee Co. Chicago, IL. pp. 19-20, 1927.

Guilford, J.P. *The Nature of Human Intelligence*. McGraw-Hill. New York. 1967.

Guilford, J.P. *Way Beyond the I. Q.* Creative Education Foundation, Inc. Buffalo, NY. 1977.

Guilford, J.P., and R. Hoepfner. *The Analysis of Intelligence*. McGraw-Hill. New York, NY. 1971.

Harbury, E. The Island of Research. *American Scientist* 54: (4) 470, 1966.

Harding, H.F. The Principles of Poor Speaking. *Scientific Monthly* 66:54-56, 1948.

Harrison, A.F., and R.M. Bramson. *Styles of Thinking*. Anchor Press/Doubleday. Garden City, NY. 1982.

Heinrich, J.S. *Creativity in the Classroom*. Science Research Associates. 1964.

Hermann, N. The Creative Brain. *Training & Development Journal* pp. 11-16, Oct. 1981.

Hersey, P., and K.H. Blanchard. *Management of Organizational Behavior - Utilizing Human Resources*. (4th ed.). Prentice- Hall, Inc. Englewood Cliffs, NJ. 1982.

Herzberg, F. Innovation: Where Is the Relish? The *Journal of Creative Behavior*. 21 (3): 179-192. 1987.

Highet, G. *The Art of Teaching*. Vintage Books. New York. 1950.

Hoagland, H. Creativity - Genetic and Psycho-social. *Perspectives Biology and Medicine*. 11:339-349. 1968.

Howe, R. *The Creative Years*. Seabury Press, Inc. New York. 1959.

Howe, R. *The Miracle of Dialogue*. Seabury Press, Inc. New York. 1963.

Hoyt, J.S., Jr. *Personal Time Management and Effective Administration*. (6th ed.). Agricultural Extenstion Service, University of Minnesota. St Paul, MN. 1977.

Hunt, M. M. Tears. *Guideposts*, October 1955. Reprinted in *Reader's Digest*, Oct. 1955. and in *Guideposts*, Feb. 1986.

Jastrow, R. Science and the American Dream. *Science Digest*, March, 1983.

Jerison, H.J. Evolution of the Brain. In *The Human Brain*, see Whittrock et al. p. 59. 1977.

JD Journal. Why People Work. Vol. 3 (1): 4-6. 1974.

Johnson, D.W., and F.P. Johnson. *Joining Together*. (3rd ed.). Prentice-Hall, Inc. Englewood Cliffs, NJ. 1987.

Kepner, C.K. and B.T. Tregoe. *The Rational Manager*, McGraw-Hill, p. 165, 1979.

Krebs, H.S. The Making of a Scientist. *Agricultural Science Review*. 6:16-22, 1968.

Lakein, A. *How to Get Control of Your Time and Your Life*. Signet. New York. 1973.

Lehman, H.C. *Age and Achievement.* Princeton University Press. 1953.

Levmore, S.X., and E.E. Cook. *Super Strategies for Puzzles and Games.* Doubleday & Company, Inc. New York. 1981.

Lewin, R. Is Your Brain Really Necessary? *Science* 210: 1232-1234. 1980.

Lippitt, G.L. *Organizational Renewal.* Prentice-Hall, Inc. Englewood Cliffs, NJ. 2nd ed. 1982.

Lock, M.C. Beating the Time Trap. In *Management a Distinct Profession.* Management Institute, University Wisconsin. 1977.

Loomer, B. Two Conceptions of Power. In *Process Studies* 6:5-32, 1976.

Loomis, E.A., Jr. *The Self in Pilgrimage.* Harper & Row Publishers, Inc. New York. 1960.

Lynch, J.H. *The Broken Heart.* Basic Books, Inc. New York. 1977.

Lyon, H.C., Jr. *Learning to Feel, Feeling to Learn.* Merrill Publishing Co. Columbus, OH. 1971.

MacKinnon, D.W. *In Search of Human Effectiveness.* The Creative Education Foundation, Inc. in association with Creative Synergetic Associates, Ltd., Buffalo, NY. 1978.

Mangrum, C.T. Providing the Right Climate for Productivity. *Supervisory Management* 26:34-40 (Oct.) 1981.

Marshak, R. The Response Grid. (Presentation to participants in the Workshop for Northeast Agricultural Experiment Station Department Chairmen. University of Maryland. 1981.

Maslow, A.H. *Toward a Psychology of Being.* (2nd ed.). D. Van Nostrand Co. New York. 1968.

Maslow, A.H. *Motivation and Personality.* (2nd ed.). Harper & Row Publishers, Inc. New York. 1970.

Maslow, A.H. *The Farther Reaches of Human Nature.* Penguin Books. New York. 1971.

Mason, L.J. *Guide to Stress Reduction.* Peace Press. Culver City, CA. 1980.

May, R. *The Courage to Create.* Bantam Books. New York. 1975.

McConkey, D.D. The Art of Delegation. In *Management A Distinct Profession.* Management Institute, University of Wisconsin. 1977.

McKim, R. *Experiences in Visual Thinking.* Brooks/Cole. Monterey, CA. 1972.

McPherson, J.H. The People, the Problems and the Problem-Solving Methods. *Journal of Creative Behavior* 2(2): 1968. (Reprinted in Parnes, Noller and Biondi, *Guide to Creative Action.* 1977).

Medawar, P.B. *Advice to a Young Scientist.* Harper & Row Publishers, Inc. New York. 1979.

Miles, R.E., L.W. Porter and J.A. Craft. Three Models of Leadership Attitudes. In *Management of Human Resources* by Pigors, Meyers, and Malm. (3rd ed.). McGraw-Hill, Co. New York. 1973.

Mintzberg, H. The Manager's Job: Folklore and Fact. *Harvard Business Review.* 83(4): 49-61. 1975.

Missildine, W.H. *Your Inner Child of the Past.* Simon and Schuster. New York. 1963. Pocket Book Ed. 1982.

Missildine, W.H., and L. Galton. *Your Inner Conflicts - How to Solve Them.* Simon & Schuster. New York. 1974.

Montague, A. *Touching - The Human Significance of Skin.* Harper & Row Publishers. New York. 1971.

Montague, A., and F. Matson. *The Human Connection.* McGraw-Hill Book Co. New York. 1979.

Morgan, J.S. *Improving Your Creativity on the Job.* American Management Association, Inc. 1968.

Morris, D. *Intimate Behavior.* Random House, Inc. New York. 1971.

Moustakas, C.E. *The Self.* Harper and Brothers. New York. 1956.

Moustakas, C.E. *Loneliness and Love.* Prentice-Hall. Englewood Cliffs, NJ. 1972.

Newell, A. and H.A. Simon. *Human Problem Solving.* Prentice- Hall, Inc. Englewood Cliffs, NJ. 1972.

Nichols, R.G., and L.A. Stevens. Listening to People. *Harvard Business Review.* 35:(5), 1957. (Reprinted by Xerox Corporation as *Effective Listening: Listener's Response Book.* 1963-64).

Nierenberg, G.K., and H.H. Calero. *How to Read a Person Like a Book.* Cornerstone Library. New York. 1971.

Nouwen, H.J.M. *Reaching Out.* Doubleday and Company, Inc. Garden City, NY. 1975.

Novak, J.D., and D.B. Gowin. *Learning How to Learn.* Cambridge University Press. New York. 1984.

Oates, W. *Confessions of a Workaholic.* The World Publishing Co. New York. 1971.

Olson, R.W. *The Art of Creative Thinking.* Barnes and Noble Books. New York. 1980.

Ornstein, R.E. *The Psychology of Consciousness.* Penguin Books. New York. 1972.

Osborn, A.F. *Applied Imagination* (3rd ed.). Charles Scribner's Sons. New York. 1963.

Osborne, C. *The Art of Understanding Yourself.* Zondervan Books. Grand Rapids, MI. 1967.

Parnes, S.J. *Creative Behavior Workbook.* Charles Scribner's Sons. New York. 1967.

Parnes, S.J., and H. Harding. *A Sourcebook for Creative Thinking.* Charles Scribner's Sons. New York. 1962.

Parnes, S.J., R.B. Noller, and A.M. Biondi. *Guide to Creative Action.* Charles Scribner's Sons. New York. 1977.

Patten, T.H., Jr. *Organizational Development through Team Building.* John Wiley & Sons. New York. 1981.

Peale, N.V. *The Amazing Results of Positive Thinking.* Prentice- Hall, Inc. Englewood Cliffs, NJ. 1959

Peale, N.V. In 1987 Let Hope Light Your Way. *Guideposts.* Carmel, NY. Page 6-7, Jan. 1987.

Peck, M.S. *The Road Less Traveled.* Simon and Schuster. New York. 1978.

Peck, M.S. *People of the Lie.* Simon and Schuster. New York. 1983.

Peck, M.S. *The Different Drum.* Simon and Schuster. New York. 1987.

Pelz, D.C., and F.M. Andrews. *Scientists in Organizations.* Institute for Social Research, University of Michigan, Ann Arbor. 1976.

Peter, G. Leadership Leads. *Cornell Chronicle.* Cornell University. Ithaca, NY. 1987.

Peter, L.J., and R. Hull. *The Peter Principle: Why Things Go Wrong.* William Morrow & Co. Inc. New York. 1969.

Peters, T.J., and R.H. Waterman, Jr. *In Search of Excellence.* Harper & Row, Publishers, Inc. New York. 1982.

Pigors, P., Meyers, A. and Malm, F.T. *Management of Human Resources.* (3rd ed.). McGraw-Hill Book Co. New York. 1973.

Powell, J. *Why Am I Afraid To Tell You Who I Am?* Argus Communications. Niles, IL. 1969.

Ranftl, R.M., *R & D Productivity.* (2nd ed.) Hughes Aircraft Co. Culver City, CA. 1978.

Ridenour, F. (ed.) *I'm a Good Man, But...* G/L Publications. Glendale, CA. 1969.

Robinson, J. *Stress and How to Live with It.* Successful Farming. Meredith Corp. 1982.

Rogers, C.R. *On Becoming a Person.* Houghton Mifflin Co. Boston. 1961.

Rogers, C.R. *On Personal Power.* Dell Publishing Co., Inc. New York. 1977.

Rogers, C. *Freedom to Learn.* Merrill Publishing Co. Columbus, OH. 1969, 1983.

Salisbury, G.W. *An Approach to the Scientific Solution of Problems in Applied Biology.* Unpublished Mimeograph. 1951.

Schein, E.H. Forces Which Undermine Management Development. (Reprinted in *Management of Human Resources,* Pigors et al., eds. McGraw-Hill Book Co. Hightstown, NJ. 1973).

Schmidt, P.F. *Coping with Difficult People.* The Westminister Press. Philadelphia. 1980.

Schuller, R.H. *Tough Times Never Last, But Tough People Do!* Thomas Nelson, Inc. Nashville, TN. 1983.

Schuller, R.H. *Success Is Never Ending Failure Is Never Final,* Thomas Nelson, Inc. Nashville, TN. 1988.

Schultz, W.N. How to Use That Wonderful Gold Mine between Your Ears - Every Day. In *Have an Affair with Your Mind.* A.M. Biondi (ed.). Creative Synergetic Assoc. Great Neck, NY. pp. 45-48, 1974.

Senge, P.M. *Systems Thinking and the New Management Style.* (A Report on the Pilot Phase of the Project). Sloan School of Management, Massachusetts Institute of Technology. 50 pp. 1984.

Short, R.L. *The Gospel According to Peanuts.* John Knox Press. Atlanta, GA. 1965.

Siegel, B. *Love, Medicine and Miracles.* Harper & Row Publishers, Inc. New York. 1986.

Siu, R.G.H. *The Tao of Science.* The M.I.T. Press. Cambridge, MA. 1957.

Smyllyan, R. *The Lady or the Tiger.* Alfred A. Knopf, Inc. New York. 1982.

Steiner, G. *The Creative Organization.* University Chicago Press. Chicago. 1965. (Cited by Dyer, p. 107, 1977)

Stock, M. *A Practical Guide to Graduate Research.* McGraw-Hill Book Co. New York. 1985.

Sutherland, R.A. *Can an Adult Change?* Hogg Foundation for Mental Health. University of Texas, Austin. 1957.

Swindoll, C.R. *Living Above the Level of Mediocrity: A Commitment to Excellence.* Word Books. Waco, TX. 1987.

Tarkenton, F. *Fran Tarkenton Demo.* (Video tape) Tarkenton Group, 3340 Peachtree Rd, Ste 444, Atlanta, GA. 30326.

Tavris, C. Anger Defused. *Psychology Today.* Pp. 25-35, Nov. 1982. (Cites her book *Anger: The Misunderstood Emotion.* Simon and Schuster. 1983)

Thomas, J.W. *Your Personal Growth.* Frederick Fell, Inc., New York. 1971.

Toffler, A. *Future Shock.* Random House. New York. 1970.

Toffler, A. *The Third Wave.* William Morrow and Co., Inc. New York. 1980.

Torrance, E.P. *The Search for Satori & Creativity.* Creative Education Foundation, Inc. Buffalo, NY. 1979.

Tournier, P. *The Adventure of Living.* Harper & Row Publishers, Inc. New York. 1965a.

Tournier, P. *Fatigue in Modern Society.* John Knox Press. Richmond, VA. 1965b.

VanDemark, N.L. Synthesis of a Scientist. From *A Symposium on Animal Agriculture.* pp. 4-21 Pub. 57, University of Illinois, College of Agriculture and Agricultural Experiment Station. Urbana-Champaign, IL. 1979.

Vaughan, F.E. *Awakening Intuition.* Anchor Books. Garden City, NY. 1979.

Von Fange, E.K. *Professional Creativity.* Prentice-Hall, Inc. Englewood Cliffs, NJ. 1959.

von Oech, R. *A Whack on the Side of the Head.* Creative Think. Menlo Park, CA. 1983.

Walsh, J. What Can Government Do for Innovation? *Science,* Vol. 205, 27 Jul. pp. 378-380, 1979.

Weisinger H., and N.M. Lobsenz. *Nobody's Perfect: How to Give Criticism and Get Results.* Warner Books, Inc. New York. 1981.

Whimbey, A., and J. Lochhead. *Problem Solving and Comprehension.* 3rd ed., Franklin Institiute Press. Philadelphia, PA. 1982.

Whimbey, A., and L.S. Whimbey. *Intelligence Can Be Taught.* Bantam Books. New York. 1975.

White, J. *Honesty, Morality and Conscience.* Navpress. Colorado Springs, CO. 1979.

Whittrock, M.C. et al. *The Human Brain.* Prentice-Hall,Inc. Englewood Cliffs, NJ. 1977.

Wickelgren, W.A. *How to Solve Problems.* W. H. Freeman & Co. San Francisco, CA. 1974.

Wilke, R.B. *And Are We Yet Alive?* Abingdon Press. Nashville, TN. 1986.

Wlodkowski, R.J. *Motivation.* National Education Association. Washington, D.C. 1977.

Woodford, F.P. Sounder Thinking Through Clearer Writing. *Science* 156: (3776) 743-745. 1967.

Woodford, F.P. (ed.). *Scientific Writing for Graduate Students.* Council of Biology Editors. 1981.

Yunich, D.L. *How to Kill Progress.* The Economic Press, Inc., Montclair, NJ. 1958.

AUTHOR INDEX

Abelson, P.H., 309

Adams, J.L., 27, 57, 59, 60, 66, 201

Amabile, T.M., 19, 20, 21, 24, 202, 204

Anderson, B.F., 48, 105, 127

Andrews, F.M., 19

Baker, H.K., 273

Benson, H., 253, 321

Bettelheim, B., 57, 134, 203, 230

Beveridge, W.I.B., 120

Bible, 65, 66, 97, 133, 158, 164, 214

Black, M., 45

Blanchard, K., 64, 139, 140, 141, 261, 262, 265, 267, 268, 276, 278, 280, 298, 299, 304

Block, J.D., 154, 174

Boyle, H., 328

Bramson, R.M., 47

Branden, N., 38, 137

Burns, D.D., 49, 77, 156

Buscaglia, L.F., 159, 160, 161

Buzan, T. 34, 37, 38, 39

Calero, H.H., 170

Capener, H.R., 187, 188

Caplan, R.D., 268-270

Chronicle of Higher Education, 15

Clark, C.H., 29

Cook, E.E., 114

Cotman, C., 21

Cousins, N., 174

Crapo, L.M., 22

Crick, F.H.C., 34

Dale, E., 17, 18, 33, 39, 60, 64, 81, 85, 89, 90, 92, 93, 133, 169, 172, 185, 212, 227, 275, 293, 302, 323, 330

Darlington, C.D., 307

Day, A.E., 319, 321

Day, R.A., 125

Deshler, G.B., 159, 163, 177, 239, 240

Doyle, M., 125, 189

Dragstedt, C.A., 200, 248

Dyer, W.G., 186, 191, 305, 306

DuBois, E.F., 165

Education Policies Commission, 44

Ehrnmann, M., 330

Emmet, E.R., 114

Ends, E.J., 261, 300, 302

Engstrom, T.W., 88

Erikson, E.H., 228, 229

Evans, L.H., 183, 184

Evans, R.I., 209

Executive Digest, 88

Fast, J., 170, 171

Ferris, M., 237, 238

Fincher, J., 36, 37

Freeh, L.A., 270, 273, 280, 282, 297

French, J.R.P., 268, 269

Freudenberger, H.J., 231, 232, 233

Fries, J.F., 22
Fromm, E., 86, 87, 144, 155, 158
Galton, L., 94
Gardner, J.W., 92, 93, 218, 228, 312, 313, 323, 325
Garfield, E., 125
Gaylin, W., 65, 67, 72, 138, 156
Goble, F.G., 23, 135, 141
Gowin, D.B., 40, 42, 45, 85, 210
Guest, E., 320
Guilford, J.P., 34
Harbury, E., 128, 129
Harding, H.F., 119, 165
Harrison, A.F., 47
Heinrich, J.S., 23, 25
Hermann, N., 41
Hersey, P., 265, 267
Herzberg, F., 20
Highet, G., 214
Hoagland, H., 42, 53
Hoepfner, R., 34
Holmberg, S.H., 273
Howe, R., 163, 320, 323, 324
Hoyt, J.S., Jr., 272, 284
Hull, R., 308
Hunt, M.M., 138
Jastrow, R., 15
JD Journal, 146
Jerison, H.J., 41
Johnson, D.W., 182, 194, 283
Johnson, F.P., 182, 194, 283
Johnson, S., 268, 304
Kepner, C.K., 87
Krebs, H.S., 230
Lakein, A., 237, 245, 248
Lehman, H.C., 21
Levmore, S.X., 114
Lewin, R., 34
Lippitt, G.L., 147, 185, 186, 194, 229, 274, 276, 277, 278, 303, 304
Lobsenz, N.M., 94, 242, 243
Lochhead, J., 112
Lock, M.C., 248, 249
Loomer, B., 157

Loomis, E.A., Jr., 227
Lynch, J.H., 174
Lyon, H.C. Jr., 81
MacKenzie, R.A., 88
Mackinnon, D.W., 8, 23, 58, 147, 204
Mangrum, C.T., 301
Marshak, R., 89, 90
Maslow, A.H., 23, 135, 136, 141
Mason, L.J., 174
Matson, F., 172
May, R., 19
McConkey, D.D., 272
McKim, R., 57
McPherson, J.H., 125
Medawar, P,B., 66
Miles, R.E., 266, 267
Mintzberg, H., 259, 260
Missildine, W.H., 94, 205, 206, 207
Montague, A., 171, 172
Morgan, J.S., 19, 27, 59, 60, 68, 69, 70, 78, 148, 149, 190, 194
Morris, D., 155, 172
Moustakas, C.E., 137, 149, 162
Newell, A., 36
Nichols, R.G., 166, 167
Nierenberg, G.K., 170
Nouwen, H.J.M., 209
Novak, J.D., 40, 45, 85
Oates, W., 251,
Olson, R.W., 114, 119, 123
Ornstein, R.E., 13, 40
Osborn, A.F., 21, 22, 56, 57, 58, 107, 117, 118, 126
Osborne, C., 67
Page, C.W., 261, 300, 302
Parnes, S.J., 56, 115, 119, 125, 126
Patten, T.H., Jr. 252, 253, 268
Peale, N.V., 64, 95, 139, 140, 141, 239, 261, 262, 268, 276, 278, 280, 298, 299, 304
Peck, M.S., 83, 91, 98, 181, 182, 184, 221
Peter, G., 262,

Peter, L.J., 308
Peters, T.J., 19, 258, 268, 276, 289, 291, 292, 295, 299, 308, 313, 319
Powell, J., 164
Ranftl, R.M., 89, 124, 248, 291, 292, 296
Ridenour, F., 230
Robinson, J., 68
Rogers, C.R., 85, 136, 175, 202, 209, 211, 212, 213, 214, 215, 216
Salisbury, G.W., 125, 126, 128
Schein, E.H., 234, 236, 241
Schmidt, P.F., 50, 221, 229
Schuller, R.H., 58, 95, 96, 240
Schultz, W.N., 34
Senge, P.M., 289
Shepard, H.A., 307
Short, R.L., 58, 201, 234, 238, 242, 244
Siegel, B., 174
Simon, H.A., 36
Siu, R.G.H., 257
Smyllyan, R., 114
Steiner, G., 290
Stevens, L.A., 166, 167
Stock, M., 125
Straus, D., 125, 189
Success, 145
Sutherland, R.A., 234, 235, 241

Swindoll, C.R., 13
Tarkenton, F., 292
Tavris, C., 74
Teyler, T.J., 34
Thomas, J.W., 175
Toffler, A., 14
Torrance, E.P., 56
Tournier, P., 71, 133, 144, 145, 146, 231, 317
Tregoe, B.T., 87
VanDemark, N.L., 43, 46, 63, 82
Vaughan, F.E., 42, 44, 54, 87, 110, 227
Von Fange, E.K., 19, 42
von Oech, R., 27
Walsh, J., 310
Waterman, R.H., 19, 258, 268, 276, 289, 291, 292, 295, 299, 308, 313, 319
Weisinger, H., 94, 242, 243
Whimbey, A., 112, 207, 208
Whimbey, L.S., 207, 208
White, J., 141, 160
Whittrock, M.C., 34
Wickelgren, W.A., 108-112
Wilke, R.B., 221, 234, 261, 302
Wimbrow, D., 140
Wlodkowski, R.J., 144
Woodford, F.P., 125, 169
Young, R.J., 187, 188
Yunich, D.L., 219, 220

SUBJECT INDEX

Acceptance-finding, 107, 123-125, 126
Action, 123, 291, 317-319:
    and adventure, 317
Administrative practices, 284, 285
Adventure:
    as motivation, 145-146
    action and, 317
Adversity, 244
Age, 21
Ages of man, 229

Alone, 155
Ambiguity, 59, 69, 148, 269
Anger, 70, 74, 234
Applied Imagination, 21
Anxiety, 44, 66-68, 71
Association with others, 154
Atmosphere:
    allow, 281
    and the four "D's," 217
    causal, 281-282
    discourage, 280

open, 217
supportive, 217, 290
Attitudes, 62-79:
    and creativity, 65
    mental, 63-64
    toward others, 63, 73-78,
    toward self, 63-65
Audience enemies, 165
Authority, fear of, 70, 75
Balance (ing), 80-101, 98-99
Barrier(s), 27-29, 307-311:
    governments as, 309-311
    mental distortions, 49-50
    perceptual, 60
    self (inner), 148-149
Behavior, group,individual, 264-267
Belief, 145
Bible:
    be new and different, 133
    love, 158
    soft answer, 164
    spirit of power, 66
    understand myself, 65
    wisdom, 97-98
    wise teacher, 214
Body language, 170-171
Boredom, 211, 231
Bracketing, 99
Brain:
    left-right, 41
    need for, 34
    structure, 34
Brainstorming, 117-120
Burnout, 231-234
Caring, 158-159
Challenge, 15, 319:
    lack of, 148
    life-long, 149
Change, 14, 317-319:
    accepting, 242
    certainty of, 14
    difficulty in making, 265
    guidelines, 304
    leader control and, 267
    leadership patterns, 266
    need for, 234-235

making personal, 241-242
organizational, 301-304
resistance to, 302-303
Child, children:
    curiosity in, 53
    live what they learn, 205
    upbringing, 203-208, 230
Chaos, in groups, 182
Choice(s) in decision-making, 56,
    86-88
Cognition (ive), 44, 49-50:
    distortions, 49-50
Commitment (ted), 238-240, 325
Common sense, 96-98
Communicate (ion), 162-173:
    and time loss, 247
    blocks, 172-173
    dialogue, 162-163
    effectively, 283-284
    essential principles for, 182
    levels, 164
    visual, 170-171
Community:
    building stages, 181-183
    true meaning, 183-185
Concentration, 41
Concept (construct) mapping, 40
Conflict avoidance, 274-275
Conforming (ity), 190:
    and the animal school, 210-
    211
Congeniality, 82
Control, mental, 82
Constructs (concepts), 40
Convergent thinking, 42
Creative (ivity):
    abilities, 20
    and aging, 21
    and education, 22
    and experience, 22
    and sex, 22
    barriers to, 27, 148-149, 201
    benefits and costs of, 30
    characteristics of, 23, 25, 142
    definition of, 18
    enhancing, 24-25

factors affecting, 28, 147
help others to be, 330-331
interacting factors, 20, 24-28
management and, 305-306
maximizing it, 330
need for, 16
organizations and, 305-306
relevant skills for, 24, 29
thinking, 43-47
traits, 23, 25, 142
Critical judgement, 148-149
Criticism, 161:
   fear of, 70, 76-77
   of education, 209-211
   willingness to accept, 242-244
Culture(al):
   and creativity, 28, 200-201
   and freedom, 200
   blocks, 201
Curiosity, 28, 52-53:
   and aging, 53
   and growth, 53
Dark pool of the unknown, 103-104
Daydreaming, 57
Decision-making, 86-90, 143, 246:
   and choices, 86-88
   and poor planning, 88
   do's and don'ts, 87-88
   participation in, 266-269
   response grid, 88-89
Deferred judgment, 118
Delayed gratification, 83-84
Delegating(ion), 246, 271-273
Dependency, over-, 75
Depression, 73, 217, 232
Design, experimental, 122, 127
Determinant situation, 104
Development and growth, 228-230
Dialogue, 162-163
Difficult person(s), 221-222, 244
Disappointment, 325-326
Discipline, 28, 82:
   self, 82-84, 148, 320-322
Divergent thinking, 45
Domain-relevant skills, 24
Downs (D's), 217

Drawing inferences, 109
Dreaming, 58, 240
Education(al), 28, 208-216:
   aim, 43-44
   definition, 85
   student reactions, 211-213
   whole-person, 85-86
Emotions (al), 28, 63-79:
   and creativity, 65
   depressing, 73
   involving others, 73
   stability, 82
   uplifting, 73
Employee participation, 268-269
Enthusiasm, 240
Environment (al), 198-224:
   and creativity, 28, 199-200,
      300-301
   organizational, 300-301
   stimulating, 261
Errors, in problem-solving, 112-114
Ethics (al):
   behavior and self-esteem, 139
   individual check, 140
   organizational check, 298-299
   power, 140
   Rotary International, 139
Evaluation, 44, 84, 137, 227:
   leader and manager roles, 278-
      279
   self-, 227-228
Examination(s), 84, 215
Excellence (ent):
   and perfection, 92-94
   and wisdom, 93-94
   companies, 290-292
Experimental design, 122-127
Eye contact, 170-171
Facilitator:
   and building trust, 214
   of learning, 213-216
Fact-finding, 107, 115, 126
Failure, fear of, 70, 148, 230
Faith, 240, 320-322:
   in ourselves, 239
Family life rules, 206

Fantasy, 57, 148
Fatigue, 230-231
Fear, 66-69:
    and imagination, 57
    of authority, 75
    of criticism, 70-76
    of failure, 70, 77-78, 148, 156,
    230
    of loss, 155
    of pain, 67, 155
    of rejection, 155
    of risking, 75-76
    or separation, 155
    of success, 227
Feedback, 157, 163-164
Feeling(s):
    angry, 70, 74
    anxiety, 66-68, 71
    bad, 72
    confused, 231-232
    depressed, 217, 231-232
    down, 217
    effects on creativity, 65-70
    fear, 66-70
    good, 72
    happy, 72-73, 134, 218, 323
    hopeful, 320
    hurt, 73-74
    insecure, 70
    jealous, 73-74
    pleasure, 72
    tense, 44, 252
Flexibility, 148
Forgetting, 36-39
Free(dom), 87:
    and believing, 56
    and choosing, 44, 87
    and conforming, 190
    and responsibility, 64, 90
    let it work, 326-327
    to learn, 212, 216
Fun-loving, 328
Goal setting, 277-278
Good(ness):
    feeling, 72
    organization, 293

Government, blocks to creativity,
    309-311
Gratification, delayed, 83
Group:
    accomplishing change, 301-
    304
    building, 181-183
    decision-making, 190
    dislikes for, 191
    dynamics, 182
    impact on creativity, 194
    meetings, 192-193
    problems in, 189, 191
    working in, 189-191
Growth:
    and creativity, 53
    and maturity, 322-325
    blocks to, 235
    interpersonal, 241
    organizational, 241, 289
    personal, 226-255, 241
Habit(s), 69-70, 87, 148-149
Half-person, 81
Happiness, 72-73, 134, 218, 323
Health, maintenance, 248-250
Hear(ing), 166-168
Honesty, 64, 84-85, 124, 162, 239:
    and creativity, 160-161
Hope (ing), 73, 239, 320-322
Humor, 174
Hypochondrical, 207
Hypothesis(es), 117-118, 120
Idea-finding:
    generation, 117, 120, 126
    stimulation of, 118
Illumination, 56
Imagination, 28, 52, 56-59:
    anticipative, 58
    lack of, 148
    vicarious, 58
Indeterminant situation, 104, 126
Individuals in groups, 195
Insecurity, 70
Institution(s)(al):
    change, 289
    drag, 309

dry rot, 312-313
growth, 289, 301-305
impact on people, 289
Integrity, 262
Intellect (igence), 32, 81:
    and creativity, 20, 23, 82
    balance and intelligence, 81-82
    importance of, 33
    structure of, 34-35
Interpersonal relationships, 28:
    and creativity, 154
    and health, 173-174
    barriers to, 176-177
    building lasting, 157-158
    relational power and, 153-154
    savvy, 82
Intuition, 28, 52, 54-56:
    and receptivity, 54-55
    let it work, 55
    the voice from within, 54
IQ and creativity, 20
It Couldn't be Done, 320
Jealousy, 73-74
Judgment(s), deferring, 118
Jumping to conclusions, 50, 113, 276
Leader (ship) 258:
    and creativity, 28, 257
    attributes needed for, 261-262
    balanced, 296-297
    dynamic, 261-262
    effective do's and don'ts, 262-263
    responsibilities of, 257, 260-261
Learn(ing):
    and tension, 44
    and understanding, 85-86
    atmosphere for, 216
    early years and, 205, 207-208
    freedom to, 85-86, 212
    memory and, 35
    principles of, 213
    to learn, 85, 150
    trust and, 214

with breaks, 39
Lecturing, 165-166
Listen(ing), effectively, 166-168
Loneliness, 156
Loss, fear of, (control, life, etc.), 155
Love (ing), 136, 158-159, 230
Lie, lying, 160-161
Male/female, 22
Man, eight ages of, 228-230
Man in the Glass, 140-141
Man for Himself, 144
Management:
    and creativity, 28, 257, 305-306
    as a new role, 258-260
    blocks to creativity, 279-285
    general practices, 275
    keeping people involved, 282-283, 285
Manager(s):
    attributes needed, 261-262, 296-297
    bombarded from all directions, 259
    motivational role, 264-266
Manipulation, 156-158
Mastery, 72-73
Mature (ity) and growth, 142-143, 322-324
Mediocrity, 13
Meeting guidelines, 193
Memory: 35-38
    increase from breaks, 37,39
    increase from review, 37-38
    rate of loss of recall, 37-38
Mental:
    agility, 43
    attitudes, 63-64, 82
    blocks, 44, 49-50
    capabilities, 42-43
    discipline, 82
    distortions, 49-50
Morale building, 217-218, 269
Motivation(al), 144, 264-269:
    and adventure, 145

and creativity, 147
and work, 145
forces, 145-147
individual, 146
leader role in, 264-269
over-, 148-149
too little, 148
Mountains of deterrents, 104
Needs:
basic, 135-136
being or growth, 135, 137
for creativity, 16
for interpersonal relationships, 154
for self-worth, 139
Maslow's hierarchy of, 135
to be right, 137
to understand, 138
to feel good, 138
Negativism, 219-222:
character disorders, 221-222
disappointment, 325-326
Neglect of child development, 207-208
Non-verbal communication, 170-172
Openness, 150, 162, 217
Optimism, 218-219
Organization(s,al), 288-314:
and creativity, 28, 291
and personal growth, 241
change and renewal, 289, 301-305, 312-313
characteristics of good, 291-293
drag, 307
dry rot, 312-313
effective, 261, 295
ethics, 298-299
growth, 289
impact on people, 289
profile of creative, productive, 290-293
top heavy, 307-308
treatment of persons, 299-300
values and principles, 298-299

Over-commitment, 232, 248
Over-coercive, 207
Over-dependency, 75
Over-motivated, 148-149,234
Over-indulgent, 207
Over-sensitive, 235
Over-submissive, 207
Others, impact on creativity, 73-78, 152-178
Pain, 67, 73, 83, 99, 155-156, 183, 227
Parent(al):
and child development, 207-208
and creativity, 203-205
child mistreatment by, 205-208
influence on children, 204
Patience, 63
Perception (ual), 28, 52, 59, 142:
blocks to creativity, 60
Perfection(ism,ist), 95, 207:
and excellence, 93
Perseverance (ing), 325
Personal needs, 135-139:
fulfilled, 252
Physical discomforts, 222
Planning, 240, 276-277:
effective, 277
for organizational change, 301-305
Pleasure, 72
Positive thinking, 95-96
Poverty, effects on child, 207-208
Praying, 240
Problem definition, 103-105
Problem(s) exercises, 108-112
Problem-solving, 102-131:
acceptance-finding, 123-125
attitudes, 107
approaches, 108-112, 121
capabilities, 100, 106
contradictions, 111
collect evidence, 122
draw conclusions, 123
evaluative criteria, 121

experimental design, 122
fact-finding, 115, 126
hill climbing, 110
idea-finding, 117, 120
in scientific research, 125-129
Salisbury approach, 126-129
skills, 107-108
solution-finding, 121
statement of, 116
sub-goals, 111
Procrastination, 235-238:
overcoming, 238
Psuedo-community, 182
Punitive, 207
Reading, 168-170
Rearing, effects on creativity, 203-208
Reasoning, 44
Recall:
with breaks in learning, 39
with reviews, 38
Rejection (ive), 207:
fear of, 155
Relating, 155
Relational power, 157
Relationships, interpersonal, 73-78, 154:
affirmation in, 161
and creativity, 174
and health, 173-174
and responsibility, 159
and trust, 159-160
barriers to, 176-177
destructive factors, 159
enhancing factors, 159, 175-176
fruits of, 175
honesty in, 160-161
lasting, 157-158
need for, 154
Relaxation techniques, 250-253
Religion and creativity, 201-203
Remembering, 36-38
Renewal, 228, 312-313
Research, pattern for, 125-129
Respect, 159

Response grid, 88-90
Responsibility:
accept, 84
freedom and, 90-92
individual, 227
in relationship, 63, 159
Risking, 75, 78
Role ambiguity, 270
Salisbury, pattern for research, 126-129
Science, and problem-solving, 125-129
Security, superficial, 69
Seeing, 170-171
Selecting creative personnel, 294
Self(-), 132-151, 229:
actualization, characteristics, 141-144
and creativity, 27-28, 133-134
challenging, 149-150
confidence, 70
development, 63, 149
discipline, 63, 80, 83
esteem, 70-71, 137, 139, 142, 161
evaluation, 63, 65, 227, 239
finisher, 150
fulfillment, 134, 141-144
love, 63
preservation, 144, 264
respect, responsibiltiy, 63, 159
renewal, 227-228
starter, 63, 150
Separation, fear of, 155
Serendipity, 52, 60
Sex, 22
Skills:
creativity relevant, 24
domain relevant, 24
Snap-decisions, 235, 276, 283
Society and creativity, 28, 198-224
Solution-finding, 107, 120-123, 126:
best approach, 121
communicate results, 124
convince ourselves, 124

inform others, 124
put it into action, 123-125
Speculating, fear of, 75
Spirit, 218-219
Stress, 219-222, 244:
    and anxiety, 67-68
    and difficult persons, 221-222
    management minimizing, 274-275
    of negatives, 219-222
Success, 71, 78, 227
Survival, 13
Task motivation, 24
Teacher (ing), 208-216:
    and learner relationships, 150, 211-216
Team(s), 180-196:
    advantages of, 187-188
    and creativity, 28
    disadvantages of, 186, 188
    efforts, 181
    effective, 184, 191-192, 295
    requirements for, 191-192
    when needed, 185-186
Tears, 138
The Man in the Glass, 140-141
Thinking, 28, 38, 41, 45:
    characteristic results of, 46
    creative, 45-46, 48
    critical, 48
    directed, 43, 45-46

fixed, 43
free, 43
positive, 96-97
restricted, 148
right and left brained, 41
styles of, 47, 220-221
Time, 244-250, 271:
    analysis of use, 246
    beat the time trap, 248-249
    best use of, 244
Touch(ing), touched, 171-172
Tradition, 69-70, 148
Trust, 159-161, 229:
    and learning, 214
Truth, dedication to, 84-85, 139, 160-161
Unconscious, 55, 58, 66
Unilateral power, 156-157
Upset, feeling, 72
Vacation, skipping, 252
Vision, 170-171
Visual imagery, 56-57
Willpower, 238-240
Whole person, 98-99
Wisdom, 28, 96-98
Work, 142, 146:
    dislikes, 191
    in groups, 189-191
Workaholic, 251-252
Worry, 57, 67-68, 235
Writing, 168-170

DATE DUE

Comments About
Breaking the Barriers to E

DR. JOÄN ROOS EGNER,
Professor of Education, Co

An appropriate reading ,
business/industry and acade..
building as a creative process give
problem solving. Our multi-cultural soc
perspective to consider alternative ways of u.
resolving issues - Dr. VanDemark has given us gu

DR. J. ROBERT COOKE, Professor of Biological Engineering.
College of Agriculture and Life Sciences...

Breaking the Barriers to Everyday Creativity is a valuable re-
source of hints and techniques for improving one's problem-
solving skills. I use it as a supplementary resource in my Bio-
logical Engineering Analysis Course at Cornell University.

DR. RONALD J. KUHR, Professor of Entomology and Director
of Research, Agricultural Research Service,
North Carolina State University...

Breaking the Barriers to Everyday Creativity is an excellent
compilation of experiences, thought and actions by a man who
has spent a career in the academic environment. His sensitiv-
ity to people's feelings and aspirations, his keen desire to have
every person reach his or her potential, and his genuine
concern for the individual are clearly delineated in this book.
As a colleague and fellow administrator, I learned much from
him and sincerely believe that many others could benefit
tremendously from reading these pages. It is a well-organized
book written in easy-to-understand language with a wonderful
message.